UNIVERSITY OF GLOUCESTERSHIRE

at Cheltenham and Gloucester

RESEARCHING
ORGANIZATIONAL
VALUES AND BELIEFS

RESEARCHING ORGANIZATIONAL VALUES AND BELIEFS

The Echo Approach

J. Barton Cunningham
Foreword by Janet Beavin Bavelas

Q

QUORUM BOOKS
Westport, Connecticut • London

Library of Congress Cataloging-in-Publication Data

Cunningham, J. Barton.
   Researching organizational values and beliefs : the Echo
approach / J. Barton Cunningham ; foreword by Janet Beavin Bavelas.
    p.   cm.
   Includes bibliographical references and index.
   ISBN 1-56720-372-8 (alk. paper)
   1.Management—Research—Methodology. 2. Industrial
management—Research—Methodology. 3. Organizational
behavior—Research—Methodology. I. Title.
   HD30.4.C86   2001
   658'.007'2—dc21   00-045850

British Library Cataloguing in Publication Data is available.

Library of Congress Catalog Card Number: 00-045850
ISBN: 1-56720-372-8

First published in 2001

Quorum Books, 88 Post Road West, Westport, CT 06881
An imprint of Greenwood Publishing Group, Inc.
www.quorumbooks.com

Printed in the United States of America

The paper used in this book complies with the
Permanent Paper Standard issued by the National
Information Standards Organization (Z39.48-1984).

10 9 8 7 6 5 4 3 2 1

Copyright Acknowledgments

The author and publisher gratefully acknowledge permission for use of the following material:

Excerpts from "The Collapse of Sensemaking in Organizations: The Mann Gulch Disaster,"
by Karl F. Weick, published in *Administrative Science Quarterly*, vol. 38, no. 3, by permission of
Administrative Science Quarterly. Copyright Cornell University, Graduate School of Business and Public Administration, Dec. 1993.

Excerpts from "Caring for the Caregivers: Patterns of Organizational Caregiving," by William
A. Kahn, published in *Administrative Science Quarterly*, vol. 38, no. 3, by permission of
Administrative Science Quarterly. Copyright Cornell University, Graduate School of Business and Public Administration, Dec. 1993.

Contents

Foreword

Janet Beavin Bavelas

In this book, Professor Cunningham presents a new framework for research on values and beliefs in organizations, integrating a variety of techniques and theories that share a novel and often unstated perspective. To understand why he has centered this approach on the Echo technique, it is useful to look briefly at the original technique, its intellectual roots, and the alternative it offers.

WHAT IS ECHO?

In a short article in 1942, Alex Bavelas described a new method for learning about a group's values from individuals in the group. Quite simply, he proposed that the researcher should ask the individuals themselves, in open-ended questions. Therefore, he studied children's school values by asking fourth through eighth grade students at two schools to answer these questions:

- "What could a child of your age do at school that would be a good thing to do and someone would praise him?"
- Who would praise him?
- "What could a child of your age do at school that would be a bad thing to do and someone would scold him?"[1]
- Who would scold him?

Each of these pairs of questions was asked several times, so that each child could contribute up to nine praiseworthy and nine scoldable behaviors. The findings revealed, for example, age differences that reflected the children's ongoing socialization into school values: Fourth-graders often attributed praise to doing assigned work and not creating discipline problems, whereas eighth-graders expected praise more for excelling or doing some special or "great" deed. There were also changes in the sources of praise or blame, with other children (peers) decreasing in frequency from fourth to eighth grade, while the school principal increased, especially for scolding.

In subsequent studies, Bavelas added a second step in which the answers written by the individuals in the group were sorted into categories not by the researcher but by representative members of the group itself. Thus, combining these two steps, the members of the group determined which behaviors (and sources of praise or criticism) to include, how these were described (vocabulary and phrasing), and the categories in which they belonged (which behaviors and sources belong in the same category). Thus, the researcher's ultimate description of the group's values was an "echo" of their own language and world view.

In some published studies and uncounted unpublished applications, what came to be called the Echo method has been used as a specific technique for capturing the grassroots view of the target group with minimum intervention by the researcher. Echo has been used to learn the values and beliefs of groups—including employees, students, nurses, psychiatric clients, and many others—in a wide range of geographical and cultural settings. It would be fair to say that over the years, Echo became known, mainly by word of mouth, as an innovative and appealing but definitely off-beat survey technique. Those who used it—and those who participated in Echo studies— were usually enthusiastic, but the method remained apparently isolated and unique, with little or no connection to mainstream research or broader methodological issues.

In this book, Professor Cunningham takes Echo out of isolation and places it in a wider context, explicating it as a wider research perspective: an *approach*, not just a technique. He gives Echo a past by showing how it developed out of a particular research tradition, especially that of Kurt Lewin. He connects Echo to the present by bringing in other researchers who, in parallel, have developed similar approaches and who seem to share similar assumptions. In doing so, he is also creating a future for the approach, offering it to organizational researchers who want to study values and beliefs in a radically different way, one that puts the researcher in closer touch with the target group. In traditional research, the researchers dictate the questions to be answered, so the respondents can only echo the researchers' language and viewpoint. In the Echo approach, the researcher listens to the individuals of interest and learns their language and viewpoint.

THE INTELLECTUAL ORIGINS

There is a clear intellectual lineage from Max Wertheimer to Kurt Lewin to Alex Bavelas. Wertheimer was a Czech who trained in Berlin and emigrated to the United States in 1933. He was a founder of the original Gestalt school of psychology (not to be confused with the 1960s therapy that took the name). Gestalt psychologists emphasized the analysis of patterns rather than pieces, and their criterion was how people actually perceived and thought rather than how experts theorized about their perceptions and thoughts. In Berlin, Wertheimer's friends and colleagues included Albert Einstein and Kurt Lewin, both of whom also fled Germany for the United States. Kurt Lewin expanded the Gestalt approach and applied it to social psychology; he was arguably the founder of American social psychology. Bavelas was Lewin's graduate student at the University of Iowa (where he developed Echo) and the Massachusetts Institute of Technology, where he joined his mentor as a colleague. He is best known for his work, started at MIT, on the mathematics of communication networks.

Beyond these professional and personal relationships, there was a strong intellectual continuity, both explicit and implicit. Gestalt psychology was, among other things, a reaction to the rigid and simplistic imitation of the physical sciences and an argument for the unique characteristics of a truly psychological science, in which the "objects of research" were able to influence the investigation and were to be respected as such. Unlike rocks, molecules, or plants, humans can speak for themselves. One implication, which Bavelas expanded into Echo technique, was that the psychologist could listen. For the same reason, Bavelas was later critical of the increasing practice of deception in social psychology experiments, describing these as "the study of what people do when they think they are doing something else." Ideally, there should be direct and honest communication between experimenter and subject, because the consensual *meaning* of the events and behaviors is central.

Another well known principle of Gestalt psychology was insistence on seeing the parts only in the context of the whole, that is, an interest in "connectedness."[2] An example is connecting the praiseworthy behavior with who would praise it (rather than just listing behaviors and sources of reinforcement separately). Rich rather than impoverished data were the ideal.

Finally, in pursuing interesting questions, Gestalt researchers tended not to be restricted by established methods. Some of the most elegant and creative experiments of the early twentieth century were designed by Gestalt psychologists, broadly defined, who did not feel limited to what could actually be done. In an anecdote Bavelas liked to tell, Lewin was describing a design he was excited about to a more traditional colleague. The colleague protested that the data could not be analyzed by any existing statistical technique, to which Lewin replied, "That's the statisticians' problem."

THE ROLE OF THE "SUBJECT"

In contemporary research, the individuals who participate in our research are typically called *subjects* (in spite of APA efforts to change the term to *participants*), who quickly disappear into *N*. Danziger has traced this usage from the late nineteenth century, with some surprising findings.[3]

In the earliest psychology labs at Leipzig, the participants were often other researchers, and "the role of data source, or subject, was [in some cases] considered to be of higher or more important status than the role of experimenter."[4] They were called "observers" or even "co-workers." In contrast, researchers in Paris labs used the term *sujet* (subject). Until the eighteenth century, this term had referred to a corpse used for dissection, then it began to mean a living person who was the object of medical scrutiny. Thus, far from being socially and professionally equal, "subjects" were clearly differentiated from researchers, who were the experts in a "rigid and well-defined role and status structure."[5] When psychology came to North America, there was a brief period of terminological turbulence from which "subject" emerged as the common term of reference. Moreover, North American researchers also moved away from the study of a selected few individuals at a time and began to use terms such as *population* and, ultimately, *N*, because of their growing statistical orientation.

All these terms remove the researcher even further from any reciprocal relationship with the individuals in his or her study. The relationship is strictly hierarchical, with the researcher as the expert and the participant the mere provider of data that fit the researcher's framework. That is, the researcher sets the questions to be answered, and any responses are constrained within them. In the typical study of values or beliefs, for example, the instances of a particular value are defined by the researcher, who assumes as an expert (1) that the value is relevant to the group and (2) that these instances define it.

Seen in this context, the Echo approach is nonhierarchical. It is built on the assumption that the individuals we study have something more to tell us than the answers to our preset questions. It assumes that they are the experts on their world, on what they value and believe, and on how those values and beliefs are manifest in their lives. In an organizational setting, it is usually the case that those in higher positions want to study those they employ or supervise; but those being studied can still be given their voice, and the others can learn a great deal about their shared organization from them. In an even greater reversal of the usual roles, we asked students to set the agenda for evaluating their professors.[6] The usual teaching evaluation surveys are written by professors. We used Echo to generate one from students, reflecting their concerns, which were often quite different but completely reasonable. As a professor, I learned a great deal from this study, which has affected and, I hope, improved my teaching.

There is an irony in current social science practices that objectify the participants and limit their responses to alternatives predetermined by the researcher. These practices are usually viewed as the most "scientific" way to proceed, yet they are not at all what most natural scientists actually do. Biologists (our fellow life scientists) in particular have a strong observational tradition in which they learn from the life forms they study. If Darwin had not been open to learning from the creatures of the Galapagos, he would have simply confirmed existing dogma. Instead, their structures and behavior shaped his theory. Taking a humbler position and finding a way to listen to the individuals we are interested in can lead to entirely new knowledge.

Acknowledgments

My interest in the Echo approach grew out of mentorship and working relationships with Neely Gardner, one of the pioneers, who coined the term "organizational development" and later taught at the University of Southern California. He was a passionate Lewinian. The spirit of this work owes much to a continuing association with another mentor, Alex MacEachern, a positively and behaviorally inclined scientist who helped me understand that values were one of the most crucial elements in understanding organizational behavior. The ideas in the book also owe much to my working relationship with Eric Trist, the founding director of the Tavistock Institute of Human Relations in London, England, who worked in the United States and Canada during the last twenty years of his life.

The more direct stimulation for this book, of course, was from a former colleague, Alex Bavelas, and a project he and Janet were working on in developing a student-generated instrument for measuring faculty performance. They described an approach to research that had history and depth, with projects that illustrated insight and change. My interest grew in several projects that I have undertaken over the last twenty years with Jim MacGregor, a student of Alex and Janet. In the book, I have attempted to show how the principles of the Echo approach are a useful framework for illustrating the unique perspectives of people who are doing work in different areas.

As I wrote this book, several people read various drafts and offered some very useful comments. John Farquharson and Joe Lischerson were especially helpful. My several meetings with Janet Beavin Bavelas assisted in giving the book its direction and depth. My wife Donna was extremely helpful in providing support as always.

PART **I**

THE APPROACH

1

Introduction

The Echo method is a way of observing, quantifying, and describing the patterns of value and influence that are felt, verbally expressed, and often acted on in human society.

The Echo Project

One has only to look at a daily newspaper to find illustrations of problems in organizations related to human and organizational performance, stress, motivation, leadership, conflict, and change. These are popular topics on most store shelves and in many university classes. Clearly, there is no shortage of suggestions and opinions on these topics. It is a case of information overload rather than underload, yet people are feeling the need for ways to resolve these and other organizational problems.

Why are we so interested in such topics when there is so much information about them? In spite of the information on these topics, people are stressed and frustrated at work. Workload and interpersonal conflict in the workplace are top problems people talk about, while absenteeism, lost productivity, and work stoppages are common manifestations. Half the decisions we make in organizations fail, even though we have more information and expertise than ever before.[1]

THE ECHO METHOD

The Echo method, as originally developed by Alex Bavelas in the early 1940s, assists in understanding problems and issues that are part of a group or organization culture. If we can describe a problem or issue using the exact terminology and sentiments of the people who are describing it, we are like the eyes, ears, and words of the people in the setting. We are representing them as they are, as an exact "echo" of what they see, say, think, or feel.

Awareness is the first step to problem solving and change. The Echo approach is a way of observing, quantifying, and describing what people value and believe. It is a way of describing the patterns of value and influence that are felt, verbally expressed, and often acted upon in groups or organizations. When we understand these patterns, we have a greater comprehension of people, are able to better communicate with them, and are more effective in developing a program of change.

Underlying the approach are two basic assumptions of human nature. First, people exhibit, in verbal and nonverbal behavior, some preferences and aversions, some obligations and prohibitions, some hopes and fears, some satisfactions and disappointments. People are assumed to feel, express, and act on their concepts of good and bad.[2] In recognizing the importance of values, one only has to look at the underlying reason that many extremists groups hold true to their purpose, no matter what the odds. This is true of all human behavior. Whether you purchase a car or express dissatisfaction with the service that you receive, you are suggesting that you do or do not value something.

When we disagree with the extremist positions of others, we are illustrating our values and beliefs, just as when we take action for a cause. Every human action illustrates the influence of a person's values and beliefs. Beliefs and values are both assumptions that describe what people hold to be true. A value is an assumption of what ought to be, while a belief is an assumption of what is or will result. While a person may value participating in a cause to change the world, he or she may not believe that participation will actually improve the environment.

Every person lives within an organization that has unique values and beliefs that are registered in the artifacts, customs, nuances, feelings, interpretations, and manners of behaving. As such, when a person talks about problems or issues experienced, he or she is reflecting values and beliefs. People are assumed to interpret events on the basis of their values and beliefs. All problems are value judgments. If we ask a hundred people, "What are some of the most troublesome problems you experience?" and seventy of them answer, "We hate teachers who come late to class," we conclude that this is an important value.

The second assumption is that values and beliefs originate in different ways. In addition to measuring values, the Echo method measures the influences that people associate with values, or who might feel or value certain things over others, and why. Many values, for example, involve social obligations or prohibitions. People might say it is a good thing to work hard and a bad thing to cheat. When we ask who would approve of working hard and would disapprove of cheating, a person might identify a teacher or mentor. Parents might have disapproved of cheating. Another person might suggest that church and community leaders were instrumental in encouraging these values. These approving and disapproving figures are called *sources,* because they are seen as giving approval and disapproval for good and bad behaviors. Patterns of cause and effect are quite different from patterns of approval, but both are patterns of influence.

Understanding people—their values and beliefs—is key to solving organizational and societal problems. In any setting, people have expectations of what should happen and how others should behave. They have likes and dislikes, as well as keen interests and pet peeves. They can be frustrated and disappointed or satisfied and happy. If we understand these nuances, we are much more likely to develop useful ideas for solving complex problems.

What Are the Tools?

I became aware of the need for the Echo approach when I observed a group of researchers administering a questionnaire among a number of aboriginal people in the Northwest Territories. The questionnaire, which sought to understand problems among teenagers, was easy enough to respond to, but it failed to represent and understand the character of the people and their culture in their terms. It produced general findings that did not offer any insights into the problems of teenagers.

The Echo method encourages the use of a number of open-ended and closed-ended questions about values, among other things. The questions used are those that emerge after understanding why people value and believe in certain things, and how they act in specific situations. Among other things, organizational respondents are asked what things they do and do not approve of, like, or agree with. The exploratory questioning is used for developing instruments and tools, which are like cultural microscopes, able to describe issues, events, and problems within the terminology that is most sensitive to the participants.

One of the Echo tools is a method of questioning in which the wording of the questions is constructed to avoid direct queries about a person's own behavior or values. The indirect method of questioning asks a person to state the values of the group without inquiring about whether the individual agrees with them. The typical questions ask for examples of good or positive aspects and bad or negative aspects of a situation or behavior. A person is asked to name the activity that fulfilled these conditions, and to identify the source from which the praise would come.

The many and varied responses are classified into categories and defined using the words of those who were interviewed or observed. Often the responses are classified by members of the respondent group as well as by the researcher, so that an exact and undistorted picture of the culture can emerge.

The Lewinian Tradition of Research and Change

The Echo approach is part of a Lewinian research tradition. While it is a useful approach for generating ideas and developing research tools, it is best understood within a tradition of research that was concerned with experimentation and social action. Although Kurt Lewin's work extended to other areas—such as the concepts of field theory—it is the work on group dynamics and action research that has had the most far-reaching practical influence. He is known for his experiments as much as for his contribution to illustrating how theory might be appropriate to initiate action.

The basic character of a Lewinian tradition of science was the eternal attempt to build a "bridge between social theory and social action."[3] He was searching for theoretical concepts broad enough to make links to other ideas in other fields. Lewin's interest in the psychological study of social issues resulted in his paying much attention to building this bridge. His work describes the challenges confronting minority groups everywhere.[4] He pointed out that every individual had a base for life—a life space—and the group is one of the most important components. The group is all important; it is the source of social status and feelings of security.[5]

The action research approach is often associated with Kurt Lewin at the Child Welfare Research Station at the University of Iowa, and the Research Center for Group Dynamics at the Massachusetts Institute of Technology and the Commission on Community Interrelations.[6] The researchers associated with the Center carried out work in a number of program areas: group productivity, communication, social perception, intergroup relations, group membership and individual adjustment, and the training of leaders and the improvement of group functioning.[7] The chief methodology was that of group experimentation and field research. Their experiments on change were carried out both in the laboratory and in the field.

The primary premise of the Lewinian tradition of research was that various methods of science can be employed in the study of groups. The researchers sought to develop a field of group dynamics dedicated to advancing knowledge about the nature of groups, the laws of their development, and their interrelations with individuals, other groups, and larger institutions. They used techniques of experimental psychology, controlled observations of behavior, and methods of social-group work. Thus, Lewin envisioned a general theory of groups for such diverse matters as family life, work groups, classrooms, committees, military units, and the community. He saw such specific problems as leadership, status, communication, social norms, group atmosphere, and intergroup relations as part of the nature of group dynamics.[8]

The Origin of the Echo Approach

The Echo approach is directly connected with the work of Alex Bavelas in the early 1940s.[9] In one of the initial studies, the goal was to understand the culture and ideology of Mennonite and non-Mennonite schoolchildren and to compare Midwestern white children with children in ten American Indian communities.[10] In the study of Mennonite and non-Mennonite school children, the experimenters investigated the social processes in which these ideologies were formed. Certain categories emerged, defining approved and disapproved behavior. The experimenters sought to investigate the sources of approval and disapproval connected with different behaviors. That is, they were able to develop several categories to describe sources of approval and disapproval. They were also able to identify how the sources of approval and disapproval related to one another.[11]

The history of the Echo method bears a similarity to the early work of Osborn, who asked children what they should do to be called good or bad.[12] Osborn classified the children's responses into several kinds of good and bad behavior, such as obedience and truthfulness. His studies compared boys and girls between two classes from two different schools.

The Echo studies, undertaken from 1966 to 1969, were concerned with understanding how people in different cultures acted and behaved. *Project Echo* was an extensive set of experiments concerned with Jewish–Gentile relations; American schoolchildren; university students from the United States, Philippines, Kenya, and Thailand; subjects in a preadolescent girls' play group; and Boy Scout groups.[13] The learning from these studies illustrates how to investigate differing human behavior. More important, the studies provide the manager and researcher with tools to investigate new and complex settings or groups.

In this book, I have traced the core principles of the Echo approach to the work of Kurt Lewin and to the ideas of Max Wertheimer and his early seminars on problem solving and productive thinking. I have tried to illustrate the importance of these principles in the way we do social research today. The principles are a useful way to integrate many contributions to research and change from people in various fields.

BEING SENSITIVE TO VALUES AND BELIEFS IN RESEARCH AND CHANGE

One of the most basic assumptions of science—that rigorous quantitative analysis yields superior choices—has come under fire for organizational problem solving. Techniques of market research, forecasting, and statistical analysis are tools of the trade for managers and researchers. One conventional view is that we can develop insightful conclusions by comprehensive analysis. If a little is good, then more may be better. Techniques like regression analysis, analysis of variance, and time series analysis are encouraging a more rigorous and statistical social science.

Rational methods, in everything from statistical analysis to goal setting, may be one of the reasons many research studies in organizations do not develop insightful discoveries. Most of the events that govern organizational issues rarely lend themselves to rigorous quantitative analysis, as the forces directing most managers and researchers are fundamentally the same as for many people in our general population. They react to many of the same pressures from culture, values and beliefs, and actions that they have done in the past.

Although conventional science is often thought of as a method of intelligence for the discovery and contemplation of new knowledge, managers have expressed the need for reality-based research in making many decisions in organizations, such as selecting employees, choosing among a number of programs or alternatives, or determining why people are dissatisfied. This more practical research requires more sensitivity and understanding of interpersonal and social issues.

The road to a more insightful understanding of many of the problems and issues we face does not seem to rest on ingenious models, advanced procedures, mathematical and statistical schemes, precise quantitative techniques, or an adherence to strict scientific principles. Understanding seems to rely on informal process, such as experience, contacts between researchers and people in the field, and immersion in the research process. Several factors are important in the process: being creative in framing the research, collaborating with people who offer different perspectives, overcoming resistance to change, and implementing changes.

Some organizational issues—relating to values, beliefs, feelings, attitudes, and social issues—seem to lend themselves more naturally to methods of research and understanding that are both quantitative and qualitative.[14] They encourage measurements similar to those in the field of medicine, where a medical practitioner is able to measure the exact level of a change—such as the number of cubic centimeters of penicillin or mercury—and observe its effect in controlled conditions.

Good physicians, as well as good managers, do not rely only on strictly defined methods and tests in their work. A good physician is also a qualitative researcher at different stages of the diagnostic process. The physician makes observations on the basis of exploration that might, after further verification, lead to working hunches about a patient's ailments. At a certain stage the physician will adjust his or her observational techniques to the unique setting of those people who have special needs or who live under certain conditions, and try to make sense of a maze of interpretations, statistical facts, observations, values, and feelings of the patient.

In fact, physicians know that a person's lifestyle, attitudes, personality, values, or other soft measures induce most of the problems that an individual faces. Understanding a person's lifestyle and personality are an important part of a physician's job, especially if the physician wants to encourage a person to quit smoking or change a diet. Changing such behavior requires changing values and beliefs.

Most organizational problems are complicated and difficult to articulate, as they are overburdened with cultural and social issues. At times people do not know why they behave as they do, except they have always acted that way. If we probe deeper, we normally find that they have acted on their values, beliefs, and expectations.

HOW TO USE THE BOOK

This book is organized so that researchers, managers, and students can use Echo strategies to encourage insight in research. It is helpful for researchers who wish to carry out a more active research process in field settings. The research tools and ideas in this book are generally designed for assisting researchers to understand values, beliefs, and behaviors. The tools allow you to design culturally sensitive research to gain culturally sensitive information. The tools allow you to see the big picture, understand the special connections between certain parts over others, and appreciate complexity.

Chapters 2 and 3 of this book summarize the general process and principles underlying the Echo approach. The process outlines the general steps in carrying out the approach, and the principles highlight the unique scientific assumptions guiding Echo research.

The Echo approach is part of a Lewinian process of research and change, a process of immersion, research and action.[15]

Immersion

Echo interviews, question sessions, and observations are part of an inductive process of understanding what people value and believe in, and what and why they might want to change. Part II illustrates ways of immersing oneself in a project to gain an understanding of people, their needs, and fruitful research directions. This part of the book outlines specific strategies for using Echo procedures in developing instruments for research. It highlights an inductive process in which researchers are encouraged to mold their methods and hypotheses after first asking questions and gaining information on values, beliefs, and behaviors unique to the people in the setting.

Research

One of the assumptions of the Echo approach is that research experiences—social experiments and questionnaires—need to be linked to the needs of people in a setting if they are to be relevant and potentially insightful. An intuitive sorting process is one of the analytical methods used for conceptu-

alizing and reflecting the problems and issues that are identified from interviews, question sessions, and observations. The process encourages a great
deal of intuition in ordering the concepts and ideas into common categories.
It also allows for methods to verify the categories. The words and phrases in
any questionnaire are highly reliable because they reflect the nuances, feelings, and perceptions of those being studied. Field studies and experiments
are designed to be sensitive to the values and beliefs in that culture. The
hypotheses developed, the instruments used, and the methods of analysis
are part of a process of understanding an appropriate direction for change.
Part III illustrates how you can create research experiences—such as questionnaire design or experiments—that are linked to the needs of the setting.
Sorting and content analysis are two approaches dealt with in this section.

Action

The Echo process is useful in communicating new information, norms,
and behaviors in an overall process of change and learning. The process is
an important part of an overall action research that is designed to introduce
change initiatives that reflect and reliably represent the culture being studied. Part IV illustrates this and how you might use the Echo approach for
communicating, developing learning experiences, or introducing organizational changes.

One of the underlying messages of this book is that it is more effective and
relevant to design research that grows out of a process of immersion that seeks
to understand the needs of people in a setting. This book illustrates the steps to
this process from beginning to end, from the very first stage, when we are
beginning to think about problems and issues we want to study.

In this book, I am suggesting that the Echo approach is a useful framework for bridging the gap between various streams of applied researchers.
Many researchers, such as Neely Gardner, Eric Trist, and others, recognized the importance of the Lewinian style (and of the spirit of the Echo
approach) in their work. Others, such as Henri Mintzberg, Karl Weick,
Gareth Morgan, and Elizabeth Kübler-Ross, are leaders in provoking us to
do research in insightful ways. I have used some of these people as examples of some of the Echo principles I am highlighting. They would not
classify themselves as Echo researchers, as they are "captains" of their own
style. However, in my view, they have something in common with some of
these principles.

This book offers a broad definition of the Echo approach in illustrating its
use in research, learning, change, and action research. It is also not a static
view, but one which has evolved and changed over the last few decades.

2

An Overview of the Echo Approach

To proceed beyond the limitations of a given level of knowledge, the researcher, as a rule, has to break down methodological taboos which condemn as "unscientific" or "illogical" the very methods or concepts which later on prove to be basic for the next major progress.

Ernst Cassirer

Scarcely a year passed when I did not have a specific reason to acknowledge the help which Cassirer's views on the nature of science and research offered.

Kurt Lewin

The creativity and flexibility made possible by using the Echo approach is connected to the Lewinian tradition of research. Treating the Echo approach as a separate entity would be like trying to apply a mechanic's shop manual in fixing a car. As a result, we present the Echo approach as part of a Lewinian research process highlighted in the work Max Wertheimer, Kurt Lewin, Alex Bavelas, and their students.

A LEWINIAN RESEARCH PROCESS
USING THE ECHO APPROACH

The Echo approach is as useful for experimental researchers as it is for those who are more qualitative in their orientation. The technique aids people interested in examining individual and group behaviors in organizations, and in illustrating how values and beliefs are important to understanding problems related to motivation, stress, dissatisfaction, and change.

Normally, researchers or managers, on their own, begin a research process by outlining the steps and methods they will use. They depend almost entirely on measures that have been used in other situations. Clients or organizational members are asked to rate their satisfaction or agreement on a range of preselected questions relating to job security, pay and fringe benefits, personal growth and development, and degree of respect and fair treatment received from your boss. A rating of 1 would indicate extreme dissatisfaction, and a rating of 7 might signify extreme satisfaction. The justification for this procedure is based on two assumptions: first, that managers or researchers are technically competent in choosing the questions or methods that are important for measuring an organization's performance, and second, that the questions they ask are understood by those who will respond.

A research process using the Echo approach usually relies on the input of people in the group or organization who are interested in having a problem studied. The measures and methods are not predefined at the beginning. They grow out of Echo interviews, question sessions, and other procedures that are used to "echo" the issues or problems that people are experiencing. This chapter offers an overview of a Lewinian research process—immersion, research, and action—using the Echo approach.

Some people begin their research process by reviewing a list of articles and reports, while others seek help from experts or colleagues who have worked on similar problems. Most researchers agree that one of the most important steps is to try to be creative in the definition of the problem, concepts, and measures to guide a study. But how?

The Echo process begins with a process of immersing oneself to understand the values, beliefs, needs, and behaviors of people who are experiencing the problem or issue. This process is designed to gain commitment and encourage insight and creativity, while also developing a framework for the research. The initial steps include the following:

1. Setting the stage for collaborative research.
2. Designing a process that encourages insight and creativity.
3. Interviewing individuals with different types of questions.
4. Interviewing groups.
5. Combining interviews with observations.

Background Note 2.1: The Process of Research

The research process is very different from the structure of the report or article that results. In our textbooks we are told that a good report has a defined structure that illustrates, among other things, a problem and purpose, a review of the literature and conceptual framework, an explicit methodology, a presentation and discussion of the results, and conclusions and implications.

There is a discrepancy between the sequence of the research process described in a report and the way it occurs. The following science fiction story, told to me by a colleague, demonstrates this:

It is decades in the future, and the U.S. has been isolated from the outside world for 50 years, since a plague killed off everyone over the age of 10, and the surviving children sealed the borders. Unexpectedly, after 50 years, the child-government summoned a delegation from Europe for "consultation." The curious Europeans landed and were greeted by men and women in their fifties, dressed in cowboy suits, little-girl dresses, and other childish outfits. Without much diplomatic delay, these children got to the point: We asked you to come because, in all this time, there have been no babies. We have done everything our parents told us; we have looked under cabbage leaves, encouraged the storks, and watched birds and bees. And we have been good boys and girls. But there have been no babies.[1]

Trying to do insightful research by sequentially following the steps outlined in a research textbook is like trying to have babies based on what children were told about creation by their parents in this story.

Setting the Stage for Collaborative Research

While a researcher usually gains access to an organization through the person in charge, other important "gatekeepers" exist, including union executives, informal leaders, strong-willed individuals, and inflexible personalities. There are, therefore, multiple points of entry that require a continuous process of negotiation and coaxing.

The process of gaining access not only offers a chance to get people's commitment to the Echo research project, but is an opportunity to gain an understanding of the criteria on which the success of the research should be judged. It is also a chance for the researcher to develop a research design to respond to the joint interests of the researcher and organization's gatekeepers.

The commitment to gather information and study an issue is motivated by problems, issues, and/or feelings of immediate concern to individuals. This commitment can be very fragmented, as individuals may be motivated to solve different problems. A researcher's initial task is to find individuals, even those with opposing viewpoints, who are committed to work together in designing the study.

The commitment to research is most visibly illustrated in a research agreement, terms of reference, or contract that illustrates the needs of people who have unique interests. This can be demonstrated in a variety of ways. It can be proposed directly by members of a joint research team who hold formal positions in the organization. Or it can be secured indirectly through members of the team who are connected to other individuals and groups who, in turn, have direct access to the organization's managers. A well-defined agreement that includes a statement of needs, goals, justifications, and expectations leaves little question as to exactly what activities encourage collaboration between researchers and organizational participants.

Designing a Process That Encourages Insight and Creativity

How might we think creatively about a problem or issue we want to investigate? Thomas S. Kuhn, in his landmark book, *The Structure of Scientific Revolutions,* used the term "normal science" to describe the research that a scientific community acknowledges as providing the foundation for further research.[2] These achievements are catalogued in textbooks. A paradigm of inquiry emerges when these achievements are significant enough to attract a following of researchers to continue the research in a specific direction. The scientist collects an array of experiences and develops conceptual categories to aid observations. Thus, when something is observed, the researcher has certain expectations about what will happen, as the questions and operational definitions are tuned to collect data to fulfil these expectations. A paradigm of research normally illustrates the way researchers understand and interpret the world, based on the beliefs, expectations, values, and cognitive styles of the researchers.

Paradigms are systems of beliefs from which people think about things. In science, we once believed that the world was flat. Everyone believed that. The discovery that the world was round introduced an entirely different way of thinking about navigation and ocean travel. Imagine: traveling around the world. New paradigms sometimes emerge when scientists have gone astray and made mistakes. Chance, random occurrences, and arbitrariness have been much more consequential than methodological correctness in provoking new ways of thinking. A piece of equipment designed and constructed for the purpose of research may have failed to perform in the anticipated manner, revealing an anomaly that cannot, despite repeated effort, be aligned with professional expectations. Such anomalies subvert existing traditions of scientific practice, leading to questions or disruptions with planned methods. Such episodes are called "scientific revolutions," as they shatter traditions.

Trying to change a person's paradigm of thinking is as difficult as trying to encourage someone to change one's lifestyle. While logic dictates the desire to do things in a new way, old beliefs and habits encourage us to think the way we have traditionally thought. In setting up a research process so it is not limited by one's paradigm of research, Kuhn suggests that we might try to think beyond the established way of thinking, making observations based on experience, just like the lay person does. Kuhn's suggestions illustrate the need for Echo methods that encourage openness to new paradigms, data, and interpretations. Begin without an established paradigm, as lay people must. Instead of defining terms and classifying things at the early stage of research, immerse oneself in a problem through interviews, observations, and other methods of sensing. Question one's self-interest, beliefs, and expectations of what one might find. Take steps to rethink the way the problem is defined.

Interviewing Individuals with Different Types of Questions

One of the best ways to get more immersed in research is to carry out a number of exploratory interviews. The Echo approach is similar to many qualitative procedures in encouraging researchers to develop their concepts and measures—their paradigm of enquiry—after they have observed or interviewed people who are familiar with the problems or issues in a study. But the Echo technique is unique in using an assortment of open-ended questions encouraging people to define what they value. A person might be asked to identify features of the organization that he or she values and does not value. For example,

- What do you value most about what your group or organization does?
- Who might best represent these values?
- What do you value least in your organization?
- Who might represent these values?
- What do you find most satisfying about the way your boss treats you?
- What do you find most dissatisfying about the way your boss treats you?

Such questions are based on the assumption that a more accurate reflection of job satisfaction will emerge when focusing on understanding what people value. Usually, an Echo interview or question session includes a set of seven or eight pairs of questions asking respondents to identify things they value and do not value.[3] The set of Echo questions are developed from a checklist of areas:

1. Respondents (for example, a person like you, an employee).
2. Event (for example, a thing to happen, a thing to do).
3. Valuation of the event (for example, good or bad, like or not like, ought or ought not).
4. Reinforcement or agency (for example, approve or disapprove, praise or blame, cause or prevent).
5. Source (reinforce or agent; for example, parents, myself, a good job, bad luck).
6. Additional context (for example, during a strike or during the political debate).

This checklist is described more fully in Chapter 6.

An abbreviated set of questions can be used in some exploratory studies for defining the concepts and measures in developing a job-satisfaction questionnaire.

- What do you generally find positive about working here?
- What might you find less positive or negative?
- Think of a time when you felt exceptionally positive about working here. Describe this situation. Why did you feel this way?
- Think of a time when you felt exceptionally negative about working here. Describe this situation. Why did you feel this way?
- What ideas or changes might help in improving this situation?
- What ideas or changes might not improve this situation?

Background Note 2.2: Using Echo Questions

In studying job satisfaction, the Echo approach offers a variety of sampling devices—interviews, surveys, Echo sessions, observation—in defining what people do or do not value. In an Echo interview, some of the questions might be as follows:

- What do you like about your work?
- What don't you like?
- What are things that your supervisor might do that you find satisfying?
- What are things that your supervisor might do that you would find dissatisfying?
- What do you find satisfying about this organization?
- What do you find dissatisfying about this organization?
- What do you find most satisfying about how your boss treats you?
- What do you find most dissatisfying about the way your boss treats you?
- Who in this organization do you find most satisfying to work with? Why?
- Who in this organization do you find least satisfying to work with? Why?

In some cases it is appropriate to ask questions that are directly related to developing an instrument or interview schedule. For example, after asking the questions listed, the researcher can ask questions like the following: What questions or items do you think we should ask to better understand this issue? What methods are more useful in understanding this issue?

The Sample of People Representing the Culture

The sampling procedure can allow for larger probability samples if the objective is to use the Echo interviews to systematically sample a culture. If the objective is exploratory in identifying items for a questionnaire, a nonprobability sample includes people who are representative of the culture. In such cases, seven to fifteen Echo respondents or interviews are appropriate.

The research for the Echo Project suggested that data from subsamples of fifteen or twenty people can accurately reflect the values and beliefs of a larger sample of one hundred or two hundred people. The samples in the Echo Project varied from as few as five people to as many as two hundred, where larger samples were used in less homogeneous groups.

A general principle is to select individuals or groups to represent the various perspectives defining an issue or problem being researched. This usually means sampling those people who are aware of the problem and have some feelings (positive or negative) about it. For assessing satisfaction of employees, the goal is to define a sample representing the total population of employees in the organization by recognizing people who were highly dissatisfied and satisfied. If the concern is absenteeism, it is sensible to sample those employees who have some record of absenteeism, as well as those who do not. The saturation principle suggests that after a certain number of interviews a researcher might not gain any more new information by additional interviews.

Interviewing Groups

Generally, Echo question sessions offer a view of the group culture as opposed to what people value and believe in as individuals. People act and speak differently in groups than they do when they are questioned individually. The sessions are also useful in focusing change. Echo question sessions are organized to include as many as ten people, where participants are encouraged to respond both individually and as a group. Echo questions can be presented on notecards or from instructions that are read aloud to respondents.

Echo question sessions and interviews are very useful for gaining an understanding of the concepts and measures to be used in developing questionnaires, goal statements, and skill requirements, and are especially relevant when group input, ideas, and commitment are needed.

Combining Interviews and Observations

Observations offer another viewpoint of an organization's culture. The observer is encouraged to take on, to some extent, the role of a member of the group and participate in its functioning. The observer is asked to experience the problem practically and personally. Observations are much more than one to three-hour interviews where both subject and researcher act in unnatural ways. This is an opportunity to see the conflicts and miscommunications that might never have been recognized by asking questions in an interview. In one study of a nuclear power plant, we had the opportunity to observe the shutdown of a unit of the plant as the operators worked to deal with many of the activities for assuring safety. We observed operators responding in a crisis-like manner to brainstorm reasons for gas leakage and possible ways to resolve them. We gained an important perspective on the problems they faced and how they relied on others when decisions were nonroutine. "Being there" certainly offered details that enhanced our ability to understand the way they made decisions.

In some cases it may be difficult to observe such exceptional events, as it is difficult to know when and where that disaster will occur. Or decision makers may be unwilling to allow observers to see their behavior in action. In such cases, Echo interviews and observations together provide a more total picture of the problems experienced.

RESEARCH

The research experience, an act of generating concepts and data to understand a problem or process, is propelled by the process of immersion that went before it. While concepts such as age, gender, and number of children are relatively easy to understand and measure, others, such as power, interest, motivation, and commitment, require an understanding of how people use them in a unique context.

Researchers are sometimes hard pressed to define concepts that are useful for understanding people in a group or organizational culture. In the same way, organizational participants are sometimes so close to the tasks that they perform on a daily basis, so enmeshed in the struggle for survival, that they have difficulty understanding how the specific concepts in their work have any relationship to generalized terms or ideas.

Using the Echo approach, the act of conceptualizing is an act of seeing the forest for the trees, visioning or seeing the long-range view, or understanding how the parts are connected to the whole. More important, it is a process of developing and operationalizing categories, concepts, and measures in surveys and experiments. Certain steps that increase the validity of the conceptualizing process include the following:

1. Using the Echo sorting and content analysis procedure in focusing research.
2. Developing surveys that echo an issue.
3. Using the Echo approach in developing experiments.

Using the Echo Sorting and Content Analysis Procedure in Focusing Research

The mass of data generated from interviews, Echo question sessions, observations, and other sources—consisting of personal statements of feelings and frustrations, examples of problems and incidents, and criteria—are the source of ideas, concepts, or ways to further our understanding. But such raw data are messy and unpatterned, without any apparent order, like a messy building site where the building materials and supplies are organized randomly around the construction area. Without some plan it would be difficult to develop a concept of the type of building that is going to be constructed.

The initial steps in developing categories, concepts, or measures consist of summarizing or transcribing the raw data or information and developing some system to reference and store the data. Copies of the interviews, Echo session responses, and observation notes can be made, and researchers might first mark each unique concept with a colored marker. An interviewer's notes can be recorded on notecards so that each card represents a concept. In some cases, the concept cards are simply separate strips of paper that represent the array of different ideas that are cut out of the interview transcripts.

The way that the statements are transcribed onto cards should reflect, as closely as possible, the manners and nuances of the people interviewed. A literal transcription is desired, making sure not to lose the context for the response. The statements are the basis for forming the concepts defining the issue or problem to be studied.

A *sorting procedure* can be used in ordering and categorizing interview statements to develop more general concept areas or categories. Sorting procedures can be used for categorizing almost any type of organizational data, ranging from tidbits of gossip to hard scientific data and statistical information. In some cases, ideas from group members are summarized and then arranged for sorting. The goal is to build a conceptual framework to focus further research and experimentation. In my view, one of the most important aspects of the Echo approach is to encourage people in the population of interest to carry out the sorting. If experts develop their own categories without the input of these people, much has been lost.

A *content analysis procedure* can be used to illustrate the frequency or importance of categories developed from sorting. The concepts used for content analysis are more relevant when they emerge so that they echo the values and interpretations of the people being researched. Content analysis is unlike statistical analysis where the researcher receives a pile of responses, ships them off to a key puncher, categorizes the variables on the basis of their statistical relationship, and massages the data by eliminating items that do not fit or vary from the norm. Content analysis is a way of ordering and sorting items or statements to represent a collective view of the issue or problem.

Developing Surveys That "Echo" an Issue

A survey that is developed from the Echo technique presents a list of values that were identified in the initial interviews, Echo question sessions, or observations. For example, organizational members identified a number of values related to their satisfaction with their supervisor, including trust, responding to concerns, and favoritism. The survey that was developed (Figure 2.1) illustrated these values and gave supervisors confidential feedback from their team members.[4] The wording of some of the questions might appear unclear to the outside observer, but the meaning is perfectly clear to the people who identified them. Echo questionnaires are developed for each group culture and the measures reflect the values they hold. For this reason, they are less useful for other settings.

Figure 2.1
Sample Echo Survey

1	2	3	4	5	6
Strongly Disagree	Disagree	Mildly Disagree	Mildly Agree	Agree	Strongly Agree

1. ____ My supervisor regularly shares information with me.

2. ____ My supervisor would be more likely to let me know when I've made a mistake than to tell me when I've done a good job.

3. ____ My supervisor trusts me to "do the job."

4. ____ When necessary, everyone on my team "pulls together" to get the work done.

5. ____ My supervisor does not respond quickly to my concerns.

6. ____ I feel my supervisor "plays favorites," which creates distrust among team members.

Using the Echo Approach in Developing Experiments

Experiments for understanding behavior and changing people are a vital step in helping change agents understand how to change an organization or group culture. They can reveal the principles for bringing about change. For example, when we use an experiment to understand the values and habits of a group of people—toward technology or a new idea or way of working—we may discover more effective ways of introducing change.

Experiments play a vital part in an overall Lewinian reiterative process of planning, experimenting, and evaluating. They assist in developing theoretical principles as much as they aid the process of change.

ACTION

The Echo approach and its principles are aimed at improving practice. Action is encouraged in several ways:

1. Using Echo principles in communicating.
2. Linking the Echo approach to the process of learning and change.
3. Linking the Echo approach to the process of action research.

Using Echo Principles in Communicating

All insights and discoveries are intermixed with a process of communicating. The content describes the important elements, while the medium is the way it is communicated. Like an orchestra playing off tune, the insights of any research may be incompatible with those who are listening to the message. The process of communication is affected by a range of issues concerned with how the insights are written, the language used, and the style of reporting.

Echo principles are easily applied in communicating and reporting. They are useful in styling a report to illustrate the values of the people in an organizational culture. The most effective reports are those that illustrate the words, nuances, and values of the people being studied. As such, steps are taken to use quotes and phrases to illustrate various perspectives on what people value and how they act.

Linking the Echo Approach to the Process of Learning and Change

Even if we already knew the answers, it is preferable to create a situation where participants can find their own answers in their own unique ways. The Lewinian style of learning and teaching is an illustration of how change occurs through involving people and giving them responsibility for their own learning, by focusing on real and relevant problems, and by questioning rather than prescribing. Learning is not one specific part of a sequence that proceeds after immersing oneself in the situation and carrying out research. The learning is ongoing and part of every step.

The Lewinian process challenges the assumption that we must have a set curriculum and defined set of skills to teach what is necessary for life. The gestalt tradition, illustrated through the works of Max Wertheimer and Kurt Lewin, stressed an attitude toward learning, a mental set, or a problem-solving orientation. This attitude did not merely stress specific subject matter, but focused on methods of teaching that were inductive and relevant to the learning needs and problems of people.

Linking the Echo Approach to the Process of Action Research

The Echo approach is extremely useful in providing data and information that can steer an action research process of change, because researchers and organizational members are involved in the definition of the research and have the opportunity to use their creativity in developing an intervention that responds to their values, beliefs, ideas, and interests.

Kurt Lewin introduced the term "action research" in 1946 to denote an approach to research combining theory building with research on practical problems, where there is a collaborative relationship between the social scientist and the client.[5] Action research aims to "contribute both to the practical concerns of people in an immediate problematic situation and to the goals of social science by joint collaboration within a mutually acceptable ethical framework."[6] As such, action research is a type of applied social research differing from other varieties in the immediacy of the researcher's involvement in the action process. It is very appropriate for implementing ideas that are generated from an Echo approach to gathering data.

THE LOGIC UNDERLYING THIS
LEWINIAN RESEARCH APPROACH

In his classic article on the transition from Aristotelian to a Galileian mode of thought, Kurt Lewin proposed answers to several questions:[7] Is it possible to determine general laws in a social science and develop precise experiments to reveal emotional life? Is it possible to study and explain inner emotional processes in the same kind of quantitative and objective way that physics does? He illustrated that it was indeed possible to be more scientific in studying single cases in the field. He based this conclusion on his perception that a fundamental change had taken place in scientific thinking since Galileo made his crucial break with Aristotle.

The decisive revolution in scientific methods was clearly expressed as early as Galileo's classic investigation of the law of falling bodies. Rather than investigating a free-falling object moving downward, he made a penetrating evaluation of situational factors, including the vertical and horizontal movements and the slope of the plain. Galileo's evaluation was as concerned about the environmental conditions as it was about the object under investigation, a change in a paradigm of inquiry.[8]

The scientific principles growing out of Galeliean science suggest that a single object or case needs to be understood in its totality, in its relationship to itself and its environment. The case is described in phenotypic (external appearance) and genotypical (genetic-conditional appearance) terms, where the frequency of a case occurrence is less important than the exact description of all the forces operating in and upon it at a given time. In predicting, the wholeness or total psychological field or life space at a given time is more important than deriving laws through observing a large number of cases.[9] In my view, this gives rise to a set of Echo principles for studying single cases in field settings.

Background Note 2.3: Aristotle's Science

The Greek philosopher Aristotle was able to offer some convincing arguments that the world was really a round sphere rather than a flat plate. His first argument was based on the fact that eclipses of the moon were caused by the earth coming between the sun and the moon, and the earth's shadow on the moon was always round, which would be true only if the earth was spherical. A flat earth would have produced a more elongated and spherical shadow. Aristotle's second argument came from his knowledge, from Greek travelers, that the North Star appeared lower in the sky when viewed in the south than in the north. The Greeks also had a third argument: One sees the sails of oncoming ships coming over the horizon before seeing the hulls.[10]

To many, Aristotle was a scientist who used something of a scientific set of principles of developing explanations for what he saw and then confirming these explanations with other evidence. The most elaborate experiments and equations of science are all focused on illustrating evidence to support theories, such as the world is round, the universe is infinite, or the earth's ozone layers are depleting. Aristotle gathered his evidence from nature, but he also relied on thought, authority, and reason. He drew his explanations for what he observed.

An "Aristotelian science" is based on the idea that the universe is harmonious and explainable with precise calculations and hypotheses. This was once the conventional view of classical physics, where prediction and repeated observations of a number or cases were the basis for establishing laws of science. The environment plays a part only insofar as it may give rise to "disturbances" that modify the nature of the object concerned. The vectors that affect an object's movements are completely determined by the object and not the environment.

A Dynamic Science

As James Glick writes, "Where chaos begins, classical science stops."[11] Being scientifically rigorous in a dynamically changing environment has challenged the physical scientist as much as it has the social scientist in organizations. The physicist can develop a linear equation to express the amount of energy you need to accelerate a hockey puck without friction or any other environmental influence. With friction, the relationship gets complicated, because the amount of energy depends on how fast the puck is already moving. "Nonlinearity means that the act of playing the game has a way of changing the rules."[12]

Millions of interrelated components in society exhibit a dynamic that is nonlinear. Any physical object is made up of a number of components, each of which encounters a number of forces that move in different directions. Components adjust and seek balance in the light of change. A hard-hit baseball can fly over the fence during the early part of the ballgame, but may be an easy catch later during the night because of the resistance from wind and the damp night air.

Any range of environmental events can provoke a point of crisis or chaos. The *theory of chaos* began in the 1960s, when it was realized that simple mathematical equations could model systems as violent as waterfalls and weather formations. The term "sensitive dependence on initial conditions" has been used to describe how tiny differences in input can easily become major differences in output. This is sometimes described metaphorically as the "butterfly effect," the idea that a butterfly's movements in some far-off Eastern country could transform the weather systems next month in London.

The forces in a social and organizational science are as real and fundamental as those that explain the laws of gravity in the physical domain.[13] Social organizations have the same dependence on initial conditions and a seemingly incomprehensible or chaotic chain of events. Organizational morale and job satisfaction may be related to a sensitive dependence on the trust of a leader or the expectation of certain promised changes. An individual's health is related to initial conditions like genetics and family background, and the influence of personality, job setting, and lifestyle. Thus, in order to understand something fully, it is important to observe its dynamic relationships as it is being influenced and changed by the environment around it. In my view, the Echo approach encourages an understanding of these dynamic relationships.

3

Principles Underlying the Echo Approach

To echo: The personification of a phenomenon or its cause; Any repetition, as of the style, sentiments, etc., of another person.

Webster's Dictionary

The following words, from Kurt Lewin, describe a challenging goal. Lewin and the group of students and scientists who worked with him were involved in a range of laboratory and field experiments, field studies, and action research experiences. The rich research tradition in which they pursued this goal is illustrated in the principles underlying the Echo approach.

Social scientists are presented with a formidable challenge. They find themselves in the midst of a rich and vast land full of strange happenings. People are killing themselves. Children are playing. A child is learning how to speak. A person who, having fallen in love, is caught in an unhappy situation and is not willing or able to find a way out. There is a mystical state, where the will of one person seems to govern another person. There is the reaching out for higher and more difficult goals, loyalty to a group, dreaming, planning, exploring the world. The social sciences are like an immense continent, full of fascination and power and full of stretches of land where no one ever has set foot.

Social scientists are out to conquer this continent, to find out where its treasures are hidden, to investigate its danger spots, to master its vast forces, and to utilize its energies.

How can one reach this goal?[1]

UNDERLYING PRINCIPLES

Lewin and the people surrounding him were committed to improving the inner value of the work and lives that people experienced. The goal was to better understand the nature of groups, their culture, and the psychological and social forces within them. Of particular importance was a spirit of exploration and adventure for opening up new paths for challenging conventional research methods. As such, the most important contributions were methodological rather than factual. In particular, the researchers were renowned in developing techniques of observation, carrying out group research in a laboratory, and using action research in field work.[2]

This chapter presents a list of principles that I have compiled based on my review of this research, my experience working with some of these people, and conversations with colleagues. These principles encourage researchers to approach issues and subjects with sensitivity, suspending preconceived ideas and letting the framework emerge after immersing themselves in the setting. They encourage us to use our experiences in articulating concepts and ideas to echo the culture of the people we are studying.

Principle 1

Begin by understanding the perspective and needs of the people who are experiencing the issues we are interested in learning about. They are the experts.

In one research project I observed, the consultants and academic researchers were assigned the task of trying to understand why people were so stressed and dissatisfied with their jobs. They designed a very sophisticated questionnaire based on a range of measures that had been used in previous studies. This, they reasoned, could be an opportunity to illustrate the linkage between two conventional theories of why people in First Nations communities were most susceptible to suicides and alcohol abuse, a way of adding to the literature.

The results of the questionnaire were difficult to interpret, because the measures did not seem to offer any insight into what might be wrong or how things might be improved. Response rates were low, participants found several measures difficult to interpret, and the framework used to communicate the results did not seem relevant. As a result, the report's recommendations did not capture a great deal of enthusiasm.

In other words, the research process offered no formula for understanding this culture. The researchers asked standardized questions that had been used elsewhere, questions that were not sensitive to the needs of the people being researched. They failed to design a research instrument and process that was sensitive to the cultural needs of the people.

Background Note 3.1: The Lewinian Tradition

The principles underlying the Echo approach span four generations of researchers, beginning after World War I at the Psychological Institute at the old Imperial Palace in Berlin. Despite the precarious economic and political times after World War I, it was an exciting period for people at the institute. Max Wertheimer and Wolfgang Köhler were breaking new ground in the formulation of Gestalt theory, which challenged a traditional idea that a phenomenon consists of aggregates of distinct parts. The Gestaltists argued that perceptions could and should be considered as organized wholes, things that are different from merely sums of their parts. The solidarity of a brick wall was something more than the sum of the bricks in it, taking on an added characteristic or quality with its distinct structure.[3]

Another generation of research is associated with Kurt Lewin, who left the Psychological Institute to come to the United States in 1933. In 1935, at the University of Iowa, he was joined by students who shared a practical interest in working on social issues. As the group of students grew, the informal relationship that had been part of life at the Berlin Psychological Institute was re-created.

The Echo approach was created by one of Lewin's students, Alex Bavelas, who developed it for a study of Mennonite children. It was often used by Bavelas as he worked with Lewin in carrying out some of the classical experiments on change and group decision making. After the technique was developed in the early 1940s, several researchers refined it and others have used it actively in carrying out their work.[4]

Another generation of Lewinian-like researchers with an Echo perspective includes Bavelas's students at MIT, Stanford, and the University of Victoria, spanning a long period from Harold Leavitt to Janet Beavin Bavelas to James MacGregor. In many cases, their students are carrying on some of the same traditions in a fifth generation.

The real experts in most organizations are the participants being researched, because they have real experiences. They can provide unique insight into how to approach a study, the measures used, or hypotheses that might be tested. The uniqueness of the Echo approach is that it allows respondents to define what should be researched. It switches the usual way in which questions are asked and answered. Respondents can identify the issues, problems, and ideas that are most relevant.

Collaborative research was the hallmark of many of the field and action-research studies carried out by Kurt Lewin and the people associated with him. One such experience involved Lewin and colleagues in an eight-year partnership at Harwood Manufacturing Corporation in a rural community in Virginia. During this collaboration, Alex Bavelas started a program of research to discover the effect of giving employees greater control over their output and an opportunity to participate in setting goals.[5] Bavelas attempted to change the informal norms of work groups regarding productivity in a garment factory.[6] The experimental group members were invited to discuss the problem of production standards and were encouraged to make their own decisions. The control groups were not required to come up with a group decision about a solution. The results illustrated that the groups that participated in decision making were more productive.

The collaborative theme in research can also be connected to some of the early investigations of problems related to wartime shortages and the use of group decisions as a way of encouraging people to eat foods that they did not normally eat but that were nutritious and in more plentiful supply.[7]

Collaborative research does not mean that people should be encouraged to be needlessly involved in the sharing of their interpretations even when they are not relevant. This collaboration assumes that members have the technical expertise and personal maturity to provide input in a constructive manner. Such research is more valuable for certain projects, possibly where the issues are more complex. Such issues require more creativity, diverse perspectives, intuition, and energy. Simpler issues usually do not require diverse viewpoints or teams, and collaboration might even be dysfunctional. There is nothing more insulting than participating in research just for the sake of being involved.

Collaboration encourages openness and the free flow of ideas. Lewin's problem solving illustrated a process of democratic informality. Each new idea or problem seemed to arouse him to think at many different levels continuously for hours, or to struggle with different interpretations. He shared his ideas immediately, even if they were half-formed, eager for comments and reactions while the original idea was still being developed.[8] A collaborative research paradigm that encourages involvement and commitment in research is one of the surest ways of developing a process for gaining the expertise of others.

Principle 2

Understanding values and beliefs is one of the best ways to understand why people behave the way they do.

Whether an individual joins a religious group or seeks to quit a job during the middle part of his or her career, the surest explanation for this behavior is what the person values. The Echo approach attempts to measure values using a range of interview methods, questionnaires, and observational methods. It seeks to help understand what people value, using a participant's words and phrases in forming concepts, questions, measures, and methods of communicating.

Suppose we wanted to evaluate student perceptions of a faculty member's teaching. Instead of imposing our questions or measures of teaching performance, we might ask students what they care about and wish to evaluate in faculty performance. Other measures might deal with faculty concerns, and still others could seek the input of peers or other groups. "If we wish to ask students to tell us what they think of teaching performance, then we will have to ask questions that are meaningful to the student."[9] We will have to know what they want to say and value.

The principle of allowing people to define what is being researched and what they value is based on a fundamental assumption that they may have significantly different views of the world and ways of talking about the same things. For example, a university professor and a student have different points of view about what is important in teaching. A lecturer who appears thorough, scholarly, and even witty to a colleague may appear arrogant, unable to answer complex questions, and insensitive to students. What a faculty member perceives as thorough may be seen as dull and irrelevant to students.[10]

The most valid frameworks or theories of human behavior reflect values, beliefs, attitudes, and expectations. Some of these measures may only be partially linked to conventional theories or ideas, but they are more directly relevant to the concepts and values that guide how people act. If we want to approach the question of what students think makes a good professor, then we have to begin to see the world through their eyes. This discourages the tendency to use the instruments of others or to develop a questionnaire by "patching" together a number of measures used in other studies. In a pure form, an Echo researcher allows his or her theory to develop inductively, based on an understanding of what people value, believe in, and experience.[11] When using respondents' input in the process of developing measures, the researcher's role changes to one of understanding and communicating rather than prescribing and compiling.

To value something means primarily to cherish, prize, esteem, and hold it dear. It is an act of passing judgment upon the nature and amount of something's value in comparison with something else. The differences in what people value are subtle and are illustrated in the importance attached to science, work, religion, family, and friendship. "To some the value of science may be military; it may be an instrument in strengthening means of offense or defense; it may be technological, a tool for engineering; or it may be commercial—an aid in the successful conduct of business; under other conditions, its worth may be philanthropic—the service it renders in relieving human suffering; or again it may be quite conventional—of value in establishing one's status as an 'educated person.'"[12]

Oscar Wilde famously observed that cynics (others have said scientists and economists) knew the price of everything but the value of nothing. The most evident paradox is that things that are extremely valuable—life-saving water and food—sell for next to nothing, although other things—diamonds and gold—sell for a fortune.

People illustrate their values through their preferences and aversions, obligations and prohibitions, hopes and fears, and satisfactions and dissatisfactions. Values are ways that people describe their beliefs and expectations, what they want or do not want. "To value means primarily to prize, to esteem; but secondarily it means to apprize, to estimate."[13] In the act of cherishing something, we are also making a judgment on the value of certain objects in relationship to others. Some values are intrinsic, are ends in themselves, and are not the object of comparison and judgment. They are essential, critical, or thought to be invaluable. Other values are less fundamental, as when we are presented with circumstances where we make judgments, choose, and establish an order of preference where things are judged in relationship to a third thing, or some other end. These are means or instrumental values.

Take, for example, a person who thoroughly enjoys conversing with a friend at one time, hearing a symphony at another, and eating meals at another. Each of these is an intrinsic value that occupies a space in life and serves its own end that cannot be substituted. There is no question of comparative value. However, there may arise a circumstance in which these ends compete or are in conflict. When this occurs, these values are no longer ends in themselves, but they become a means to realize something else. If a person has just eaten and the opportunity to hear classic music is a rarity, he or she will probably prefer music to eating. In the given situation, music is given a greater preference. In the abstract, apart from the needs of the situation in which a choice has to be made, the degree or order of the value is not important.[14]

While some values are ends in themselves (terminal), others are means to other values (instrumental).[15] Good things to do might be called instrumental values, while good things to happen might be called terminal values. Instrumental values relate to other criteria or orders of preference. For example, employee-related instrumental values might relate to pleasant personal interaction, interest and motivation, or helpfulness and teamwork. Employer-related values could describe an employee's ability to learn, aptitudes, attendance and promptness, dependability, and good work habits. These values are interpreted in relationship to an employee's or employer's unique criteria or preferences. Such evidence suggests that the life space or job space of employees is different from that of employers.[16]

Participation may be implemented in an organization because participants value involvement and group decision making. Such a value has intrinsic worth and is not open to discussion, rarely open to criticism, and seldom open to change. Beliefs have a similar quality, in that they are also an assumption about what we accept as true and usually take for granted. Participation may be valued as something important to do, although we may not believe that it will not work with a particular group of people. Beliefs about participation may become emotionally charged when the person's lack of participation challenges our values.

We can learn about values by comparing what people say about what they like and dislike, what they find desirable and less desirable, and what they think is good or bad to do. Ask people to give some examples of people they like and do not like. Ask them to think of music they like and dislike. Then ask them to describe the characteristics of such people and music. Such comparisons force people to articulate their values about the type of people and music they like.

When we make judgments, we are likely to describe and react to extreme positions, especially negative ones, whether we are discussing people, music, events, feelings, or roles. Allowing people to make comparisons between positive and negative feelings encourages them to conceptualize and formulate their values. When individuals make judgements by seeing both extreme positions, they have the opportunity to define how they feel in reference to both positive and negative values.

People can more easily articulate their values if they are encouraged to compare something they desire with things they do not want. Such an understanding encourages people to compare something with its polar opposite. Some psychologists have used this principle to describe how people make observations or understand their world.[17] In other words, we form our constructs of how we see things by the comparisons we make on an everyday basis. Other psychologists have used this principle in developing scales that study values, as in the good–bad ratings of the Semantic Differential Scale.[18]

Although oppositeness can be a prominent feature in some questioning, free-response questions are encouraged in areas where people are asked for their attitudes, opinions, or examples of behaviors.[19] These are areas where people might be asked for opinions about the future or events that might affect them.

Principle 3

Recognize the range of information that individuals can offer: behaviors, opinions and attitudes, suggestions and goals, and values and beliefs.

Gareth Morgan's insightful book, *Images of Organization*, suggests that all our interpretations of organizations are really metaphors.[20] He presents an old Indian tale of six blind people and an elephant. The first person feels the tusk and suggests the animal is like a spear, while the second person, on feeling the elephant's side, proclaims it to be like a wall. The third person, who feels the leg, thinks it is like a tree, while the fourth person describes the elephant's trunk as a snake. Feeling the elephant's ear, the fifth person thinks it is like a fan, and the sixth, grabbing the tail, says it is much like a rope. If the elephant was set in motion, these understandings would be even more complicated. The man clinging to the leg would experience an elliptical forward motion and the man holding the tail would be whipped about in the air. The others would be jerked and jolted, and splashed and splattered with water and manure. Each person has a unique metaphor for describing the elephant.

As with the blind people, our actual experiences with organizations and life are unique interpretations or metaphors. Getting information on different perspectives is like getting the six blind people together to develop a collective picture of the elephant. All any person can do is tell us what an organization is like for him or her, or to give us a metaphor to describe it. Understanding is enhanced not by the most appropriate metaphor, but in using different metaphors to offer unique interpretations, as any given situation can be seen from various perspectives.

Ask a person what he or she feels and thinks and you will probably get many ideas, opinions, feelings, and self-perceptions. Ask a number of managers the following question: "What are the skills and strategies you use for motivating people?" In many cases, they may tell you that they allow people to participate, that they seek to empower them, and that they listen to their employees. If you recorded these statements, would you have an accurate statement of what these people value and do? Hardly.

When I asked a manager the principles he used in managing, he responded by saying that he was generally a participative manager, that he sought input from his employees, and that he had an open-door policy to encourage participation. His employees had a different story. Most people tell us what they want us to hear in revealing their idealized self-image. Their comments are also limited by their personal biases. When I asked this manager a different set of questions, based on the critical incident technique, I was able to gain some insightful information on how he managed and the principles he used. I asked him to identify examples of incidents that illustrated how he managed, dealt with conflict, and so forth.

Figure 3.1
Information Iceberg

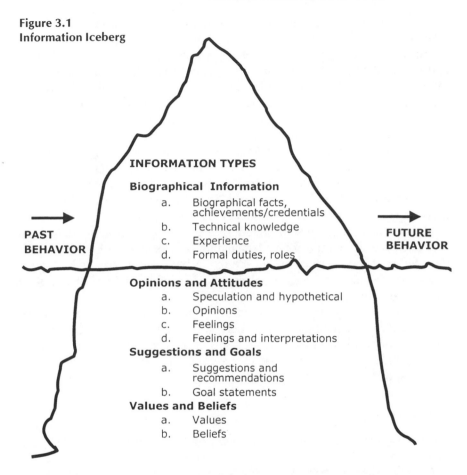

INFORMATION TYPES

Biographical Information

    a.   Biographical facts, achievements/credentials

    b.   Technical knowledge

    c.   Experience

    d.   Formal duties, roles

Opinions and Attitudes

    a.   Speculation and hypothetical

    b.   Opinions

    c.   Feelings

    d.   Feelings and interpretations

Suggestions and Goals

    a.   Suggestions and recommendations

    b.   Goal statements

Values and Beliefs

    a.   Values

    b.   Beliefs

PAST BEHAVIOR

FUTURE BEHAVIOR

There are various types of information—both formal and informal or identifiable and unexposed—in any setting. Each represents a different metaphor to describe that setting.

Figure 3.1 illustrates a picture of the "information iceberg" to display the various types of information we might gather. Like polar icebergs in the North Atlantic, the top and most exposed parts of the information iceberg represent the smallest part of the total mass of information. Formal documents and definable records represent only about 10 percent of the possible information we might gather, while the remaining 90 percent is unexposed and hidden from view.

The iceberg illustrates a range of metaphors that might be used to describe any person or setting. The top part of the information iceberg represents what is easily identifiable and definable: the organization's reports, budgets, mandate, mission, and so forth. It describes the biographical facts, technical knowledge, and descriptions of actual experiences. Biographical data can describe age, marital status, and position. Achievement questions might refer to grade point average, publications, honors, and achievements.[21] The information at the top part of the iceberg is very reliable, but may only be a partial perspective on future behaviors. The understanding gained from such information requires an inferential leap in predicting behavior. While biographical facts, such as gender, age, and knowledge of budgeting, are very reliable measures, they will not necessarily predict what people will do.

The middle section in the iceberg, just below the imaginary waterline, illustrates a range of information about opinions, attitudes, suggestions, and goals. Truly, it represents a much larger amount of information than one would find in an organization's formal documents. This information is found in an organization's informal network, is more speculative and conversational, and may not reflect what the person actually does.

The information at the very bottom of the iceberg, relating to values and beliefs, is the most valid for understanding how people will act in the future. Some of the information outside the iceberg summarizes past experiences, actual incidents, and actual cases. This information is also a good indicator of future behavior.

The iceberg suggests that some information—some metaphors—may be more basic in predicting behaviors. That is, values, beliefs, and critical incidents (of past behaviors) may require a smaller inferential leap in understanding future behavior, because they are not opinions, judgments, or personal dispositions.

Principle 4

Encourage a democratic and informal process of problem solving.

All researchers face times when they are stuck and unable to find a novel or insightful way to define the information they are investigating. When people finally see the answer to a complex problem, they experience something of an "Aha!" feeling. They are able to break loose from their habits and see things in a new way.

"Start strong, and the trick is to go through the doors you can open—not to kill yourself trying to go through where you can't open the doors."[22] This slogan, by Kurt Lewin, illustrates a practical approach to solving problems. His "democratic informality" encouraged a process of lateral thinking, such as what one would find when ideas emerge from free-flowing discussions. Instead of proceeding step by step in a sequential manner, lateral thinking involves (1) the deliberate generation of alternative ways of defining a problem and a solution, and (2) the challenging of assumptions. This might involve defining the problem from a number of perspectives, using different theoretical frameworks to investigate a problem, and having unique and opposing viewpoints to solving the problem.[23]

Lewin looked for relationships, gestalts, influences, and patterns that were linked to others. He used various charts and displays to try to illustrate the relationship of one energy field or force to another. In the same way, the Echo approach encourages people to try to understand the reasons why certain things occur. It seeks to measure the influences that people associate with values. While people might illustrate values of working hard or treating customers well, the Echo approach encourages questions designed to understand why people feel this way or who has influenced this value. Asking the question "why?" can expose such influences. This question has been well documented as part of a conflict resolution process of asking parties to define their interests.[24] The question evokes an understanding of the history behind the problem, the underlying interests, beliefs, and assumptions.

At least five variables—role, event, valuation, source, and reinforcement—are useful as a checklist to encourage an understanding of why people value the things they do. When we ask who might approve of being polite, one respondent might say coworkers, while another might indicate parents. When we ask people to identify some of the positive events that have made them feel good, one respondent might indicate an incident concerning pay, while another might describe how he or she was treated by a supervisor. These approving influences are called *sources,* and are the reasons or influences for people feeling satisfied or being polite toward customers. They indicate why a person's values are shaped in unique ways.

Another understanding of influence grows out of asking questions such as, "What is a good thing to happen? Who or what would cause it? What causes good things to happen to me?" These and other types of questions elucidate a pattern to illustrate the relationship between a value, an influence, and a belief. The sources of social approval and disapproval are assumed to be held in common by a certain group, and the most important sources are those mentioned more often by most people.

Principle 5

Respect people for what they value and believe in.

People in any organizational or group culture have unique expectations, values, and beliefs. Respect them for this uniqueness. The only way we can learn about people in another culture is by allowing them to express their ideas and values in their own terms. The framework for understanding must emerge from them.

In another field, I think the work of Elizabeth Kübler-Ross nicely demonstrates how we can gain insightful knowledge if we allow people to express themselves in their own terms. In her book, *On Death and Dying,* she describes the changes in emotions, thoughts, and feelings experienced when a person is told that he or she will die or that a loved one will die. The first reaction may be a temporary state of shock from which the person recuperates gradually, but, "when his initial numbness begins to disappear and he can collect himself again, man's usual response is 'no, it cannot be me.'"[25] Other stages in this experience include rage and anger, bargaining, depression, and acceptance. Death can contribute to personal growth in the one who dies or in those who are left behind, although not everyone who is dying ever reaches a level of acceptance. Many who have witnessed massive deaths and destruction, during wartime or disease, have emerged from their experiences with "growth and humanness greater than achieved through almost any other means."[26] Acceptance provides the foundation for being able to die meaningfully and for subsequent growth in oneself and others. Any sensitive person may not ever be immune to the feelings of anger, depression, and sadness at the death of a loved one. However, it is possible to become more at peace with the thought and be able to deal with it in a productive manner.

Kübler-Ross's findings were very insightful because they echoed the feelings and emotions of those who face death and dying. The vivid examples allow us to become involved in the feelings that the words evoke. As we read her work, it is impossible not to tune into our own emotional reactions to the stories, accounts, and situations she describes. She has opened our eyes, whether "we" are a dying patient, a close friend or relative of someone who is dying, a member of the helping professions or academic community, a person with a desire to learn, or a researcher interested in understanding the principles of provocative and meaningful research.

When she began her studies, she was searching for ways to keep her students awake and interested during a two-hour lecture. In order to bring some relevance to the subject, she followed the lecture with an interview with a sixteen-year-old girl suffering from acute leukemia. The students in the class manifested more fear and nervousness than the dying girl. Much later, the seminars became a weekly occurrence. The students who filled her Death and Dying seminar came for many reasons. Many showed an interest and commitment and, although feeling some discomfort and anxiety, they tried to find ways of understanding these frustrations. The sufferers presented no problem either: "They were 'grateful' to be useful, and overcame their initial shyness and willingly expressed their grief and other difficulties with their imminent death."[27]

For many years, Kübler-Ross continued to ask terminally ill people to serve as teachers for her and her students. After attending the Death and Dying seminar, a minister summed up his feelings about how he would approach his future clinical counseling duties. Perhaps the following statement serves as a personal addendum to the above principles of research:

I consider this opportunity a totally new experience for me and one that I anticipate with a mixture of excitement, curiosity and dread. I will take five "rules" with me into this experience, "rules" that I know will change as I experience myself in relation to these "rules":

Number 1: Concentrate on the dying [person] not as a case history, but as a part of a one-to-one relationship. This attitude requires disciplines which are new to me. First, I must try to be myself. If the dying [person] repulses me, for whatever reason, I must face up to that repulsion. I also must let the other person be himself, without projecting my own feelings of repulsion or hostility. Since he [or she] really is a human being, I suspect he [or she] needs the same type of love and care that I do.

Number 2: Honor the sanctity of the human being. Just as I have "secret" values, fears, joys, so does he. His God, Christ, and value system have been hard won over a lifetime of curiosity, struggle, and hope, as have mine. My faith is that when we talk to each other about ourselves, we will find something in common. And the commonality is that "wondrous ingredient" that allows people to share their lives. That sharing is the realization of our humanness.

Number 3: Honoring the sanctity of the individual forces the counselor to let the patient "tell him [her]" how he [she] feels. The minister must, in this situation, "let the [person] be." This simple rule does not imply granting all of the [person's] demands and jumping whenever the patient wants the counselor to jump. If the counselor is honest, he will face his bias and accept it as his personality rather than apologize for it and try to hide it. The belief that "I know what is best for the patient" is not true. The patient knows best.

Number 4: I must continually ask myself, "What kind of a promise am I making to this patient and to myself?" If I can "realize" that I am trying to save this person's life or to make him happy in an unendurable situation, then I believe that I am typically human and hopefully can stop trying to attempt both. If I can learn to understand my own feelings of frustration, rage, and disappointment, then I believe I have the capacity to handle these feelings in a constructive manner. It is in this realization that human wisdom lies.

Number 5: My fifth and last rule, the rule that covers all four others, is expressed in the Alcoholics Anonymous Prayer:

God grant me the courage to change the things I can,
the serenity to accept the things I cannot change,
and the wisdom to know the difference.[28]

CONCLUSION

The principles underlying the Echo approach encourage a dynamic process of research in which it is highly unlikely that the researcher will know in advance the exact theory that will be used and developed. The definitions of the problem, the propositions to be tested, and the methods to be employed undergo modification as interim results are validated or invalidated in practice and in experimentation. The principles outlined here illustrate how we might do this.

PART **II**

IMMERSION

4

Collaboration: A First Step
in the Echo Approach

Motivation alone does not suffice to lead to change. This link is provided by decisions. A process like decision-making, which takes only a
few minutes, is able to affect conduct for months to come.

Kurt Lewin

Commitment to change grows from a decision-making process that illustrates trust, clear expectations, active involvement in decision making, and
a willingness to respect the values of others. This chapter highlights a process for developing commitment to change in settings where various parties
have vested interests.

The collaborative research project at Harwood involved several significant organizational experiments, research that was in stark contrast to that
led by Frederick Winslow Taylor, an American industrial engineer often
called the father of scientific management. Lewin's interest was propelled
partially by his interest in work as something that had "life value," a capacity to give meaning to the person's entire existence. For Lewin, it was
important that a new job includes ways of making the tasks richer and more
satisfying.[1]

Lewin saw beyond Taylor's system of specialization and standardization that aimed to achieve greater industrial efficiency through scientifically combining the best skills of various workers with established standards of production. The atmosphere of informality and participative decision making surrounding Lewin's work was in stark contrast to Taylor's detached observations, time and motion studies, and pseudoscientific principles. Lewin was popular with production workers as well as supervisors, even though such employees might be more naturally suspicious of outsiders, foreigners with a German accent, people with minimal industrial experience, or anyone who tried to improve their work methods.[2]

Alex Bavelas developed the Echo approach while a graduate student with Lewin at Iowa. The approach was the undercurrent of the way he implemented a program of collaborative research at Harwood. That is, Bavelas asked questions, encouraged group members to identify their difficulties and suggestions, and allowed them to be active in analyzing and making decisions on the advantages and disadvantages of different methods. He asked individuals and groups to make decisions on the procedures and methods that should be used. The decisions had a "freezing" effect, as individuals had made a commitment to follow through. Alex Bavelas and John French, who succeeded him at Harwood, were able to enroll many of the 600 plant workers and almost all of the managers in one experiment or another over the years 1940 to 1947.

ENCOURAGING COMMITMENT TO CHANGE

Ideally, we would hope that people would be open to meet and talk about issues and problems affecting the way they work and live. However, commitment and interest in research and change is often affected by the politics of research. People may be interested in different problems and issues, or they may have a general unwillingness and lack of ability to work with others.

It is possible, although rare, for every member of a group or organization to be motivated to participate in a research project. More than likely, some people, possibly 5 percent, might be enthusiastically supportive, while others might be unenthusiastically skeptical. This is true when researchers design questionnaires in the field or when experimenters work with student groups. Some people will resist the research while others will be more keen to participate. The task, therefore, is to encourage greater commitment from the people who are uninformed, unenthusiastic, or too busy to be interested.

Proposition 1

Commitment to a collaborative relationship is encouraged when people trust the researcher and the process.

Even when an organization's leadership has provided formal commitment, an Echo research project might be resisted by important gatekeepers—union executives, informal leaders, strong-willed individuals, and inflexible personalities—who refuse to fully participate, do not trust the researchers, or have no interest or commitment to the research. Low response rates, lack of openness in responding, inadequately completed questionnaires, and instruments that are not sensitive to the issues are just a few examples of problems that occur when there is a lack of commitment or trust. While formal agreements to do the research will legitimatize a project, informal access and trust is crucial if we want participants to identify with the issues and assist in resolving them.

Imagine your feelings after participating in Milgram's experiment on "obedience," in which your task was to administer shock to a victim who was, apparently, complaining, crying, and telling you to stop.[3] You continue and ask yourself, "Can I trust the researcher? Is he or she really justified in doing this?" You begin to feel uncomfortable with what you are doing, but you continue to obey the experimenter and block out the cries for help. After the experiment is over, the researcher tells you that the victim was not feeling the pain, but was just acting. When you leave the experiment, how do you feel about what you did? How do you feel about the researcher? Would you trust this researcher again?

A breakage of trust is like a cancer. It sows the seeds of a distrust that will spread rapidly to others. It is obvious from Milgram's description that most of his subjects were concerned about the victims and did not trust the researcher. This distress might have resulted from concern about his or her research ethics as well as the thought of what was being done to their victims. The experiment was probably not a convincing parallel between Milgram's experiments and the authoritative relationships in Hitler's SS, as Milgram suggested. The SS were more committed to their leaders and the cause, while Milgram's subjects displayed intense emotions about what they were doing. One has to wonder how subjects felt during and after the experiment? Can Milgram gain insightful information when subjects did not trust him? Do subjects act naturally in a research setting when they do not trust the researcher?

In one project I observed, a manager offered the following comment on a researcher who reported her interview in an inaccurate way. "I was shocked when I found out what she had said about me. I just couldn't believe it. She quoted something that was completely out of context. When I talked to her the next day, she was sorry that I felt the way I did. But the damage was done as far as I was concerned. My name was in a report and I had not agreed to having my views expressed to others. . . . I'd never trust her again." An Echo project relies on trust. Participants are more likely to identify their values and needs when they trust the researcher and have an interest in the project.

Background Note 4.1: Milgram's Experiments on Obedience

Stanley Milgram's experiments on obedience try to illustrate a very important social problem, the social consequences of destructive obedience. In them, he tries to draw a parallel with Hitler's Germany, where subordinates carried out orders to execute millions of people. Milgram points out that "Gas chambers were built, death camps were guarded, daily quotas of corpses were produced with the same efficiency as the manufacturer of appliances. These inhuman policies may have originated in the mind of a single person, but they could only be carried out on a massive scale if a very large number of people obeyed orders."[4] Here is a statement from Milgram's abstract:

The article describes a procedure for the study of destructive obedience in the laboratory. It consists of ordering a naïve S to administer increasingly more severe punishment to a victim in the context of a learning experiment. Punishment is administered by means of a shock generator with 30 graded switches ranging from Slight Shock to Danger: Severe Shock. The victim is a confederate of E. The primary dependent variable is the maximum shock the S is willing to administer before he refuses to continue further. 26 Ss obeyed the experimental commands fully, and administered the highest shock on the generator. 14 Ss broke off the experiment at some point after the victim protested and refused to provide further answers. The procedure created extreme levels of nervous tension in some Ss. Profuse sweating, trembling, and stuttering were typical expressions of this emotional disturbance. One unexpected sign of tension—yet to explained—was the regular occurrence of nervous laughter, which in some Ss developed into uncontrollable seizures. The variety of interesting behavioral dynamics observed in the experiment, the reality of the situation for the S, and the possibility of parametric variation with the framework of the procedure, point to the fruitfulness of further study.[5]

In the experiment, subjects were observed to sweat, tremble, stutter, bite their lips, and dig their fingernails into their flesh. The following is his description of the effect of the experimental condition on one of his subjects:

I observed a mature and initially poised businessman enter the laboratory smiling and confident. Within 20 minutes he was reduced to a twitching, stuttering wreck, who was rapidly approach the point of nervous collapse. He constantly pulled on his earlobe, and twisted his hands. At one point he pushed his fist into his forehead and muttered: "Oh God, let's stop it." And yet he continued to respond to every word of the experimenter, and obeyed to the end.[6]

After the experiment was over, Milgram indicated that procedures were taken to assure that subjects would leave the laboratory in a state of well-being. The researcher arranged a friendly reconciliation between the subject and victim, and efforts were made to reduce any possible tensions.[7] The impact of the experiment on respondents has generated a great deal of discussion. One might wonder what procedure could dissipate the type of emotional disturbance described.[8]

Proposition 2

Commitment in a collaborative relationship is encouraged when there are clear rules and expectations.

Clear rules and expectations are important in Echo projects. Even boxers who are entering a fighting ring have an understanding of the rules. When a professional boxer meets a street fighter, the rules are not clear. A street fighter might feel that kicking and pulling hair is appropriate, while the trained boxer might expect that the fight would be carried out using the "rules of the boxing ring." A willingness to fight fair will not establish a clear set of expectations because different people will have unique opinions of what is fair.

Even in wars, people attempt to establish rules for fighting fair. There are expectations that nuclear weapons and poison gas should not be used and that civilians and prisoners should be humanely treated. While the world has tolerated wars as a necessary evil, they have tried to establish codes of being fair and just. Stiff moral condemnation is applied to those who have broken the rules of war, such as Hitler's atrocities against the Jews during World War II and Saddam Hussein's rape of the environment and firebombing of the Kurds.

If the relationship is not defined, people will make assumptions that are likely to be incorrect. A well-defined relationship has clearly understood norms and values for working together. People are clear on the rules, codes, and norms to be practiced.

I was recently involved in a research contract to assist a number of satellite organizations to merge under one structure, with a new building, technology, and reporting relationship. When management hired me, the union postponed the scheduled meetings, asking for representation by a union consultant. In the two months that followed, the union restricted my access to the people in the organization I wanted to consult with. In response, management was unwilling to meet with the union consultant because of difficulties they had with her in two previous initiatives that had to be abandoned. In the initial workshops that were finally held, union members were distant, unresponsive, and impolite. Management members were equally indifferent when the union consultant offered comments or suggestions.

The solution to this problem was evident: Focus on the issues rather than on our differences. The union consultant and I developed a relationship that highlighted our joint interest in getting the two parties working together. While we recognized that we represented different parties, we were "singing from the same song sheet," and did not have any major disagreements about how to carry out the research to assist the amalgamation. We worked together in facilitating a discussion that highlighted some of the problems with previous amalgamation efforts and encouraged the two parties to brainstorm ideas for assuring the success of the present project.

Over several meetings and informal discussions, the group came up with a number of ideas for working together, including running joint workshops, sharing information, and developing "terms of reference" to communicate their expectations and values. In fact, they developed two joint union–management committees, a steering committee to guide the project and a working committee to carry out the research and implementation. Over the next two months we worked with the union and management members of the steering committee to develop a five-page terms of reference document that summarized the project's purpose, the principles underlying it, the structure of the steering committee, evaluation procedures, and the schedule for the work. The process of developing the terms of reference was as important as the operating principles that resulted. The steps we took were able to overcome long-standing disagreements and skepticism toward us and the process.

Proposition 3

Commitment to a collaborative relationship is encouraged when group members make decisions that illustrate they are responsible for the project.

The idea for an initial experiment on group decision making at the Harwood Manufacturing Corporation came partially from earlier food-habits experiments in which housewives had carried out decisions they had shared in making. Groups who made the decision themselves had changed their eating habits in a much more significant way than groups whod had been trained by a nutritionist. In beginning these food-habits experiments, the research team of Margaret Mead, Kurt Lewin, and the Iowa researchers wrestled for hours over the research approach before finally deciding on using the Bavelas test. They developed Echo questions like, "What is a good meal for a boy to eat?" and "Who would praise him for it?" From questions of this sort, they obtained new information about customs and maternal and paternal moral roles in the Iowa version of American culture. They obtained details illustrating that "the Father presided over meat and butter, Mother over green vegetables and fruit juices, while deserts and soft drinks were wholly delightful and approved by no parent at all."[9]

Group decision making was a key strategy that Alex Bavelas used in trying to get workers at Harwood to improve their productivity. In unstructured and informal meetings, lasting approximately thirty minutes, people were encouraged to discuss their difficulties and their ideas for improving productivity. The group openly discussed the advantages and disadvantages of different methods that individuals used. When they came up with ways to overcome their difficulties, management agreed to help make the changes. The group later decided to increase its output of seventy-five units to eighty-seven units, a level they had never attained before, and still later to ninety units. This output was maintained even when other groups in the plant showed no significant increase.

The series of studies at Harwood—relating to self-management, leadership training, changing stereotypes, and overcoming resistance to change—illustrated how group decision making and humanizing the workforce were used in getting commitment to research and change.

Proposition 4

Commitment in a collaborative relationship is encouraged when there is an interest in knowing others as "people."

An atmosphere of informality and fun extended into Lewin's home and into other endeavors. Group members were loyal to each other and their interest in knowing other people as "people." This was an important part of their collaborative experience.

Personal relationships are a part of any research relationship, as much of the time we spend conversing with others is spent discussing our values and interests in work, society, politics, and life. When a participant says that she was happy the government intervened in the postal strike, what is she saying? Very likely, she might be saying she disagrees with the postal strike. With a little more probing, we might begin to understand this person's values and attitudes toward government intervention, unions, pay increases in the public sector, and the post office in general. Such informal communications help in getting to know other people as people. They help us understand what people value and believe in, the most important elements of an Echo project.

Questions that can assist group members understand common values in a team project might include the following: What do I want to accomplish? What don't I want to see happen? What do others want to accomplish? What would they not want to see happen? What are things that might help us complete the project? What are some of the constraints that might keep a healthy research relationship from developing? Such questions encourage a joint statement of what people value in a new project. This might be a first step in trying to clarify expectations and in developing commitment.

Background Note 4.2: Getting to Know People as People

The conflict in Ulster has gone on for years, and in mid-November 1999, the parties had been especially fractious in trying to negotiate an agreement to set up a new government. Under the guidance of U.S. Senator George Mitchell, the political parties were sitting across a narrow table in a modern drab office. "The meetings were very harsh, filled with recriminations," the former U.S. Senator recalls. "They would say, 'I don't believe you. You're wrong.' They were pointing their fingers in each other's faces. They were directly calling each other liars."

On Good Friday the previous year, this group had signed an accord to "make peace and run an elaborately balanced government together." The deal floundered. The two bitter opponents—David Trimble of the Ulster Unionists (UUP) and Gerry Adams of Sinn Fein—hardly knew each other and had no mutual trust.

Mitchell decided a change of scene was vital, so he moved to the secluded home of Philip Lade, the American ambassador to London. He placed everyone in comfortable chairs and asked for a news blackout. After the first day of talks, Mitchell asked them to return for dinner at 8 P.M. Twenty people filed into the ambassador's sumptuous dining room.

Mitchell asked that no business be discussed. "It was surreal," recalls one of the participants. Slowly, the ice began to break. They talked about fishing, their families, opera. "It got to be—not friendly, but an acceptable atmosphere," says Mitchell.

The next day the working discussion was more productive. Two weeks later they moved back to Belfast for intense negotiations. Mitchell patiently listened until the UUP and Sinn Fein talked themselves out, lowering the volume through their own unflappability.[10]

A useful exercise in getting to know other people as people is to begin an informal conversation during a coffee or lunch break. Focus the conversation on things you do outside of work. What did you do on the weekend? What movie or play did you recently see? What is a recent book that you read?

When working in any group, it is always useful to take stock. This might be achieved by beginning the meeting with questions like this: What are some of the things that have worked well? What are things that have not worked well? What are things we can do to improve? Relationship building begins by clarifying expectations and setting the ground rules or the norms and values that will define the way the group will work. Understandably, the relationship issue may be taken for granted in many interviews or conversations between close friends or people who know each other on an intimate basis. When relationship issues are communicated, people have an opportunity to get to know what others value and believe in.

Background Note 4.3: Working Alone or Collaborating?

Since it is often difficult to work with other people, some of us may feel that we would be just as effective if we could work alone or do things ourselves. After all, people like Estée Lauder and Bill Gates illustrate such acts of individual genius.

"Even as the lone hero continues to gallop through our imaginations, shattering obstacles with silver bullets, leaping tall buildings in a single bound, we know there is an alternate reality."[11] In *Organizing Genius*, Warren Bennis and Patricia Biederman illustrate that there is rarely only one face to success. What might seem to be individual achievement is most often the result of the synergy of a number of people working together. These results should hardly surprise us. We live in an increasingly complex and technologically sophisticated society, where most urgent projects require the coordinated contributions of many talented people. One person can rarely do it all, no matter how gifted, talented, or energetic.

Review some of the successful entrepreneurial experiences of people like Estée Lauder, Sara Breedlove, Anita Roderick, Henry Ford, Ferdinand Porsche, Walt Disney, and Jack Warner. Most of these are seen as examples of individual entrepreneurship. Look further at their lives and you may find a significant other, a mentor, or even an antagonist who propelled these people out of solitude to reach for something much beyond what one could do alone. Estée Lauder worked closely with her family and son Leonard, while Sara Breedlove relied on her daughter and husband to establish a national hair-care business. Anita Roderick, the entrepreneur behind The Body Shop, worked closely with her family. Henry Ford counted on the great inventor, Thomas Edison, for some important innovations, and Porsche worked with his son to design and build the sports car that still bears the family name. Jack Warner worked with his brothers Sam, Harry, and Albert in creating Warner Brothers.

TAKING STEPS TO BEGIN A COLLABORATIVE PROJECT

Collaborative work within teams of researchers and clients was an important part of the Lewinian research approach. Clients worked with researchers in making decisions on the way the research would be carried out and helping to implement some of the norms of an action science.

A healthy collaborative relationship does not evolve naturally, but it can be encouraged when researchers are clear on each other's expectations and interests. A useful process that I have used for encouraging collaboration is suggested in Fisher and Ury's classic book, *Getting to Yes*.[12] They remind us that all relationships are potentially conflictive and involve negotiations of some sort, whether we are negotiating how to carry out research, designing a new community program, or improving our working conditions.

Relationship issues are potentiality the most troublesome in any group, because they involve human emotions of trust, understanding, and respect. Most people, whether researchers or organizational participants, have strongly felt feelings on appropriate research methods, questions to ask, or objectives that the research might achieve. Useful steps include developing an awareness of common interests and values, defining the problem and issues, identifying the constraints that might affect the study, and outlining norms and values a team might follow in carrying out a research project.

Responding to Interests Rather Than Positions

In one project to design and implement a gender-neutral job evaluation plan in a unionized environment, the union held to their position of wanting a union plan, while management wanted their plan. Each party held to their position and, over a ten-year period, the project floundered, even though each party was interested in seeing it carried out.

In defining the interests and values underlying each group's position, we asked each group why it wanted its unique plan. The union's interests were, "We perceive that a union plan is more fair," "We do not trust a management designed plan," and "We think management plans are more difficult to use." Management's interests were, "We feel that the factors in a union plan are slanted towards union factors," and "We think a management plan might be more fair."

The "why?" question encouraged the parties to identify the interests underlying their positions, interests that related to fairness, involvement in the design, criteria or factors that recognized their needs, and so forth. Even after articulating these and other interests, both union and management were still skeptical, but they were willing to continue the process of searching for a plan that would best meet both party's interests (needs and values).

Suppose you wanted to identify the interests of team members in participating in a project to understand the challenges, needs, and competencies of managers in the public sector. In the first step, ask why team members or organizational participants want to participate. This question usually illustrates a number of interests related to learning about managers, completing an excellent project, and being rewarded for work that is well done. A next step is to identify each individual's interests or needs in completing the project.

What motivates me in this project? What is not important to me? These questions usually illustrate what people are prepared to do in completing the project. For example, some team members might articulate their time commitments, their unwillingness to work late into the night to achieve an unrealistic deadline, and a desire to carry out a project in an orderly manner.

A clear understanding of the underlying interests—values and needs—helps focus a research process so that people will commit themselves to it. Whether a person is a team member in a project or a manager in a field setting, there is a need to feel that a project responds to one's interests.

Understanding the Research Problem or Issue

When researching many organizational problems, researchers often find themselves in situations in which respondents express a great deal of anger, frustration, or misunderstanding of their managers or programs. The researcher is sometimes forced to take on the role of the counselor before being able to develop an understanding of any facts underlying the issues. Surfacing and responding to feelings and issues—emotional comments and feelings of frustration, anger, or misunderstanding—is a first step in understanding that most factual issues are linked to strongly held feelings.[13] People also need to articulate their values, opinions, positions, and viewpoints.

Imagine a situation where your friend is trying to sell his classic Aston-Martin, which he bought ten years ago for $50,000. Just recently, he spent another $60,000 to have the car restored, in addition to three years of his time. He has an emotional commitment, and no amount of logic will convince him that someone would not appreciate the work he has put into the car. However, since the market value is only $70,000, it is very likely that he will find it very hard to separate his emotions from logic in trying to sell his car. How would you help him disentangle his emotions from the facts?

First you have to separate the people from the problem. When different people—researchers or organizational participants—are emotionally involved in something, they may have difficulty seeing the facts underlying an issue. Having a clear understanding of the problems or issues is an important step to keeping the project focused. This is best achieved by asking key participants to give anecdotal examples of the problems or issues as they have experienced them, giving attention to facts and feelings that might help explain the issue more fully.

The following are examples of questions we asked a number of managers before we initiated a process of designing a new job evaluation plan for managers in a nonunion environment. That is, before beginning, we tried to develop a clear understanding of the problems, needs, and interests that managers perceived, their expectations of what a new plan would and would not do, and the features of a plan that they valued and did not value.

We'd like to begin by trying to develop an understanding of how you feel about the present job evaluation plan and how a new plan might be designed. We're trying to interview a number of people in different positions who might offer different perspectives on this job evaluation experience and what job evaluation might look like in the future in this organization.

- From your perspective, how would you describe the present job evaluation process? What are some of the main problems that it has? What are some examples of these problems? What are some of the good things or things that work well with the present job evaluation plan? What are some examples of things that work well?
- What do you think a new job evaluation system should do to respond to any problems? What do you think a new job evaluation system should not be expected to do?
- Can you think of some examples of factors that you would like to see in a plan? Can you think of some examples of factors that you would not like to see in a plan?
- What are some of your interests in a new job evaluation plan? What are examples of interests or needs of others you fear might shape the development of the new job evaluation plan?
- What are some principles and norms you feel we should use to guide the development of the new job evaluation plan? What are some principles and norms you feel we should not use in guiding the development of a new plan?
- What ideas or solutions would you like to see explored in developing the new plan? What are some ideas or solutions you feel will not assist in developing the new plan?
- What are some strategies we might use in implementing the plan? What strategies would be less effective?
- What would make you support a job evaluation plan? What would make others support a job evaluation plan?

These questions, with added probes, offered a realistic perspective on the challenges, issues, and values underlying this group of managers. Most admitted that they found their existing plan difficult to interpret and hard to understand. Some felt that they understood parts of the plan but were unable to explain it to others or use it without the assistance of an expert consultant:

We could not complete the process by ourselves. We had to have a consultant to help us come up with the right evaluation. If we did it ourselves (independently) we would arrive at many different answers.

Almost everyone admitted a lack of familiarity with the job evaluation plan, the factors, or how they are evaluated. Respondents indicated that the job evaluation committee has not met in nearly two years, and committee members expressed a lack of confidence in explaining the system or how it should be used.

No one really understands the system or how to use it. "I don't know what the factors are. Don't know what I have to do to get to another level. Don't know why my job's paid what it is."

These statements illustrate practical examples or symptoms of problems as perceived by different people. They were extremely helpful in focusing the study on the problems or issues that needed to be addressed in the study.

Alternatively, when researchers do not have the opportunity to interview or survey people in the organization to be studied, they might ask themselves a number of questions in developing an understanding of the problems or issue to be researched. Here are examples of such questions we asked students when they were charged with the task of developing an understanding of the challenges, needs, and competencies of managers in the public sector.

- From our perspective, how would we describe the challenges, needs, and competencies of managers in the public sector? What are some examples of these challenges or problems?
- What are some of the key issues managers have to address in the particular organization we are studying? What are examples of these issues?

The use of such questions encourages researchers to clarify the purpose of the study and the problems and issues it may uncover. The surest way to clarify what needs to be done in a project is to be clear on the problems and issues it will address. Clarity increases when we articulate the problems or need for the study in a proposal, set of principles, guidelines, or terms of reference to steer the research project. Such a document is extremely useful in projects where there are people with divergent interests or low trust, or where a research assignment is extremely complex.

Identifying Constraints in Carrying Out the Project

The understanding and imagination of a project team is particularly useful in identifying some of the potential obstacles affecting the project. To do this, they might ask themselves a series of questions: What are potential conflicts that might develop among us? What are our personal time constraints that might affect the project? What are some of the worst things that might happen in carrying out this project? What are some things that might cause this project to fail? What are some of the things that are crucial in making sure this project is a success?

Brainstorming and other idea-generation activities are useful in identifying constraints that the team will have to respond to in the short and long term. Participants can prioritize these threats in terms of their Probability, their Impact, and the researcher's ability to Control or manage them. This PIC analysis may indicate that certain events are highly probable and have a great impact, and that it is necessary to act to control them. As a rule of thumb, researchers need to be concerned with only those events they have some possibility to control and that have some probability of happening.[14] A strategy for working together might have mutually agreed upon mechanisms for resolving problems and constraints.

Developing a Team Charter

We try to create a Lewinian-like atmosphere among graduate students who are charged with undertaking team projects in organizations. To do this, participants are asked to write a team charter as a mechanism to clarify expectations. They end up with two to five pages of notes that describe their mission, vision, and philosophy. The process, in many cases, seems to encourage productive group work.

A mission statement—a group's purpose for existence or raison d'être— helps a group focus its energies in responding to key stakeholders, or the persons or groups that place a claim on a team's resources, time, or outputs. Since the key to success in most groups is the satisfaction of stakeholders, an understanding of the stakeholders' needs is a basis for judging and evaluating success.

The vision is a picture of the future that we are trying to achieve or create in this collaboration. A vision is usually future oriented, inspirational, needs an effort to achieve, and is democratically agreed to. It is like a gardener's vision of a new flower garden. The person who is creating a flower garden has a vision of what is wanted, but is faced with the features of the landscape, the costs for renovation, and personal desires to achieve the goal.

A philosophy statement describes the values related to how we will operate or treat each other. The following is an example of a philosophy statement that provides a statement of one group's values:

- Of all the environmental influences that will affect this team project, the most powerful ones are the interpersonal relationships between team members, described by our interest in others as people, our willingness to help others, and our enthusiasm.

- We feel that part of this team's effectiveness is based on our willingness to take time at team meetings to review and revise our team charter and evaluate our team dynamics, roles, and goals.

- A key element in our team's functioning is our ability to trust each other. At its most basic element, trust is maintained by doing what we have committed ourselves to and following the norms and practices we have agreed to.

- As a team, we aspire to be highly effective in demonstrating teamness, learning, and excellence.

Ground rules or working norms help the group define their expectations and how they will treat each other on a day-to-day basis. By articulating expectations, we are able to identify how meetings will be chaired, who will take notes, how process issues will be monitored, and when we will seek help in resolving conflicts or disagreements.

THE PROCESS

A collaborative experience relies on trust, clear expectations, active involvement in decision making, and a willingness to respect the values of others. This can be achieved in many ways, one of which is through a communication process that leads to a team charter. In the same way, a team charter will not guarantee the success of the collaborative experience, as a most important process is the ongoing feedback and discussion of group functioning. As such, the process of discussing norms for working together— through developing a charter or informal discussions—is more important than any formal statement of them.

EXAMPLE: WRITING A TEAM CHARTER

The team charter might include a mission statement, vision, underlying values, and working norms. Before writing your mission statement, answer the following questions.

What. This can be expressed in terms of what makes you distinct (i.e., the products, services, or needs you address).

Who. Who are some of your key stakeholders or people that you have to respond to, such as clients, superiors, and influential people?

Why. Why do we have the goals and motivators we have? These goals might be related to doing well, learning, or developing one's career.

Where. Where do we do our main activities?

How. How are we carrying out these activities?

"How" and "where" questions provide a description of the physical work space and equipment you will use.

Your vision for the project evolves from a definition of your values and the possible things you might do that are quite different from what you do now. A vision might be futuristic, inspirational, an idea or picture that motivates, and/or agreed to by team members.

• What do you want this project to do and be for you? What don't you want this project to do for you?
• What do we want to achieve in this project? What don't we want to achieve?

The philosophy statement contains a list of values you would like to work by.

• What are things we might do to work well together? What are things we should not do?

• What are some of the positive things that might happen if we work well together? What are less positive things and how do we avoid them?

Each team member might make a list of his or her expectations of himself or herself and others in relationship to their roles within the team and their roles in relationship to the clients. After agreeing on these expectations, each team member is asked to list the consequences for not meeting the expectations.

Designing a Process That Encourages Insight and Creativity

Get a good start and you've got a chance to win. Get a bad start and
you've got dirty air for the whole race.

Sailor's creed

Some of the most serious threats to insight and creativity in research come
from the failure to deal with the uncertainty of the search process, inappropriate search generators, or using frameworks or theories that are not
appropriate for the problem. These threats may result from adopting a theory
or framework before we fully understand a problem or from failing to appropriately frame the problem. This chapter is based on one assumption: A
most important aspect of an insightful research project is its initial focus or
starting position. It illustrates some of the preliminary steps that might be
useful in setting the stage for using the Echo approach.

The Echo process encourages creativity, much like we might witness in
conventional science where scientists are trying to unravel a problem or
make a discovery. Accounts of the trials and successes of Nobel prize win-
ners and others provide a view of the search process in the field of science.
These experiences suggest that process of scientific research might be analogous to searching for a diamond in the dark.[1] Imagine that you are searching

for a diamond in a huge, dark room. What do you do? One option is to grope blindly in the dark hoping to chance upon the diamond. This might be an effective strategy if you have a rough idea of where the diamond might be. But you might change this strategy if, after several attempts, you fail to come up with an idea of where the diamond is. You might abandon your search and begin to search for the light switch, which, if the light could be turned on, would reveal the location of the diamond immediately.

Most scientists who have made insightful discoveries have experienced an analogous situation. They believe they know just what to do, only to discover they are "groping in the dark," or following an idea or theory that is going nowhere. This is a conception of problem solving as a heuristic search through a problem space (dark room). Re-representing the problem is equivalent to turning the light on, or to looking at the problem in a different way. The change of representation is like a paradigm shift, a new point of view or approach to problem solving.

Maurice Allais, who did some pioneering work on the theory of markets and efficient use of resources, wrote, "On the whole, my work has been a response to the need I have felt to understand concrete reality and to provide satisfactory answers to the questions suggested to me by the obscurities, contradictions, and gaps in the existing literature. My work has thus been a long, and often painful endeavour to steer away from the beaten paths and dominant ideas of my time."[2] Stigler describes this process as follows:

This endeavor is not that of a graceful intellectual gymnast: on the contrary, the scientist is stumbling about in a jungle of ideas or facts that seem to defy system or logic, and usually he [she] fails to emerge with anything but scratches. The dangers of the search include the chance that a gifted rival will reach the goal, and the danger is not reduced by the fact that the rivalry is conducted under what for able and ambitious competitors are unusually chivalrous rules.[3]

These feelings of discomfort, contradiction, and stumbling in an uncertain and ambiguous jungle of ideas are the breeding ground for discarding old models and theories. Such feelings are sometimes unpleasant. One's mental discipline and attitude in responding to these feelings of uncertainty are key in encouraging insight and creativity.

INSIGHT AND CREATIVITY IN SCIENTIFIC RESEARCH

A review of how insightful discoveries have occurred in scientific research reveals comments like serendipity, chance, persistence, conflict, and politics. Note how velcro and cyclosporine were discovered.

Velcro has turned out to be one of the world's most versatile and flexible fastening methods. The hooks and loops that are part of Velcro fasteners have been used for applications that range from children's running shoes to steel products. The idea for Velcro emerged in Switzerland in the 1950s when George deMestral returned from a walk and noticed that his jacket was covered with cockleburs. After noting how strongly the cockleburs hung to his coat, he examined them under a microscope and discovered that the cockleburs were covered with hooks that had become embedded in the loops of the fabric on his coat. Nature had designed this process so that the cockleburs would become attached to passing birds and animals in enhancing the reproducing process.

The first efforts of manufacturing hook-and-loop tapes were slow and tedious, but many improvements were made. Pure polyester tape was later used to prevent damage from ultraviolet light, chemicals, and moisture. Later, steel and other synthetic fabrics were designed so that fasteners could be designed to withstand temperatures of 800 degrees Fahrenheit.

In 1976 a pharmaceutical breakthrough occurred that reversed the bleak record of transplant surgery. It happened when Swiss researchers were examining soil samples in search of a new antibiotic. By chance, they found a fungus that produced a powerful immunosuppressant, a substance that blocks the body's defense mechanisms from rejecting foreign tissues. The new discovery, now known as cyclosporine, received its first clinical trials in 1980. A surge of transplants followed, and the chances of survival of a successful graft increased.

The discovery resulted from a practice of some pharmaceutical companies of encouraging their employees who travel abroad to collect and test soil samples that might have antibiotic microorganisms. In the early 1970s, microbiologist Jean Borel of the Sandoz Corporation in Basel, Switzerland, began investigating samples from Wisconsin and from Norway. Both samples contained two new strains of fungi that produced a water-insoluble substance. The substance, named cyclosporin A, did not have strong antibiotic properties, but it had an unusually low toxicity and strong immunosuppressive effects. Jean Borel persisted with his work, even though the management of the Sandoz Corporation wanted him to discontinue it.

Jean Borel's later tests indicated that immunosuppressive effects could be demonstrated in all the animal species tested. However, little or no drug could be found in the bloodstreams of humans who digested the gelatin capsules. For Borel, the problem was the method of ingesting the drug.

He performed a test on himself by drinking a cocktail consisting of a mixture of pure alcohol, water, and an emulsifying agent. He felt tipsy but, two hours later, it was possible to identify a concentration of the drug in his bloodstream. Later, olive oil was used in orally ingesting the drug.

With cyclosporine, there is almost twice the chance that liver, kidney, and heart transplants will succeed. These advances signify dramatic improvements since South Africa's Barnard performed the first heart transplant in 1967, when his patient died only eighteen days after receiving his new heart.

Cyclosporine has also been helpful in treating parasitic diseases. It was accidentally discovered that the drug is able to kill schistosomes, the worms causing the tropical disease schistosomiasis. It also inhibits the malaria parasite.

The conclusion that we might draw from these and other stories is that creativity and insight in scientific discovery is often a romantic experience, a rags-to-riches story, or chance. An alternative view offered here is that "creativity in the early stages of science is a way of thinking that can be learned and practiced."[4] Creativity at the beginning of the research experience might have a logic of its own, requiring mental discipline in thinking and reasoning. Insightful discoveries are more likely to occur from a creative, flexible problem-solving process.

ATTITUDES THAT REDUCE CREATIVITY DURING THE EARLY STAGES OF RESEARCH

How might we think creatively about a problem or issue in social research? Janet Beavin Bavelas, in *Permitting Creativity in Science*, illustrates a number of ways that creativity in the early stages of science might be hindered.[5]

Dismissing Casual or Deviant Observations

As Janet Beavin Bavelas reveals, discoveries can result from everyday observations that we often dismiss. Even casual observations can lead to discoveries. Kurt Lewin, for example, noticed that a waiter could remember everyone in his group and what each person ordered. However, he forgot everyone completely as soon as the bill was paid. This observation eventually yielded the classic "Zeigarnick Effect," in which interrupted tasks are remembered better than completed ones.[6] We do not usually expect that novel ideas can be found in everyday life, in restaurants, or in common places.

The common tendency is to dismiss ideas that are not well articulated, just as we often ignore people who offer deviant or unusual ideas. It is most difficult to accept the comments of others when we are launched on a path that we think is promising. Comments or ideas that may suggest we make a change are hard to accept in all areas of life, including our writing style, mannerisms, or appearance.

A good way to understand how things really are is to listen for rumors, opinions, and statements that are different from what we might expect and want to hear. Ask others what they think of these deviant ideas. In other words, listen and reflect on deviant comments and ideas before rejecting them.

Vertical and Categorical Thinking

Discoveries are often hindered because we too quickly categorize, classify, or rely on past experiences in explaining what we observe.[7] The term "vertical thinking" was coined by Edward deBono to describe a tendency to define a problem in a single way, then pursuing that definition without deviation until some kind of solution is reached.[8] No alternative definitions are sought. This is like the researcher who gathers information and develops solutions that are consistent with the original paradigm or framework for viewing a problem.

In improving the design of watches, for example, researchers who are vertical thinkers will continually try to improve upon their original designs. This led the Swiss researchers in the 1960s to continually improve with research to discover better ways to manufacture the gears, bearings, and the mainsprings. When lateral thinking Swiss researchers invented the electronic quartz movement at their research institute in Neuchâtel, Switzerland, it was rejected by Swiss manufacturers. It didn't have a mainspring, bearings, almost no gears, and it was battery powered. They were so confident that the idea would never make it that they let their researchers showcase it at the World Watch Congress that year. The rest is history. The Japanese picked up the idea. By 1980, the Swiss had lost their market share, collapsing from 65 percent to less than 10 percent. Their huge profit domination had dropped to less than 20 percent. Between 1979 and 1981, fifty thousand of the sixty-two thousand watchmakers had lost their jobs.[9] I have tried to use the Echo approach as a way to avoid vertical and categorical thinking. That is, I encourage the categories or ideas to evolve from the field or perspectives other than my own.

Depending on Conventional Concepts or Theories

Social science ideas are indexed more by concepts than by events or phenomena. Words like planning, organizing, and staffing are used to describe what a manager does, and textbooks have been arranged to illustrate these practices. The field of management was captured by a stereotype of managerial behavior, reinforced by teachers and researchers. We even invented a term, "POSDCORB"—planning, organizing, staffing, directing, coordinating, reporting, and budgeting—to help us remember the concepts defining management.

When we observe management in action, we see an entirely different process, as we learned from Mintzberg's classic study of the nature of managerial work.[10] When he observed managers, he found entirely different behaviors, such as performing ceremonial duties, reading numerous reports, and spending hours listening and communicating. Mintzberg's research illustrates how easy it is to be misled by the conventional concepts and theories one might find in textbooks and research articles. Continuing to use these concepts discourages researchers from searching for new concepts that might more accurately describe a situation.

What concepts, theories, and literature should a researcher rely on when beginning a study? Janet Beavin Bavelas illustrates this tendency with the words of Sir Peter Medawar,

Too much book learning may crab and confine the imagination, and endless pouring [*sic*] over the research of others is sometimes psychologically a research substitute, much as reading romantic fiction may be a substitute for real-life romance. . . . The beginner must read, but intently and choosily and not too much. Few sights are sadder than that of a young research worker always to be seen hunched over journals in the library; by far the best way to become proficient in research is to get on with it.[11]

People who worked within a Lewinian tradition were very committed to suspending their values and beliefs and concepts as best they could in entering a new situation. They sought, first, to define what people valued, believed in, or acted on.

Being Overly Critical

Most insightful ideas, when they are initially stated, may sound vague, ill-defined, and incomplete. They are likely to be subject to remarks such as the following:

"That would never work."
"That would be impossible to implement."
"What would you do about this problem?"
"I think that has already been tried before somewhere else."
"Is that practical?"

These are very natural remarks that, if allowed at the early stages of the research, are likely to increase the likelihood that a new idea might be rejected before it has a chance to fully develop.

Some people are more predisposed to criticize or pass judgement on an idea, provoking others to respond to their critical questions rather than encouraging them to develop the idea. A person's mental disposition or style illustrates his or her style for problem solving.

Because a new idea is likely to be loose and conceptless, it is likely to be resisted or rejected unless time is taken to consider it seriously. The way the problem is presented can have a powerful impact on the judgments that other people make, particularly where there is some uncertainty about the potential outcomes. The researcher's initial task is to discover ways to present ideas—by developing trust in the open exchange of information—so that comments stimulate rather than inhibit creative thought.

Charging Ahead Too Quickly

Most researchers feel the pressure to get on to later stages of research so that they can develop their instruments of data collection and begin work. It seems more efficient to get on with it rather than wasting time thinking and trying to be creative. Certain principles guide us in moving quickly to define our problem and objectives:

Whenever something is complex, simplify it.

Whenever we face uncertainty and ambiguity, clarify the situation.

Never, never say I don't know.

Ambiguity, vagueness, and lack of definition are frustrating and painful. The lesson is to learn to tolerate them rather than seeking closure too quickly. The pressure to get on to later stages of the research—where concepts are developed and tested—is something to be resisted.

Living with ambiguity, vagueness, and uncertainty may be more important than making a quick decision or prematurely defining the study's direction or problems. This may be equivalent to the first principle of "brief" or "strategic" psychotherapy, which is, "Our problems are caused by our efforts to deal with them."[12] In other words, the pressure to define things leads to applying our methods too quickly, with the inevitable consequence of setting us back.

The ability to see something new or to change one's representation is often associated with the tolerance for uncertainty, failure, and accident, especially for problems that are complex, changing, or messy.[13] Living with opposition and tolerating uncertainty may be more valuable than defining a problem statement or set of constructs that immediately reduces the opposition and uncertainty. An individual's willingness to tolerate ambiguity may encourage an openness to seeing many varied ideas, some of which might be novel.

These suggestions will not pave the way for creative and insightful research. Rather, they help to encourage people to begin research by trying not to dismiss casual observations, have preconceived ideas, depend on conventional theories, charge ahead too quickly, or be overly critical.

ATTITUDES THAT INCREASE CREATIVITY DURING THE EARLY STAGES OF ORGANIZATIONAL RESEARCH

The nine-dot puzzle (Figure 5.1) is a famous example of problem solving where most people, after discovering the answer, feel an Aha! experience.[14] In the puzzle, people are asked to join the nine dots with four or three straight lines. If you haven't done the puzzle, try it. One answer is illustrated in Figure 5.2.

Some people see the answer right away. Others try to join the lines within the box. Figure 5.2 is a four-line solution to the nine-dot problem. Several three-line solutions also exist. One three-line solution is to draw a line joining the left edge of the top left dot to the right side of the bottom dot and continue the line downward until you reach a point where you can begin to

Figure 5.1
The Nine-Dot Puzzle

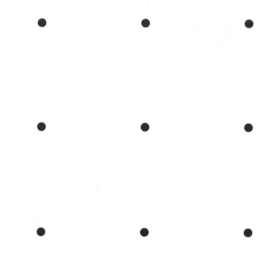

draw your second line upward, joining the left side of the center circle on the bottom to the right side of the center on the top. Continue upward until you reach a point where you can begin to draw the third line downward to connect the right side of the top right dot to the left side of the bottom right dot. Many other three-line solutions exist. Try folding the paper to join the lines.

The puzzle illustrates how problem solving sometimes occurs. People believe they know what to do, only to discover that the lines they draw within the box do not solve the problem. They may draw several lines and then try to think of other ways to solve the problem before they switch from the search for a solution within a given representation to a search for a new representation altogether. Some will make an insightful discovery without help. They will experience a subjective Aha!

A similar problem-solving process often occurs for social researchers. Herbert Simon's skepticism and criticism that theories of rational decision making did not correspond to fact was followed by an alternative definition of "bounded rationality," which described how a decision maker searched for decision alternatives. Rather than optimizing, the decision maker sought "satisficing" goals and developed mechanisms of learning and adaptation.[15]

Simon's idea was insightful, and offered a better explanation of decision making in practice. He came upon the idea in a rather cyclical trial-and-error way, where he grew to reject old ideas of rational decision making because of his discomfort with them. He was provoked in several ways, from doubt that such ideas could improve practice to his awareness that decision making in practice was very different from the accepted view of rationality.

Figure 5.2
One Solution to the Nine-Dot Puzzle

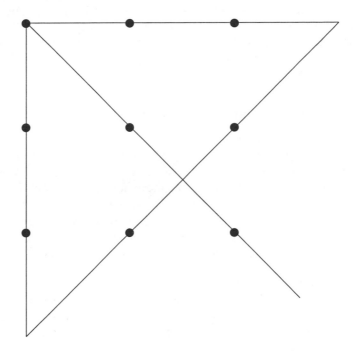

Simon's creative search might illustrate an "attitude" of searching involving asking questions and a desire to understand everyday occurrences. It is an attitude that might be encouraged by preparing oneself to handle ambiguity, uncertainty, and adversity.

How can one duplicate such an attitude? Here are some strategies illustrated in the Lewinian tradition of research, tactics that encourage us to understand and echo the needs of the setting as part of the process of developing ideas in organizational research.

Beginning with the Field

It is noteworthy that most literature references describe general trends, accepted practices, and conventional explanations. The continuing reliance on the literature and experts amounts to reshuffling old ideas already in the field. This, by definition, is limited by however we might be able to recombine these ideas, the result being a new permutation of old ideas, at best.

Instead of going to the literature or experts, try to describe and understand a problem or issue by the way it is described by people in the field. The assumption is that conventional concepts and categories are less relevant for provoking insight, because they encourage the verification of previous theories rather than encouraging new ways of representing something. The field provides an opportunity to view problems or issues in their natural setting, not defined or categorized as concepts or academic constructs. Instead, events and ideas are presented as they occur, randomly and uncategorized. It is like trying to find a new constellation from among the many that have already been identified.

Fitting the Inner Requirements of a Problem

Max Wertheimer's seminars and his book *Productive Thinking* illustrate how a genuine solution fits the inner and intrinsic requirements of the problem and is guided by the direction of the task.[16] In a genuine solution, every step is determined by its function in the whole structure of the problem situation. Wertheimer suggested that solutions range in terms of their goodness, foolishness, and sensibility. In a bad solution, the steps are made in a random fashion and are not intrinsically related to the whole process. In a genuine solution, the whole process has a unitary character; it moves in a consistent direction from start to end.

The productive thinking process is not necessarily as smooth as his formulation suggested. He was describing an ideal that neglected various factors, just as Galileo's laws of falling bodies deal with pure cases and neglect friction and various other factors. In some problems, solutions result from a trial-and-error process.

To illustrate this, Wertheimer contrasted two kinds of solutions. In one, an ape's behavior illustrated consistent movement in the direction of achieving the goal of obtaining food outside the enclosure in which the animal was kept. Another animal moved at random and seemed to find the food by accident. Although both behaviors achieved the goals, one was random, and was not focused on solving the problem. The other had a consistent and unitary character guided by the goal.[17]

Wertheimer asked the seminar participants to explain the characteristics of a good and genuine solution and of a bad solution, a discussion that suggested a bad procedure was senseless and structure blind because the steps dropped out of the blue and were not determined by the whole qualities of the task. The steps were arbitrarily arranged and had a structure that was alien to the problem. The procedures might be externally related, perhaps because the researcher was familiar with them, because they were deemed to be more acceptable, or because they were new.

In contrast, a genuine procedure involved sensible thought processes. The steps were conceived and carried out in accordance with the structure of the task and the steps worked in the direction of a better structure. In an ideal case, there were no wasted steps or detours. One went straight toward the goal in a direction determined by the inner requirements of the task.

Every step was determined by its function in the whole problem situation and was not arbitrary. Grasping the structure of a problem and the related structure of the solution is an important step to developing a genuine solution. A genuine solution involves real understanding of the problem.

While the characteristic of good and bad solutions may seem difficult to define, Wertheimer illustrates how they can be easily recognized in particular cases. The structure of the problem may be part (sometimes the crucial part) of the problem-solving process. Once the structure is seen, the difficulties disappear and the various data and observations click or fall into place in the proper relation to each other and to the solution. There are, however, problems that do not readily reveal their structure even after they are solved, perhaps because of their complexity or because they are subwholes in the solution.

Seeking the Collaboration of Others

The Lewinian tradition of research as described by Alfred Marrow in *The Practical Theorist*, encouraged openness and informality. Within the institute in Germany, Lewin's students formed close-knit groups and informal relationships. One such relationship was called the *Quasselstrippe*. In German, *quassel* means rambling on, while *strippe* is a string. The Quasselstrippe was a group in which people felt they could talk freely. This group met at the Schwedische Café across from the institute. "Animated conversation, bad puns and much laughter prevailed at lunch at the Quasselstrippe, with Lewin joining in the fun as much as anyone."[18] One or another of the dozen students surrounding him would either report on current research or propose a project. In Iowa City, a group of students congregated in the Round Window Restaurant, where they had the top-floor room where students could buy or eat their own lunches. The Iowa students sometimes called the group the "hot-air club."

In these discussions, one contribution would build upon another and group-formed ideas emerged for a testable hypothesis or an enthusiastic consensus on how a new area of investigation should be explored. None of the group ever felt he or she was on stage when presenting ideas or projects. People worked as if they were among peers, sharpening ideas from other's comments or recruiting assistance.

The group of people surrounding Lewin was never very large, as membership changed as new students arrived, presented their work, wrote their theses, and departed. Seminars were often held at Lewin's home, in a room with brown-stained wooden walls and a floor littered with sheets of brown wrapping paper on which people drew their diagrams in colored chalk.

Commitment to collaborating with others in a Lewin-style seminar group is initially motivated by common interests in focusing on problems and issues that people feel are important. Interest in getting people to meet together to discuss research is often very fragmented, as individuals may be motivated to work on their own individual problems. Since membership in a collaborative working group is voluntary, many people may not feel inclined to participate.

For a collaborative experience to develop, each person must be clear on the goals or norms of working together. Norms might encourage attendance, humor, informality, helpfulness, unselfishness, and a genuine desire to help others.

Using Examples and Analogies

Ask a person to describe something and they will offer an opinion. Test this out by asking managers to tell you about how they manage. Ask parents about their parenting style. In most cases, they will tell you they were participative managers or that they never yelled or shouted at their children. Their employees and children may offer a very different opinion.

Analogies and examples encourage an in-depth description of real issues, rather than a person's opinions and interpretations. In using analogies, it might be feasible to ask questions like, "What does this remind you of?" or "When have I felt like this before?" Analogies can be developed by completing the sentence, "This situation is like a . . ."

Other tactics encourage writing about critical incidents, in which participants articulate how they acted or behaved rather than what they perceived or felt. The critical incident technique has been used in uncovering the types of events new employees see as critical in communicating an organization's culture, for discovering the training needs for youth, and for identifying critical leadership competencies of manufacturing supervisors.[19]

The purpose of analogies and examples is to provide a rich background of uncategorized experience so researchers can begin to think differently about how to solve a problem. The value of this is illustrated by Janet Beavin Bavelas:

When you do not know anything about bird songs, you seldom hear them. But once you begin to learn about them, you suddenly hear birds where there was silence before. Perception is active, not passive, driven by schemata or cognitive classes. Similarly, once you begin to have a critical mass of examples of your vague idea, it will suddenly assault you from all sides; you will be unable not to see it. In my area, every social encounter, every novel or short story, every movie becomes full of exactly what it is I am currently most interested in. This hyper-tuning, this exaggerated observation is invaluable, not as evidence, for it is totally, hopelessly biased, but for helping to answer the important question, what class does this belong to.[20]

Encouraging Reframing

Some people are more creative than others in changing their framework for problem solving. Like a patient who refuses to believe a physician's terminal diagnosis, there are reactions of unwillingness to accept and adjust and to continue not to change one's behavior. The reactions of denial and anger sometimes prevent people from making any adjustment. Other people are more able to make adjustments and to change.[21]

Getting locked into a framework for solving a problem is analogous to getting your car stuck in the snow on your driveway. I watched my son try to take our car out of the garage and drive it up the snowy driveway onto the road. In six to eight attempts, he shot out of the garage at top speed, only to stall, spinning wildly on the hill. After he took a break, he came up with an idea of having his friends weigh the back wheels down by sitting in the back seat and trunk of the car. He drove straight up the hill.

In this case, my son was spinning his wheels literally and figuratively. He was, initially, locked into one framework for solving a problem, trying harder and harder to get up the hill. Then, frustrated, he took a break and returned later with a new framework for solving his problem. He laughed, suggesting, "I've got to do something different. It takes an idiot to try something over and over again and expect different results."

Analogously, in our thinking, we sometimes start spinning our mental wheels; that is, we work harder and harder at a frustrating problem, but succeed only in getting into a condition where it becomes more difficult to solve it because we are stuck in a rut. We become more determined that our approach will work, and more hopeful that it will.

"Why is it that some people, when they are faced with problems, get clever ideas, make suggestions and discoveries? What happens, what are the processes that lead to such solutions?"[22] There are many answers to these provocative questions from Max Wertheimer, one of which suggests that problem solvers rely on inappropriate past experience. A creative solution might emerge if problem solvers or researchers are able to refocus or reframe the issue in different ways. This might involve defining the problem from a number of perspectives, using different theoretical frameworks to investigate a problem, and relying on different and opposing viewpoints.[23]

Allowing Creativity to Occur in Different Forms

Creative thinking is a fluid process, based on the way a person thinks. Insightful ideas are sometimes molded and refined from single, dramatic events, while others are part of a long process of unravelling. The problem-solving process may illustrate different types of concentration, discipline, and completion of details. In the field of poetry, Stephen Spender writes about two kinds of concentration: One is immediate and complete, the other is plodding and only completed in stages.[24] He indicates that some poets scarcely need to revise their works, while others evolve after long periods of revision.

Mozart thought out symphonies, quartets, and even scenes from operas in his head as he went about his day. Then he transcribed them in their completeness. A more plodding concentration is illustrated by those who write in stages, feeling their way from rough draft to rough draft. This type of concentration was illustrated by Beethoven, who wrote fragments of themes in notebooks he kept beside him, working on and developing them for years.[25] Although Mozart's form of concentration may seem more brilliant and dazzling, Beethoven's is equally as impressive when the results, and not the process, are what are being judged.

Some theoretical development might be consolidated with a Mozartian type of concentration. Most research problems that are complex and involve a large number of different people and perspectives might be more naturally consolidated with a more plodding Beethovenian model for those who are less gifted with the Mozartian talent. Spender's comments about his Beethovenian process might be appropriate for the field researcher:

Myself, I am scarcely capable of immediate concentration in poetry. My mind is not clear, my will is weak, I suffer from an excess of ideas and a weak sense of form. For each poem that I begin to write, I think of at least ten which I do not write down at all. For every poem which I do write down, there are seven or eight which I never complete.

The method which I adopt therefore is to write down as many ideas as possible, in however rough a form, in notebooks (I have at least twenty of these, on a shelf beside my desk, going back over fifteen years). I then make use of some of the sketches and discard others.[26]

ENCOURAGING INSIGHT

An insightful idea usually results from being creative in thinking "outside the box." A person who is trying to solve a problem is often a creature of habit, using principles or "rules of thumb" he or she has used in the past. These habits are obvious when we search for our misplaced house keys. We will try to find the keys in ways we are familiar with, using general heuristics (When something is lost, think of the last time I had it) or specific heuristics (I've often left my cars keys in my coat). Such search processes are often selective, constrained, or based on what we did in the past.

A desire to be more creative is often provoked when things are not working, and when events and people challenge the conventional way of seeing something. However, any new idea or framework is more likely to be insightful if it is encouraged by a creative attitude that maximizes the use of field involvement, collaboration, examples and analogies, real concepts, and a diversity in creative styles. Such an attitude is certainly more productive than one that is based on unfounded habits or beliefs.

Unlike the alchemists, who spent all their time and energy on mixing various kinds of matter in special ways in the hope of producing new kinds of matter such as gold, people who are more successful in quickly finding new ideas are able to reframe more quickly. They have much in common with a good carpenter, who may never be perfectly flawless in implementing his or her methods, but is able to correct and adapt them in making sure that the final product appears flawless. In the same way, the Echo approach, as used by Alex Bavelas and others, was seen as a way of encouraging creativity and insight. It was an attitude much more than a set of strategies that they followed in a procedural way. The strategies I have listed are only some of the ways this attitude might be encouraged.

6

Interviewing Individuals with Different Types of Questions

I keep six honest serving men
(They taught me all I knew)
Their names are What and Why and When
And How and Where and Who.
                    Rudyard Kipling, "The Elephant's Child"

The importance of different types of questions in interviews was underlined as early as the Hawthorne studies in the 1930s. These studies were primarily concerned with trying to understand how various aspects of the organization's design affected morale and productivity. Almost everything researchers did—increased lighting, decreased lighting, more and less rest, food, and coffee—resulted in performance increases. The results seemed the same whether they introduced something new or took it away.

Interviewers who tried to unravel these results got superficial, specific responses to the structured interview questions they asked.[1] Frustrated, the interviewers tried a radically new approach in which they asked a series of open-ended questions about what the employees did on their jobs. The employees launched into long tirades to which the interviewers patiently listened. More important, the researchers gained surprising understandings about human relations from the open-ended interviews.

TYPES OF INTERVIEW QUESTIONS

I have used the information iceberg to outline several types of questions that a person might ask to understand why people act the way they do.

1. Biographical characteristics
2. Opinions and attitudes
3. Suggestions and goals
4. Values and beliefs
5. Past behaviors

Figure 6.1 illustrates these various types of questions.

The most exposed part of the information iceberg, which represents the 10 percent above the imaginary waterline, illustrates the most reliable information, as it is easily coded and verified. It summarizes questions relating to biographical facts, achievements, or technical information, all which are measurable and verifiable. Biographical data can describe age, marital status, and position. Achievement questions might ask for grade point average, publications, honors, and achievements. Technical knowledge questions ask about a person's technical capability to carry out a task and can include questions on general performance. Experience-based questions highlight human capabilities, such as a person's ability to type, write a memo, or fly an airplane. Such biographical and experience questions, although potentially very reliable, require an inferential leap in predicting behavior.

Most of the information at the top of the information iceberg can usually be gathered through methods other than interviewing. Since some of these questions are usually cumbersome to ask in interviews, the information might be better collected in other ways, through organization records or other forms.

Below the imaginary waterline are a variety of questions that are important in understanding interpersonal and organizational behavior. The information gathered from them is more difficult to verify and gather, in addition to being potentially more unreliable. If the questions are not carefully asked, individuals will give different responses to the same questions.

Answers to the first two sets of questions—relating to attitudes and goals—do not always help us understand how people will act in the future. Since attitudes are a psychological predisposition to respond positively or negativity and goals reflect intentions, they are only slightly more relevant than biographical questions in understanding behavior. We are all aware of cases where a person's attitude toward something—such as dissatisfaction with a job, marriage, or country—did not noticeably change their behavior. That is, some dissatisfied people are very productive people in their jobs and lives. In the same way, a person's intention to act—quit smoking, go on a diet, relax more—does not predict that he or she will act in that way.

Figure 6.1
Interview Information Iceberg

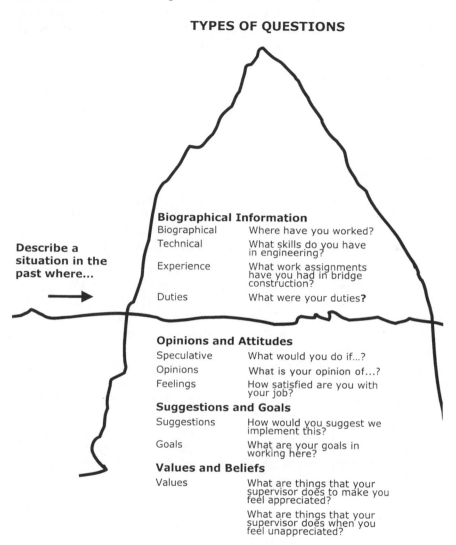

TYPES OF QUESTIONS

Biographical Information

Biographical	Where have you worked?
Technical	What skills do you have in engineering?
Experience	What work assignments have you had in bridge construction?
Duties	What were your duties?

Describe a situation in the past where... →

Opinions and Attitudes

Speculative	What would you do if...?
Opinions	What is your opinion of...?
Feelings	How satisfied are you with your job?

Suggestions and Goals

Suggestions	How would you suggest we implement this?
Goals	What are your goals in working here?

Values and Beliefs

Values	What are things that your supervisor does to make you feel appreciated?
	What are things that your supervisor does when you feel unappreciated?

The sets of questions relating to values and beliefs are the core of the information iceberg. Values are assumptions about what people find worth pursuing in life, while beliefs are assumptions that people hold to be true. Values and beliefs represent the core of interpersonal and organizational behavior, and are most difficult to understand and the most hidden from public view. Yet they are the most relevant to understanding what the person will do in the future, just as they are the most basic in predicting the flow of the iceberg. In most cases, people act in accordance with their values and beliefs, a fact that is illustrated when people are driven to do something—work hard, climb mountains, or kill other people—because of values and beliefs.

The set of questions reflecting past behavior—those displayed outside the iceberg—are also quite relevant for helping us understand what people will do in the future. That is, one of the best ways to understand people and how they will act is to find what people did in the past under similar conditions.

While there are many types of questions to enhance our understanding of people, the Echo approach suggests that values, beliefs, and behaviors can offer a valuable perspective.

PROBLEMS AND PROSPECTS IN USING OPEN-ENDED, UNSTRUCTURED INTERVIEWS FOR UNDERSTANDING INDIVIDUAL BEHAVIOR

Pundits are very critical of open-ended interviews. They point out that different schoolteachers might feel very confident about the accuracy of their assessment of five children, yet their evaluations offer radically different conclusions. "I think this child is gifted," says one teacher. "This child has behavioral problems," says another, "and needs help."

Selection panelists are often bemused by the lack of consistency in their judgments of a candidate's potential in a selection interview. Several selection officers, all of whom have very different judgments, can interview the same applicants. One candidate may be ranked as first by one selection officer and fifty-seventh by another.

Insightful questions in interviews can provide a rich assortment of information. Much of the information we gather in interviews is messy and difficult to interpret. Here are some problems that occur when we ask questions in interviews:

- The "Yea-Sayer" Bias. Some people want to be nice and create a favorable impression. They don't want to tell you that what you are doing is not right. They are "yea sayers." Ask these people a discerning question and they will agree with you. The tendency to agree with all or most questions asked is particularly prominent when people are asked to assess a new product, program, or idea that was previously unfamiliar. It's like a honeymoon. During the first few days, everything is great.
- Social Desirability Bias. Some questions are more likely to get a positive response. We tend to overestimate how many times we exercise because exercise is socially desirable. In the same way, most people will likely say that they are participative managers because that is a desirable characteristic, even though their peers might believe they act like Genghis Khan.

- The Halo Effect. A recent event may affect our judgments of what is important. Imagine how a person might respond to a question about a new program or product if he or she had recently had a good experience with your company's staff. Imagine how a person might respond if he or she just had a bad experience and were treated impolitely or curtly.

- The Four-Minute Rule. Ask yourself about the last person you met. How long was it before you made a judgment of whether you would like him or her? In the same way, many of us make judgments about a person very quickly, without fully understanding the problem. We make a judgment about people very early in most interviews, usually within the first four minutes.

An interview is an opportunity to get information from the respondent in a face-to-face situation. On the surface, the most sophisticated way to respond to these problems is to structure an interview or questioning process so that subjects or applicants respond to the same set of questions in the same order. Structure increase accuracy, reliability, and validity.[2] But a predefined structure of questions might also decrease the insight and depth of understanding of a problem. It is especially difficult to develop a penetrative understanding of an organization's culture from structured, standardized questions.

The Echo interview is an open-ended, unstructured interview. The style of open-ended, unstructured interviewing encourages a process that is very similar to any discovery process encouraging search, self-analysis, and creative insight. The open-ended interview can be valuable for understanding an organizational problem as perceived by the individual participants. It can be used for developing theories or hypotheses that are valid for the situation, as a first step in the construction of measurement instruments, in developing a statement of goals, or in constructing a sense of cultural feelings and interpretations. The goal of such a process, ultimately, is to create a manageable understanding of the numerous problems, feelings, and insights people have.

Any discover process is usually rather open-ended when people have an opportunity to explore ideas and thoughts. In an open-ended discovery-like interview, people are encouraged to delve deeper in exploring their experiences. An interviewer guides them by reflecting comments, summarizing statements, and providing an atmosphere for an open, trusting discussion.

A major element in the Echo open-ended process is a commitment to learning about people on their own terms. The task is to find out or discover what is fundamental or central in what people value and the way they think and act. The interviewer's job is to create the environment to do this.

Persons who participate in interviews are more likely to provide insightful responses if they are allowed to structure the interview in their own format. The open-ended style of interviewing implies that an individual's world cannot be described by tightly structured questions. The interviewee can best describe his or her world within a structure of questions that encourages exploration.

ECHO QUESTIONS FOR UNDERSTANDING
VALUES AND BELIEFS

John Dewey's classic book, *Democracy and Education,* illustrates how the use of language is an extension of the principle that things gain meaning by being used in a shared experience or joint action. When words do not enter in a shared experience, either overtly or imaginatively, they are simply stimuli with little intellectual value. There is no conscious purpose or meaning. The "plus sign may be a stimulus to perform the act of writing one number under another and adding the numbers, but the person performing the act will operate much as an automaton would," unless the person realizes the meaning of what is done.[3] With the Echo approach, values and beliefs are thought to be the most valid statement of the meaning that people ascribe to certain things, events, or people. The approach offers a way of understanding values and beliefs underlying what people experience and say. The method suggests that problems and issues within a setting can best be defined by identifying the values that people have toward them. Its purpose is to generate reliable, culturally unbiased information about issues and events facing a group of people. Any set of concepts, questionnaires, or measurement tools that are developed from this process have a shared meaning for that culture.

There are several types of questions that can be used to understand values and beliefs, most which ask several positive and negative open-ended questions on an issue. A respondent may be asked to answer several positive and negative questions: What is a good thing to do? Who would approve? Some of the corresponding negative questions might include the following: What is a bad thing to do? Who would disapprove?

Usually, about seven to ten positive and corresponding negative questions are asked in each interview or Echo session, although this may vary depending on the issue. In constructing such questions, the following checklist might be considered:[4]

1. Role of the Respondent. For example, a person like you, an employee. Who are some people, like you, who have a positive influence? Who are some people, like you, who have a negative influence? Role specifications in Echo questions could be you, a person like you, a person like your friend, a person like your neighbor, a member of your class, a person older than you, a person living in another country, a person you would not like, or a person very different from you. An alternative to using such specifications is to ask completely unspecified questions: What is a good thing to do? What is a bad thing to do?

2. Event. For example, a thing to happen, a thing to do. What are some things that you would like to happen? What are some things you do not want to happen? What are some things you would like to do? What are some things you do not want to do?

3. Valuation of the Event. For example, good, bad; like, not like; ought, ought not. What are some positive things you would like to happen? What are some negative things you would like to happen? What are some good things you like to do? What are some bad things you like to do?

4. Reinforcement or Agency. For example, approve, disapprove; praise, blame; cause, prevent. What are some things that might have caused this to happen? What are some things that might prevent this from happening? Who would approve? Who would disapprove?

5. Source. Reinforce or agent; for example, parents, myself, a good job, bad luck. Are there people in authority who might have encouraged this to happen? Who might have discouraged this? What might have caused this to happen? The goal of these questions is to identify the source of the events.

6. Additional Context. For example, during a strike; during the political debate. Are there events that might have influenced this to happen during the political debate? Are there events that might inhibit this from happening during the political debate? The goal of these questions is to make the other five questions more specific. Another kind of additional context is the specification or future time or conditional mood, to modify the event. Past tense "happen" questions tend to elicit satisfactions or disappointments. Conditional "happen" questions, about things that could happen, tend to elicit hopes and fears.

Complex questions might be considered. For example, simple questions might include the following: What is a good thing to do? Who would praise you? Who would scold you? These questions might be combined into a more complex question: What is a good thing to do so someone (source) will praise you (reinforcement), but your friends in the club will scold you?

Before Echo interviews and question sessions, the questions should be tested on an equivalent group of people to those who will be sampled. Question cards, printed instructions, biographical data or forms, and supplemental forms can be revised in response to feedback from participants.

It might be appropriate to ask questions that are directly related to developing an instrument or interview schedule. For example, after asking the questions listed, the researcher might wish to ask questions like the following: What questions or items do you think we should ask to better understand this issue? What questions or measures are of less value in understanding this issue?

ADAPTING ECHO PRINCIPLES FOR UNDERSTANDING ORGANIZATIONAL EXPERIENCES AND BEHAVIORS

Since the Echo approach suggests that we need different types of information to understand people, it is often useful to use different questionning techniques such as the critical incident, behavior description, and repertory grid.

Critical Incident Technique

The importance of the critical incident technique is highlighted when we ask someone to tell us about what managers do. This simple question has been asked of managers by children, staff specialists, university students, and scholars. Ask managers and you are likely to be told that managers plan, organize, coordinate, and control, just like Henri Fayol said in 1916.[5] The views that managers have of themselves are reinforced by textbooks, teachings, and a whole field that suggests that good managers are able to plan, organize, coordinate, and control. So when we ask managers what they do, they say they do just that. Is this a case of social desirability, or just a bad question?

When we observe management in action, we find something entirely different, as was pointed out by Henry Mintzberg in his classic book, *The Nature of Managerial Work*.[6] Mintzberg and others observed that management is something entirely different when we observe it in action. They exploded a myth and illustrated how poor questions have reinforced this misunderstanding. Managers perform a set of roles to handle the extreme variety and pace of their work. These roles include interpersonal roles (as figurehead, leader, and liaison), information roles (as monitor, disseminator, and spokesperson), and decisional roles (as entrepreneur, disturbance handler, resource allocator, and negotiator).

There are other examples of undiscerning questions like "What do managers do?" I have asked many such questions. What skills are important for a manager? What suggestions would you offer others to be more successful? How would you motivate your teenagers? Such questions encourage others to offer their opinions and commonsense truths. Sometimes these opinions are based on very little information.

Psychologists during World War II had a similar problem when they asked field commanders, officers, and soldiers how to improve the performance of bomber and tank crews. They observed that when an officer or crew member was asked to describe the behavior of an effective tank crew, he responded with a list of traits or vague descriptions, such as courage, leadership, know-how, and the like. Some psychologists began to ask for examples of problems or critical incidents of effective and ineffective performance. The critical incident technique emerged as the interviewers began to learn to ask for examples of incidents that the bomber and tank crews experienced. The officer or soldier replied with examples of effective or ineffective tank crew performance. These stories about specific tank crew behavior helped to identify performance problems and improve tank crew effectiveness. The term "critical incident" was used for such stories because they illustrated real events describing specific effective or ineffective performance.[7]

Critical incidents provide data reflecting behavior. They usually are not opinions. Opinions, as such, illustrate a person's attitudes and ability to articulate. In describing an incident, a person usually does not rely on opinion or intelligence. A person relies on memory of past observations rather than opinions or judgments of certain events.

A list of critical incidents provides a flavor of the issues or problems that are more important to the responder. This provides a pool of important incidents described in the interviewee's terms, in addition to the feelings and perceptions of how they are viewed. Such a pooling of incidents gives a wider perspective on the variables underlying an event, or at least one that is more inclusive than responses to general questions.

Critical incidents might be used to understand topics such as motivation, communication, leadership, or other general areas. The questions can be used to define values and beliefs, or they might provide a perspective on what people experience. The following are examples of questions seeking to identify critical incidents about motivation. These questions sought to understand the characteristics that maintained and sustained motivation for entrepreneurs:

- Can you give me an example of a time when you felt especially satisfied or motivated? Describe the situation. What motivated you? What turned you on?
- Can you give me an example of a time when you felt especially dissatisfied or unmotivated? Describe the situation. What was it about this situation that you found demotivating or dissatisfying?

These questions can provide a rich pool of incidents, feelings, and perceptions, but only if they are asked within an appropriate sequence, and with the appropriate probes.

Probing is a way to continue the same line of questioning by searching for more information. Soliciting examples and explanations from the person being surveyed can expand responses (Could you give me an example? or Could you give me another example of this?). Information from other sources, such as observation and survey techniques, might be sought in the probe. Such probing asks for more in-depth information and personal experiences that could not be obtained from the interview (Are there other data or people who might offer a similar [or different] perspective on what you have just said?). The language of the interview is the respondent's language expressed in the jargon he or she has become familiar with. It is not predefined by the questions or phrases the researcher uses (I'd like to understand the terms you use to describe this).

The critical incident technique has been used in a variety of settings. It was used in uncovering the types of events new employees see as critical in communicating an organization's culture, for discovering the training needs for youth, and for identifying critical leadership competencies of manufacturing supervisors.[8]

One of the major drawbacks of the critical incident method is that it relies on a person's ability to remember something. Some people have more intense feelings toward some issues and may be more likely to recall them. As a result, the technique relies on the interviewer's ability to uncover some of those things that might be forgotten.

Behavioral Description Interviewing

Here is an example of a set of questions often asked in selection interviews:

- Why do you want to work for this organization?
- What qualifications do you have that make you feel that you will be successful in this job?
- This position involves a lot of contact with the public. How do you feel about your skills in dealing with people?
- This position involves working closely with others. How did you get along with others in your previous employment? Have you had any problems getting along with coworkers in the past?
- What are your goals and visions of what you would like to do in the next few years?
- What are some of your strengths and weaknesses?
- If you had to try to get the cooperation of someone, how would you do it?
- If you had to deal with a member or the public who was angry, what would you do?

Most people who are applying for a job will prepare for these questions. These are classic textbook questions that simply tell you that the person was prepared for the interview. These questions reveal very little about what the person is really like. A person's goals and visions are simply his or her aspirations. A person's goals do not tell you about how he or she works on a day-to-day basis. Hypothetical questions about gaining cooperation and handling difficult people illustrate that the person might be up to date with the most recent management literature. They do not tell you whether he or she will be successful in gaining cooperation or in handling difficult people. Do we expect that a person will really tell us his or her real weaknesses? Would we expect a person to tell us that he or she has been unethical or fired for incompetence in a previous organization? No, of course not. The person would word the answers to reveal his or her most positive side.

In short, such questions reveal very little about the person's behavior. Those that answer such questions well are those who are more verbal, more prepared, and more able to give a pleasing initial impression in interpersonal situations. These characteristics may have nothing to do with what you want.

Behavioral description interviewing is a form of critical incident interview that has been used in employee selection. It is based on the often-quoted principle that one of the best predictors of what a person will do in the future is what they did in the past.

Reliable and valid evidence of past performance can assist in predicting the future.[9] Here are some examples of questions that help in understanding a person's past behavior:

- Tell me about an accomplishment during your last job that you were very happy with. Describe this. Where did you get the idea, how did you plan it, how did you implement the plan, how did you deal with some of the major obstacles?
- Tell me about your typical workday. For instance, what happened yesterday? I'm trying to find out some nitty-gritty details of your day-to-day work period. That is, from the time you come into the office until the time you go home.

Some of these questions can focus on specific aspects, such as motivational leadership, communication, conflict, and so on:

- Could you give me an example of a situation you have faced where an employee was performing well? Describe how you dealt with this situation? What did you say to the individual? What did the individual say and what are some of the things that occurred?
- Could you give me an example of a time when you carried out a task in which you had to coordinate a number of people in developing and implementing a plan?
- Could you give me an example of a time when a colleague came to you and asked you to help them with a personal problem?
- Could you give me an example of one of the projects you have completed that you think best demonstrates your leadership ability?
- Could you give me an example of a time when you have had to fire somebody for poor performance? When you had to fire somebody even though they were performing well?

These questions, when they are followed with further behavior description probes, can provide approximations of what the person did. They ask the individual to describe the exact behavior that occurred in the particular work setting.

Each of these questions should be followed by questions asking for examples of events illustrating the other extreme. For example, behavior description questions set up a format so that an individual can describe extreme cases. For instance, what is the most, least, last, toughest, worst? These are superlative attitudes. They assume that future action is best predicted from superlative attitudes, values, and behaviors that occurred in the past. In this sense, they are more realistic than questions that relate to opinions and commonsense truths.

Questions about past behaviors are very useful for an understanding of organizations, as they describe observable events and acts. In principle, these questions seem easy to get good information on, since they ask a person to summarize an event or experience. Difficulties with the reliability of the information arise because of memory loss, remembering less significant events, highlighting the most recent ones, threatening questions, or confidential questions. Such statements, however, are valid to the respondent.

The Repertory Grid

In 1954 a psychologist by the name of George Kelly offered a new theory of personality based on the idea that every individual characterizes his or her world through a series of constructs. These constructs are the basis by which an individual interprets the world. Kelly's form of psychotherapy sought to help people become clearer on the constructs that defined their worlds. Disturbed people were unclear and confused. Healthy and undisturbed people had greater clarity on the constructs that ordered their worlds. In order to help people order and define the constructs within their lives, Kelly developed what is known as the Role Construct Repertory Test, or RepGrid (Repertory Grid).[10] Even though the RepGrid was originally created as a way to help psychotherapists, it has since been adapted for a variety of studies, especially in identifying skills and characteristics of people and organizations. The interviewee is asked to make a comparison of people, tasks, organizations, or characteristics he or she is familiar with. The interview process encourages the development of a set of concepts and terms that describe these comparisons. In other words, the interviewee is being encouraged to comment on something (skills or characteristics) by making a number of comparisons with other cases.

In developing a list of characteristics of managers, the interviewee is first asked to identify six managers whom he or she is familiar with and can make a judgment about. The person is also asked to identify the worst and best manager imaginable. This can be a real person or a general impression of what the worse or best would be like. Each of the six names (or pseudonyms, if the person does not want to identify them) can be written on notecards.

The interviewer then initiates a series of comparisons by choosing three notecards (on a systematic or random basis) and placing them in front of the interviewee. The interviewee is then asked to describe a characteristic that is common in two of the cases but is different in the third. After the construct is identified, the interviewer will probe to have it described more fully, with questions such as, "What does this mean?" or "Could you give me an example of this?" More than one characteristic might emerge from each set of comparisons.

Several such comparisons are made in developing a list of constructs such that each is described on a continuum: lack of clear direction versus clear direction and vision, low customer satisfaction versus high customer service orientation, and so forth. Interviewees might also be asked to rate the importance of each characteristic in comparison with others and to assess each person on the basis of these comparisons.

In one study, after completing five RepGrid interviews, I combined the data into an overall list of concepts. After a great deal of refinement, seventeen concepts emerged to provide a picture of the responses to the general question of what characteristics describe this sample of Singaporean organizations. That is, we developed a list of categories for each case and then sought to develop a more common list of criteria, recognizing the intent and meaning of their descriptions. The categories were intended to represent items that had common and similar meaning. For example, one of the categories described "training," but different people used unique terms. Some people described it as being trained and educated to do one job, while others thought of it as formal training sessions that taught on-the-job procedures.

The RepGrid style of questioning has been used in a wide variety of studies, including studies measuring the change in how graduates perceived their environment after they left school and found employment. The elements for comparison in this study included nonwork environment, likes and dislikes, and personal heroes and villains.[11] Another study used the RepGrid technique when three parks were compared to find out how they were alike and unlike the third. This was continued until a list of constructs was compiled and subjects were asked to distinguish the importance of the constructs. They were then asked why they made these judgments, until a set of primary values was revealed.[12] Another research study attempted to measure changes in self-image among a group of MBA students by showing comparisons of the impact of courses.[13] It has also been compared to cognitive mapping as a research tool.[14]

THE PROCESS OF INTERVIEWING IS
AS IMPORTANT AS THE QUESTIONS ASKED

Most of the interviews associated with the Echo style of research are rather open ended, so participants have the opportunity to explore ideas and thoughts in response to certain general questions. The researcher encourages an exploration of ideas and issues by reflecting and summarizing comments while providing an atmosphere for openness. The emphasis is on stimulating participants to talk about ideas, interests, needs, and values. In conducting the interview, participants are encouraged to talk about the problem or issue underlying the research, exposing feelings about the situation and providing an environment where the interviewee can explore the problem and come up with his or her own interpretations.

I feel that there is a circular pattern in most interview responses, as a respondent may offer a superficial answer at first but later may offer a deeper response with some more thought. It is almost as if people talk in circles. In the initial statement, the respondent might address the issue superficially and then stray momentarily to another topic. He or she might even laugh or digress rather radically to another topic. Such digressions are rather common and a good interviewer allows them to happen. One of the first steps in understanding might be in asking, "What do you mean?" or "Tell me more," or "Can you give me an example?"

Listening and Paraphrasing

How do you check to make sure that you understand another person's ideas or information as he or she intends them? How do you know that the remarks mean the same to you as they do to the other person?

When we listen to another person, we usually do so at one of four levels. We might actually *ignore* what the other person is saying, because we already feel we know what they will say or what is important. We may *pretend* to hear, while nodding our head and using phrases like "uh-huh," "hmmm," or "right." We might practice *selective listening*, tuning out during certain parts of the conversation while hearing others. We do this when we are in a boring lecture or when someone is talking too much. We might also practice *attentive listening*, paying attention to the words and phrases, the energy level in the words, and the gestures and inflections.[15]

Empathic listening is not active listening, reflective listening, or other strategies that involve rephrasing or paraphrasing what others have said. Such listening strategies only reflect on the ideas and phrases that participants use. Empathic listening is a higher form of listening. It asks that you get into the other person's head and try to understand values and beliefs. Put yourself in the other person's shoes and try to find out what he or she values and believes in and why. Understanding values requires a different style of questioning and listening. The essence of empathic listening is not sympathy or feeling sorry for someone. It is that you understand the person and his or her values and beliefs. You understand the person so well that you can predict his or her actions.

Empathic listening involves more than registering or cataloguing another person's values and beliefs, as well as their feelings, thoughts, problems, or needs. One of the tests of listening is being able to restate the other's words as the person has stated them. If the person accepts this, there's an excellent chance that the interviewee has listened and understood the messages. A reflective summary is a way of summing up the feelings another person has expressed, disregarding the factual details and incidentals. It involves making summary statements of what the interviewee has said, pointing out important phrases of the discussion as voiced by the interviewee, and rephrasing what the interviewee has expressed, using such terms as "you feel that" or "you value that." Paraphrasing thus is crucial in attempting to bridge the interpersonal gap. It increases the accuracy of communication and the degree of mutual and shared understanding. It conveys your interest and concern to see how others view things.

People sometimes think of paraphrasing as merely putting the other person's ideas in another way. They try to say the same thing with different words. Such word swapping may merely result in the illusion of mutual understanding.

Silence during Interviews

Effective interviewing relies on the proper use of pauses. In one case, I observed a high school girl who sat through several group counseling sessions uttering no more than three or four words a session. At the end of that time she had apparently resolved her difficulty, faced up to the fact, and learned to attack the problem in a problem-solving manner. She no longer had an adjustment difficulty in her schoolwork or with her fellow classmates. This probably is an extreme case. Nevertheless, pauses can be constructive, a time when the interviewee is collecting thoughts, struggling to find adequate expression for them, and clarifying true feelings.

The respect for silence is a key skill to enhance the process of interviewing. Silence may occur for various reasons. The interviewee may require time for thinking. Confusion can create silence either because of the issues dealt with or because of the interviewer's probes. Silence may also occur due to the interviewee's uncertainty of the interviewer's expectations. The interviewee may be silent because he or she is resisting what he or she considers to be probing. There are short pauses when one is simply looking for thoughts.

The purpose of the Echo interview process is, ultimately, to create a manageable description of the numerous values, beliefs, behaviors, and other information that might affect the research or give it a clearer direction. Ultimately, it shapes the research project so that it is more focused in getting commitment from people who would otherwise be less interested.

In any interview process the interviewer will use different types of questions. Different questions will get at different levels of information: Some are more appropriate for defining criteria or measures for further research, and others assist in probing and developing a deeper understanding of the problem and need for change. Some questions will seek to develop an understanding of interests, values, and commitment. Other questions might be used to help understand how participants feel that the project might be focused to respond to their needs.

The success of an interview grows from trust much more than from interviewing technique. It involves gaining respect, genuineness, understanding, acceptance, and empathy. Curiosity and exploration are more likely to be aroused in a free and secure environment where people are clear on expectations, and where the research project articulates their values and beliefs.

HOW QUESTIONS FOCUS A POINT OF VIEW

"Every decision to observe something, or to ask a question, or to meet with someone constitutes an intervention into the ongoing organizational process. If I interview someone about his [or her] organization, the very questions I ask give the respondent ideas he [or she] never had before."[16] This statement, by Edgar Schein, suggests that the very process of formulating answers forces the respondent to define a point of view that the person may never have thought of before. The term "experimental effect," first coined in psychology, implies that the experimenter or researcher, in the very act of research, is introducing a variable that changes the nature of the situation.

I feel that the manner in which the questions are asked and the type of questions play a key role in encouraging people to think differently about the people doing research. They can increase or decrease anger or hostility toward organizational issues, as well as increase or lower expectations for change, simply because the interviewer acted in certain ways.

The Echo approach encourages a process of inquiry to assist the respondent, as much as to gain information for the researcher. The process of inquiry itself may act on the respondent, as some respondents report changes in themselves as a result of being interviewed. Many interviewees report great benefit from the self-analysis that was set in motion. Some individuals report making life-changing decisions in the middle of the interview. Most important is the inquiry might start a process of change in the whole institution.[17]

EXAMPLE: USING ECHO QUESTIONS FOR UNDERSTANDING COMMUNICATIONS PROBLEMS IN A NUCLEAR POWER PLANT

In trying to understand the communication problems that might occur in the control room of a nuclear power plant, here are examples of some of the questions we used in understanding "working relationships."[18]

Considering the various communications linkages that you have just identified for the different parts of the shift, we would like to ask some questions about the nature of your working relationship with each of these individuals or groups. For each of these individuals or groups:

- Could you give some examples of things that this individual or group does that you find helpful to you in your job?

- Could you give some specific examples of things that this individual or group does that are not so helpful to you in your job?
- What are some things that you might do which they might consider helpful in their job?
- What are some things that they might do which they might consider less helpful in their job?
- Describe a time when you felt especially good about the working relationships in this organization. What happened? Why did this happen?
- Describe a time when you felt especially bad about the working relationships in this organization. What happened? Why did this happen?
- What do you find satisfying about your working relationships with people in this organization?
- What do you find dissatisfying about the working relationships with people in this organization?
- Who in this organization contributes most to establishing a positive working relationship? Why?
- Who in this organization contributes most to establishing a negative working relationship? Why?
- What do you find most satisfying about the way your supervisor treats you?
- What do you find most dissatisfying about the way your supervisor treats you?
- What does your supervisor do which you find especially pleasing?
- What does your supervisor do which you might find especially displeasing?
- What are some positive things you would like to happen in improving the working relationships?
- What are some negative things you would not like to happen in the working relationships?
- Are there people in authority who might help improve your working relationships? How might they do this?
- Are there people in authority who might not help improve your working relationships? How might they do this?
- Are there events (conflicts, budgets, etc.) which have positively affected your working relationships?
- Are there events (conflicts, budgets, etc.) which have negatively affected your working relationships?

The first set of two questions produced 264 examples of things people were doing that were helpful or not helpful. These were classified into twelve categories. The questions represent a variety of types of Echo questions that, after pilot testing, might be used for understanding this issue. Each question could be followed by specific probes, such as the following: Who would approve? Why did this happen? How might this be prevented?

7

Interviewing Groups

> Dynamic wholes have properties which are different from the properties of either their parts or the sum of their parts.
>
> Kurt Lewin

An individual behaves differently in a group than when not in a group. Kurt Lewin's experiments revealed that neither the personality of the person alone nor the nature of the social situation by itself is adequate to interpret behavior. Group standards and norms set in motion powerful pressures to conform and go along, and any individual who attempts to deviate is often pressured to conform and to work within the norms. The group is therefore a psychologically organic whole, rather than a simple collection of individuals. The group interaction is something of a gestalt, a whole containing dissimilar parts. "The whole of the group is different from the sum of its parts: it has definite properties of its own."[1]

GATHERING DATA ABOUT GROUP VALUES AND BELIEFS

The Echo question session[2] is similar to a focus group meeting[3] in encouraging a group-interviewing format that is an opportunity to collect data from the interacting group. The Echo question session is unique in trying to measure group and individual experiences as well as group pressures, norms, and values. In particular, the Echo question session is particularly useful for encouraging organizational change.

The Echo question session seeks to encourage creativity and critical thinking from a number of open-ended questions that provide diverse perspectives on a topic. Participants might be encouraged to respond to questions that probe for an understanding of various aspects of a program or idea, such as the purpose or the way a program is designed, administered, or delivered.

Questions might include the following: What are some of the opportunities this organization faces? What are some of its threats? What are some of this organization's strengths? What are some of its weaknesses? What ideas or projects might we pursue to respond to strengths, weaknesses, opportunities, and threats? What are some of the most important problems we have to deal with now? What are some problems we might have to deal with, given the changes that are occurring? What ideas and skills will we need to change? A good guide creates a natural progression and encourages participants to develop consensus about the most important issues.

Questions might also probe for concrete and detailed accounts of participants' experiences. This means locating the specific examples, reasons, or issues underlying a person's attitude, values, or beliefs. An emphasis on examples of experiences provides a rich description of what and why things happened, and how the situation might be averted. The goal is to try to elicit experiences or reference to the experiences of others, rather than opinion. Participants might be asked to identify what they find satisfying and dissatisfying, and what ideas they have for change or improvement:

- What are some of the things which are satisfying about . . . ?
- What are some of the things which are dissatisfying about . . . ?
- Can you offer an example of an experience when you were very satisfied with the . . . ?
- Can you offer an example of an experience when you were very dissatisfied with the . . . ?
- What are some ideas for improving the . . . ?

The interviewer might encourage respondents to move back and forth between positive and negative questions. What are some of the things you find most demotivating? What are things that you find very motivating? Question guides that provide only one perspective—negative or positive, past versus future, individual perspective versus organizational perspective—might discourage exploration.

Most focus group discussions assume that the moderator will not be an expert or offer comments in the discussion. In this sense, the moderator's role is one of tracking the discussion to assure that all topics are dealt with in each group and are adequately reported. It is also important to summarize the discussion at certain junctures and to be able to list the most important issues that might guide further work or exploration.

The skills of a moderator go beyond those needed in the individual interview. Good listening, summarizing and reflecting, flexibility, and empathy are truly important skills of all interviewers. Group interviews require unique skills, as the interviewer must keep one person or coalition from dominating, while encouraging recalcitrant participants to be more involved. In addition, the moderator must be able to summarize important points and seek consensus and encourage a direction. While providing an agenda is an important means of focusing a discussion, the moderator's role is to focus the agenda, while being flexible enough to modify it when items might be inappropriate. In focus groups the agenda is more than a listing of topics people should report on, and it may not be as necessary to follow the agenda explicitly. Rather, the agenda is the direction offered at the beginning of a meeting, just like a sailboat might set an initial course during a race, only to have it modified by shifting winds and unpredictable actions by participants. Participants need to know the agenda is being modified or altered in favor of a revised agenda item that is more in touch with their needs.

While verbal tracking means summarizing the discussion within certain topics or time periods, it also means that the moderator must be able to link the discussion to those that occurred under previous topics or even in previous sessions. Because tracking leads the moderator to refer to previous material, it provides a mechanism for moving the discussion, as well as developing consensus and crystallizing what actions need to be taken. This is especially true as a technique for defusing comments that reflect a participant's ego or interests. The tactic might be illustrated by statements such as this: "The main agenda item at this time is to focus on 'our strengths.' We might again highlight some of the weaknesses you comment on later on in this session. As we can see, the main strengths we have mentioned include. . . . Are there any others we feel are important to mention?"

Given that most interacting groups may be steered by group forces or by more charismatic or dominating individuals, the session allows for data to be gathered from individual members, before, during, and after the session. In one session on revising the curriculum of a school of public administration, we asked participants for examples (on yellow comment cards) of management problems they experienced that students should be prepared for, trends that will make it difficult to manage, skills that are most appropriate, and learning methods that would be useful in teaching these skills. The seventy participants were divided around seven tables so that each group had a cross-section of students, senior managers, and faculty. After completing their individual responses, a moderator led a group discussion and participants were encouraged to write additional ideas during this session on red comment cards. During a plenary session, participants were encouraged to offer concluding statements on blue comment cards about "anything they wanted to talk about which might not have been covered in the sessions."

USING GROUP INTERVIEWS TO ENCOURAGE ORGANIZATIONAL CHANGE

The Echo question session highlights the gestalt idea that a group is an organic whole, rather than a simple collection of individuals. As such, a highly attractive group in an organization or community can bring great pressure to bear on its members. Kurt Lewin discovered that if a group sets its standards and goals, there are pressures on individual members to conform. The further a person attempts to deviate from the norm in a highly cohesive group, the stronger the pressure for the person to work within the group's norms.

Lewin concluded that it is futile to try to change any one person from one pattern or another unless the entire group is involved. Rather than disturb the relationship to the group, the individual will as a rule take considerable risk, even at substantial financial sacrifice, to conform to the group. Thus, the behavior of a whole group may be more easily changed than that of a single member. This willingness to stick together (cohesiveness) is an essential characteristic of any group. Indeed, without it, it is doubtful that a group could be said to exist at all.

A cohesive group is held together if the positive forces of reciprocal attraction are stronger than the negative forces of repulsion. Among other things, the group activities must strengthen the individual's chances to achieve one's goals. Over a period of time, certain standards and norms develop and each member expects that others will conform to these standards. The extent of conformity varies with the degree of cohesiveness. What makes a group cohesive is not the similarity of the members, but their interdependence. Out of this dependence on others to achieve goals, a readiness arises to share chores and challenges, and even to reconcile personality clashes.

A group does not have to be composed of members who are greatly similar; it may be a gestalt, a whole containing dissimilar parts. For example, according to Lewin, "a man, wife, and baby within one family may show greater dissimilarity to one another than the man to other men of his age and social class, or the woman to other women, or the baby to other infants."[4] He remarked that dynamic wholes have properties that are different from the properties of either their parts or the sum of their parts. This does not mean that the "whole is greater than the sum of its parts." The whole is not necessarily superior, nor does it add up to more.

Lewin spoke often of the hopeful role of group dynamics and action research in human affairs. He was often involved in carrying out group experiments, many of which were about change in overcoming values and prejudices. Underlying these experiments on change was the use of Echo question sessions to identify why people resist change, and why they hold the values, norms, and beliefs they do.

The analysis of the dynamics of a group was a key part of the first experiments on changing food habits among six Red Cross groups of volunteers organized for home nursing. The objective was to increase the use of beef hearts, sweetbreads, and kidneys during a period of wartime shortage. Considering the deep-seated aversions to such foods, a change of this sort was much more difficult, perhaps, than the introduction of a vegetable such as spinach or escarole.[5]

The researchers began their work by developing an understanding of what foods the family eats, what they find to be attractive and unattractive or the positive and negative forces that affect a family's food habits. The positive forces toward buying a food might relate to a buyer's like for a food, knowledge of the family's likes and dislikes, and ideas about what food is essential. The opposing forces might be due to the lack of readiness to spend a certain amount of money, a dislike of lengthy or disagreeable forms of preparation, unattractive tastes, lack of fitness for the occasion, and so forth. Food is bought if the total force toward buying becomes greater than the opposing forces.

As in the case of the movement of bodies in physics, the balance of positive and negative forces determines the possibilities of change, even though the "body" being acted upon is a human thing (the behavior of a group of people). As in physics, the forces are not of the same magnitude. The result, illustrated in Figure 7.1, is a series of positive and opposing forces of varying strengths (represented by arrows of varying lengths). Introducing a change requires a change in a state of equilibrium between positive and negative forces. Food is bought if the total forces toward buying are greater than opposing forces.

This equilibrium principle is analogous to the way adrenaline and white corpuscles are immediate responses to injury or illness in our bodies. In the same way, the body's internal thermostat assists in helping to adjust to changes in temperature through shivering or sweating. In groups, there is a constant inertia or resistance to new changes affecting individual habits and group norms. This does not mean that groups do not change, but they continually try to adjust to it.

After a food is purchased, the direction and strengths of the forces will change. The force against spending money will be reduced and the person will be doubly eager not to waste the food. The force against wasting money will have the same direction as the force toward eating this food.

The example illustrates that the buyer of the food has the function of a gatekeeper to what the family eats. Changes in the food habits in the family depend on the person buying the food. Changes in the attitudes and desires of children and spouses will affect actual food habits only to the degree that they affect the buyer of the food.

Figure 7.1
Forces Affecting Whether a New Food Is Bought

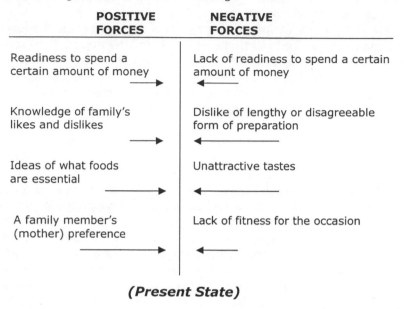

POSITIVE FORCES	NEGATIVE FORCES
Readiness to spend a certain amount of money	Lack of readiness to spend a certain amount of money
Knowledge of family's likes and dislikes	Dislike of lengthy or disagreeable form of preparation
Ideas of what foods are essential	Unattractive tastes
A family member's (mother) preference	Lack of fitness for the occasion

(Present State)

The experiments on changing food habits involved six groups of thirteen to seventeen members. In three of the groups, attractive lectures were given that linked the problem of nutrition with the war effort and emphasized the vitamin and mineral value of the three meats, giving detailed explanations with the aid of charts. The health and economic aspects were also stressed. The preparation of these meats was discussed in detail, as well as techniques for avoiding the characteristics to which there were aversions (odor, texture, appearance). The lecturer was able to arouse the interest of the groups by giving hints of her own methods for preparing these "delicious dishes" and her own success with her family. Only 3 percent of the women who heard the lectures served one of the meats never served before.

In three of the other groups, Alex Bavelas initiated an informal Echo question session that encouraged participants to elaborate the obstacles participants like themselves might experience. What were some of the general and specific obstacles to changing toward sweetbreads, beef hearts, and kidneys? What is a good food for a boy to eat? Who would praise him for it? What were some of the things that people might do so that family members did not dislike the meats? From such open-ended questions the researchers obtained information about customs and maternal and paternal family roles. After identifying obstacles and concerns, the groups and the nutrition expert offered remedies and recipes for preparation. The follow-up study illustrated that this group questioning and decision-making procedure encouraged 32 percent of the participants to serve one of the meats they had not tried before. Subsequent experiments—encouraging the use of evaporated milk, cod liver oil, and orange juice for babies—showed results that were even more dramatic. During the course of these studies, the concept later known as "group decision" was developed.

The questioning process encouraged participants to articulate their fears and obstacles and ways to overcome them. The most important aspect of the procedure was the active participation and involvement of participants and the chance to express motivations (values) corresponding to different alternatives. The act of decision making has the effect of freezing a person's motivation to act.

The experiment illustrated how it was easier to change the culture—the underlying values and beliefs—of a group working together than to change single individuals. One of the reasons "group-carried changes" are more readily brought about seems to be the unwillingness of the individual to depart too far from group standards. The person is likely to change only if the group changes.

Changes accomplished by reducing restraining or negative forces are likely to be more sustaining than changes induced by additional or positive forces, especially if they respond to fears and obstacles. Fears and obstacles illustrate values that illustrate why people will resist a change. Negative forces that have been removed will not push for a return to old behaviors and ways of doing things.

Change as a Three-Step Questioning Procedure

Kurt Lewin defined the change process as involving steps of unfreezing the present norms for performing, moving to a new level, and freezing the new norms at the new level. Here are some questions that encourage participants to experience unfreezing, moving, and freezing.

Unfreezing is something of an emotional catharsis, to remove prejudices and break away the shell of complacency and self-righteousness.[6]

- What are some of the things or norms you do not like about the . . . ?
- Give me an example of times when you felt extremely dissatisfied with . . .
- What are some of the obstacles?

Moving is an awareness and understanding of the new and more appropriate norms of performance.

- What are some things or norms that you feel are working well?
- Give me an example of times when you felt extremely satisfied with . . .

- What are some of the opportunities?
- What are some of the ideas or solutions?

Freezing of the new norms involves setting new norms and behaviors.

- What are things or norms you would like others to do?
- What are things or norms you would not like others to do?

BALANCING PRACTICAL AND RESEARCH REQUIREMENTS

In some question sessions there is clearly a greater priority on getting feedback and developing creative solutions than on being systematic in data gathering. Since it is very difficult to accomplish both objectives in one project, being clear on the need for the question session and the purpose is a first step.

While a random sample is often most appropriate to avoid bias in data collection, it is often useful when introducing organizational changes to select on a political rather than a random basis. The need to get input from informal leaders, union representations, top management, or other key employees in a change experience gives a higher priority to being politically sensitive than scientific.

The selection of the moderator can influence the quality of any question session. Some people have discipline to listen without interjecting their opinions, a warmth and liking of people, a sense of humor, and an ability to detach themselves from the issues. They recognize that the purpose is to obtain information and not to teach or preach. For others, acquiring these skills requires effort, a desire to learn, and coaching.

The way the question session is introduced can influence the moderator's work. Problems emerge when the moderator gives excessive attention to potential problem areas, striving to get other positive or negative comments or paying attention to details. Moderators need to know when to probe, when to ask follow-up questions, and when to encourage quieter participants and restrain dominant ones.

The question session relies on effective questions and data handling. Usually this involves no more than ten to twelve questions with probes. Depending on the orientation of the question session (whether it is focused on data gathering or organizatonal change), the questions should offer a balanced perspective of positive and negative experiences, ideas and desired behaviors, and obstacles and opportunities to implement any changes.

The question session encourages responses from both individuals and groups, before and during the session. It seeks to understand both group and individual experiences and can be a useful device in getting commitment to change.

EXAMPLE: A MODERATOR'S NOTES FOR
AN ECHO QUESTION SESSION

We are generally interested in better understanding how our graduate program might do a better job. More specifically,

- How can we make sure our graduate program is delivering a service or a product which is of high value to the users (the various organizations making up government service)?
- How can we make sure our graduates are competitive with others who are graduating from other programs?

In responding to these questions, one of the essential issues is the curriculum and how it is taught.

- What are the skills we should be teaching?
- Are there innovative ways of teaching them?
- Are employers happy?
- Can we do better?

The process that the school has embarked on in looking at the curriculum includes a range of activities, including focus surveys, focus groups with managers, and so forth. We have already developed a vision.

The school aspires to be the leading Canadian community of students, practitioners, alumni, faculty, and staff developing knowledge through teaching, research, and professional development emphasizing innovative management of public policy and services.

The school offers a number of programs

- Aboriginal Studies (etc.)
- Diploma Program (etc.)
- Philippine Program (etc.)
- Executive M.P.A. (etc.)

In the midst of all these programs, we wanted to take the opportunity to rethink our graduate program to see if it needs change. We want this program to be a cutting-edge program to lead the future rather than follow what others have done. In our discussions, we had several questions we could not answer:

- Could we be more innovative in the delivery of the program?
- Should we be more management oriented instead of policy oriented?

- Could we emphasize team teaching as a strategy to improve our teaching effectiveness?
- Can we better integrate our courses with each other and with the needs of specific organizational problems?

Many of these questions are difficult to answer, since we do not know what government will be like in the future and we dare not go too far in our design of a new program without checking out what might be happening in the environment.

- There are dangers of making a decision without being aware of the environment. (Five-minute film clip from *Butch Cassidy and the Sundance Kid*.)
- Interpretation of film clip.

  Professors teaching classes which are out of touch with environment.

  Students charging out in the environment without the proper skills.

Our goal today is to develop a better understanding of our environment, and we have asked you as experts in the field to use your collective wisdom to help us understand what the future might look like and how we might respond. Think of the school as looking for a new paradigm for teaching (have example of a paradigm lock).

During the morning session, we are interested in five questions. (Each question has individual probes.)

1. What are the most difficult problems you have experienced in your management?
2. What problems will we have to be prepared for, given the changes in government?
3. What trends will make it difficult to manage?
4. What skills are most appropriate?
5. What learning methods are most appropriate to address these new skills?

Individuals are given twenty minutes to answer these questions on note cards. Subgroups of twelve people are systematically divided so that each group has different levels of managers. Each group is given one-and-a-half hours to develop a group response. A plenary session is held during the last hour of the morning session.

During the afternoon session, five questions were addressed:

- What are some of the school's opportunities?
- What are some of its threats?
- What are some of the problems with the program?
- What are some of the positive aspects of the program?
- What ideas or projects should we pursue in the near future?

8

Combining Interviews
and Observations

Ah, Watson, you see but you do not observe.
                                    Sherlock Holmes

What people say they will do may be very different from what they will actually do. Understanding what people do involves much more than listening and recording interviews of perceptions, attitudes, behaviors, values, and beliefs. Given that only a small percentage of our communications are represented in words we say, we know very little by the spoken word alone.

The most obvious device for learning about the nature of individuals or groups is to watch them in action. Indeed, chroniclers and reporters throughout history have employed observational procedures. This is perhaps shown most impressively by social anthropologists in their reports of the behavior, culture, and social structure of primitive societies. Several classical scientists—from Aristotle's observations of the heavens from the island of Lesbos to Herodotus's chronicled observations of the Greco–Persian wars—have used observations as a way to substantiate their ideas, experiences, or travels.

PARTICIPANT OBSERVATION

An early classical study of group behavior in 1937[1] is an excellent example of how other researchers used Echo principles in understanding the perspective and needs of people and their expertise. W. F. Whyte moved into one of the slums of Boston to begin a three-and-one-half year study of social groups, political organizations, and racketeering. He gained admittance to the social and political life of the community and faithfully kept notes of the various happenings that he observed or heard about. His detailed accounts of the structure and culture of the Norton Street gang and the Italian Community Club generated a number of hypotheses about leadership, status, mutual obligations, and group cohesion.

Direct contact in a setting for an extended period of time provides an opportunity to gain data presented as a history of a group, through their stories, feelings, and experiences.[2] The descriptions can be the eyes, ears, and feelings for those who read them.

Observations are much more than one- to three-hour interviews where both subject and researcher act in unnatural ways. Participant observation allows the observer to take on, to some extent, the role of a member of the group and participate in its functioning. The observer has the same experiences that others do. This is an opportunity to see the conflicts and miscommunications that might never have been recognized by asking questions in an interview. In one study of a nuclear power plant we had the opportunity to observe the shutdown of a unit of the plant as the operators worked to deal with many of the activities for assuring safety. We participated with operators, responding in a crisis-like manner, brainstorming reasons for gas leakage and possible ways to resolve them. Being there certainly offered details that enhanced our ability to understand the way they made decisions.

Some exceptional cases, like the decision making during a disaster, cannot be observed because it is difficult to know when and where that disaster will occur. Or decision makers may be unwilling to allow observers to see their behaviors in action. In such cases, interviews may provide a more total picture of the problems experienced.

Participant observers can play various roles. At one extreme, the observer might be an onlooker seeking to implement an explicit scientific structure. At the other extreme is the observer who enters the setting as a participant with a genuine openness and unstructured approach. Observational questions can be posed in an exploratory or sensing fashion to gain insights for theory or further testing. They can be used to supplement other data sources, such as interviews, questionnaires, and unobtrusive measures. Or they might be used as the primary data-collection device for testing hypotheses in action. In general, the purpose depends on whether one is testing a research hypothesis or carrying out an exploratory study.[3]

More structured observations rely on instruments and procedures for observing, and include questions about who talks to whom, how many interactions were initiated by the person, how many times the individual left his or her desk, and so on. Researchers can develop a set of reliable measures for systematic observation and recording of what is observed. They are not encouraged to observe behaviors other than those originally defined in the procedures.

An onlooker observer usually makes no secret of the investigation, often making it explicit that the research is the overriding interest. The purpose is to observe and to move "where the action is."

Most observational designs will be of the onlooker variety and suffer from the bias associated with "being intrusive." Not interrupting the natural setting is a key requirement for understanding the persons involved, their behaviors and perceptions, and the dynamics of the physical and social environment. The goal, then, is to become accepted and respected in a way that encourages people to be as natural as possible. The term "naturalistic" suggests that a researcher does not interrupt the setting while trying to understand the persons involved, their behaviors and perceptions, and the dynamics of the physical and social environment.

It is not always easy to observe and record important events simultaneously as they occur. There may be too many things happening at one time or it may not be possible to predict when important events will occur. Problems develop when two or more activities occur simultaneously, as when a manager spends time with an employee to communicate a new idea, but also spends time trying to understand a production problem.

Observations offer an opportunity to participate in the daily life of the group or organization in question. Ideally, one does not interrupt the natural sequence of events. However, observer effects are probably inevitable in any study. These problems are vividly obvious as one tries to observe the problems and issues faced by drug addicts or prostitutes. There is an obvious problem of entry and being accepted as a "true participant observer." Members of some groups are likely to be very leery of those who want to observe them, while there are obvious questions of risk for the researcher. "Going native" might be extremely dangerous.

Observers need certain skills and personal attributes, such as the ability to listen and establish a rapport. The stronger the personal relationship, the greater chance researchers will be able to observe people as they really are. The goal is to become known as a "regular" and start to know and understand people as they normally are.

The limitations of observations, because of sample size, inaccuracies, or omissions, are well known.[4] Observation studies are subject to at least two classes of error: *control effect* and *biased-viewpoint effect*. Control effect occurs when the measurement process becomes an agent working for change.

In the act of observing, the participant may influence the setting. A biased-viewpoint effect occurs when the observational instrument may selectively expose the observer to the data. The observer may selectively summarize aspects of the situation or shift the calibration of the observation measures. There may be a tendency for the observer to be disposed toward exotic data, and to be more likely to report on those things that are different from his or her own viewpoint.[5] The only way to control such errors is to look for confirmation from different perspectives.

USING ECHO PRINCIPLES WHEN OBSERVING

By far the most influential observational study in the emerging theory of group dynamics focused on group atmosphere and styles of leadership.[6] This was a study which used Echo-like questioning to answer questions like, "What constitutes good and bad leadership?" and "What are some of the influences upon the group of different styles of leadership and group atmospheres?" Groups of ten- and eleven-year-old children met regularly over a period of weeks under the leadership of an adult who induced different group atmospheres: democratic, autocratic, and laissez-faire.

The effects produced in the behavior of the group members were large and dramatic. Autocratic group members were more aggressive and blaming and, at the end of the experiment, some of the autocratic groups destroyed the things they had constructed. When members moved from one group to another, their aggressiveness changed to what was occurring in the group. Interestingly, rather violent "explosions" resulted when some of the group members who had reacted submissively to an autocratic leader were given a new, more permissive leader.

The research, although original and insightful, was subjected to criticism because it manufactured emotionally charged political ideologies and values. However, it did illustrate how the creation of miniature political systems in the laboratory can demonstrate their power to influence people. Almost immediately after the study, researchers began related projects to further understand the group processes of communication, status, social norms, leadership, and so forth.

Within the Lewinian tradition of observation, researchers sometimes find themselves observing people in the laboratory, while in other cases they find themselves in the field. Many of Janet Beavin Bavelas's arranged experiences illustrated observations of people in laboratory settings. She brought people together to observe them talking, because she was interested in learning about the ordinary conversation that takes place in spontaneous dialogue with friends, family, coworkers, neighbors, strangers, and so forth. It didn't matter where she observed these dialogues, as these interactions are the same in the field as the laboratory.

The task of carrying out an observation is similar to one a fire inspector would be charged with in trying to unravel the details of how a fire destroyed a building. The fire inspector is presented with a mass of partially destroyed and randomly arranged materials. The most important data are those with the most potential for uncovering the cause of the fire. Thus, most data-collection efforts have to respond to choices of what to observe and collect information on.[7]

Studies illustrating Echo principles have much in common with the work of a fire inspector.[8] They proceed through steps, including carrying out exploratory observations and interviews, developing more comprehensive ways to observe and analyze, picking ideas that are more relevant for further research, and verifying interpretations.

Carrying Out Exploratory Observations, Recordings, and Interviews

In preparing for observations and record collecting, researchers usually have some broad questions in mind. As experience with previous disasters provides an understanding of what to look for in the rather chaotic remnants of a building, the fire inspector is able to probe in certain directions over others.

The initial stages of an exploratory, inductive process are characterized by searching for leads and exploring hunches about what might be occurring. In Janet Beavin Bavelas's teams, these observations might be supplemented with open-ended questions probing for what is happening, or with brainstorming sessions to try to develop hypotheses for further research.[9]

The initial observations become the basis for forming concepts to guide subsequent evaluations and, in certain cases, to conduct other observations or experiments. These concepts are formed in much the same way that a researcher gathers ideas in interviews or question sessions by sorting the various pieces of information into categories or themes. Such observational procedures borrow strongly from ethnography, an anthropological method encouraging researchers to become immersed in a setting to understand the key patterns.

In carrying out the initial observations, choices have to be made about what and who to observe, and what features of an interaction are more salient to observe. One can always fall back on some accepted theory or concept in trying to guide the initial observations. Some ethnographers have guided their research to understand more about the activities that describe a culture. In organizations, one might assess goal achievement, management functioning, group dynamics, functional theory, efficiency, or others.

Janet Beavin Bavelas's team began one project by observing the communicators of listeners and how they added to the conversation of narrators. The research assistants were "charged" with the feeling that their investigation could lead to something "really neat." Although they were not given any structure or direction on what to observe, they were asked to "watch closely what people are doing." They were clear on their general purpose and the context for what they were doing, as their research was focused on understanding how the listener shapes the direction of the conversation. While most previous research had focused on the speaker and how the listener responded, they knew that the hearer was dealt with as a figment of the speaker's imagination and not as an active coparticipant. In some of the previous research, listener responses seemed to be quite generic, illustrated as nodding and generic vocalization (e.g., "mhm," "uh-huh," or "yeah").

The researchers saw a set of specific responses—gasping in horror, mirroring the speaker's gesture, or supplying an appropriate phrase—that were tightly connected with what the speaker was saying at the moment. They learned that listeners become conarrators by illustrating and adding to the story. In recalling a life-threatening experience (a close call), narrators often moved quickly between horror and humor, both dramatizing the danger and making fun of it (because it ended well). Listeners were able to do this even though they, as strangers, had no previous experience with the story. They were able to contribute specific and appropriate details, moment by moment.[10]

How did Bavelas's research team come up with the idea that unique patterns in communication existed? The researchers did not try to follow any specific procedures, guides, or criteria to structure their initial observations. The observers were not trained on what to observe, except to watch for what was happening. They worked within assumptions that conversation was an integrated and richly patterned activity that participants do both rapidly and skillfully. "Our observational methods were inductive. We believed that we learn from watching how people talk and listen, and then we can test this knowledge experimentally. We also felt that the narrator and listener's conversations had to be lawlike, that the investigation will uncover something neat. There's the feeling, 'Oh boy, we're going to find out what really is happening.'"[11]

Using Interviews to Get New Ideas

During any observation, questions arise about what people are doing or what events mean. Understanding is often aided by interview questions that ask people what and why they are doing something. For example, in trying to understand the communications that occurred during a shift turnover in a control room of a nuclear power plant, we asked several questions:

1. What occurs in the time period before the shift change?
2. What are the major communication linkages which you have with others at the end of the shift (last hour or so)?
3. What would be the mode of communication usually used (i.e., phone, radio, face to face, etc.)?

4. Approximately how long and how often does this communication occur and how?

5. Could you give some reasons why you would communicate with this person or group? Could you give some examples?

On the basis of these observations, more selective questions were asked. Considering the questions on communications linkages during different parts of the shift, we asked operators to identify the nature of their working relationships with each individual or group.

1. For each individual or group

   a. Could you give some specific examples of things that this individual or group does that are helpful to you in your job?

   b. Could you give us some examples of things that this individual or group does that are not so helpful to you in your job?

2. In your working relationships, there are times when miscommunications occur, which may or may not lead to problems. For each of the individuals and groups identified earlier

   a. Could you give us some examples of miscommunications that have occurred, in which, for instance, something you said was misinterpreted by the other person, or you misinterpreted something they said?

   b. Is there a time in the shift when these types of miscommunications tended to occur more frequently?

   Beginning of shift

   Middle of shift

   End of shift

Observing an operator carrying out an activity may not indicate what he or she felt was being done and why it was important, or how it relates to other overall activities. Thus, the interview questions were an opportunity to provide a perspective on why these events occurred.[12]

Interviews also verify what is happening and, more important, why it is happening. They help the observer see the actions in context, so participants do not have to recall or interpret why they are doing something. Observations, when combined with interviews, provide a two-facet approach to understanding, in which the data from one method can be used to verify another method.

Recording

Seemingly, video recordings are the easiest way to record an observation, allowing researchers to make initial observations, brainstorm ideas or possible hypotheses, and then rewind the tape to view it again. The observations can become more focused after a process of viewing and brainstorming, a process that relies on creativity and the ability to see new anomalies.

Note-taking methods are commonly used in anthropological studies where researchers describe key activities and events in a form to illustrate how it occurs naturally. When a second observer is present, they can compare their records with each other and address anomalies. If there are differences, observers can go back to the setting to "observe again." When an observer is forced to work alone, the observer might try to describe the actual events in a chronological sequence without making interpretations, using an observer guide. If the goal is to develop hypotheses, the most prudent principle is to try to echo what is relevant and interesting in what people said and did.

Picking Ideas That Are Most Relevant for Further Research

One of the observer's most important choices involves picking the thread or theme to follow from the many that are presented during any observation.

Grouping or Sorting Things Together

One technique often used by Kurt Lewin was to put things that belong dynamically together, and separate out things that do not belong. These groupings—such as between the narrator and listener, or between a worker and a machine in assembling a toaster in factory—might recognize those activities that go together at particular times and those that routinely follow one another in sequence.

For every grouping of events or activities, questions arise: Where do the causative energies originate? What are the forces that link these activities together? What are the causes or sources for a person's behavior? Lewin created a conceptual system based on a "person" in a complex energy field where tensions arise when there is a need or want. It is their striving for discharge that supplies the energy for, and is consequently the cause of, all mental activity. To see the whole before the part and to pay constant attention to the operative forces might be taken as the key proposition underlying Lewin's work. These fields of activities that group together constitute "dynamic wholes."

The recognition that most things can be grouped or connected together does not constitute any proof that there is a functional interplay between specific activities. More in-depth understanding might be gained by trying to understand how the whole is connected to its parts; that is, what are the forces—positive and negative—in each grouping.

Illustrating Dynamic Relationships

Behavior, as Kurt Lewin emphasized so often, is a function of the person and the environment. This interdependence he displayed in a formula as $B = f(p,e)$. Behavior of every kind, including wishing, thinking, achieving, and striving, is a product of a field of interdependent variables. He called the field the "life space." It embraces needs, goals, unconscious influences, memories, beliefs, events of all kinds, and anything else that might have direct effect on behavior.

Background Note 8.1: Lewin's Jordan Curves

Behavior is a function of life space, or $B = f(LS)$. Lewin proceeded to conceptualize through topology the life space and to represent it as a "Jordan curve," an irregular close curving line that his Berlin students called little "eggs." Everything inside the figure was the person and the totality of possible facts that are capable of determining the behavior of an individual. The space outside the curve represents the nonpsychological world of either physical or social facts. The Jordan curve is the map to guide the psychologist.

Nonpsychological $\left(\quad E\ (P)\ E\quad\right)$ Nonpsychological

(P + E = Life space, L)

Whether these Jordan curves express behavior, they highlight the importance of trying to illustrate or map the chain of events or relationships of various activities.[13]

After sorting the observation notes, transcripts, or other information, it is possible to illustrate how they relate to each other. The maps, topographical diagrams, and charts are a tool for encouraging discussion. Different people can offer their own interpretations of the forces affecting a grouping of activities, what is occurring, when, and why. This is like a road map that illustrated how activities, events, or concepts are linked and interrelated.

Asking Questions and Brainstorming

One of the best strategies for encouraging creativity is to ask questions to encourage people to define the problem more explicitly. What are examples that illustrate this issue? What analogies and metaphors illustrate what the problem is like? Research team members are usually very willing to brainstorm their ideas, and this may be the best way to encourage a creative process.

Lewin, of course, was a Gestaltist, as was Max Wertheimer and many others who worked within this research tradition. Lewin was most concerned with asking the question that is most important for practical purposes—namely, "What must one do to obtain a desired effect in given concrete cases?"[14] He was convinced that it was important to spend time figuring out what the inferred determinants of behavior may be and how they may be tested.

Observing From Different Perspectives

Kurt Lewin often relied on everyday common observations. For example, Lewin was watching people in a cafeteria as they reached over the pies that were near to try to get the ones that were more distant. This led to testing an idea that "the grass on the other side of the field is greener," or the "effect of a barrier on a valence (desire)." They had the cafeteria staff place pies in order, while keeping track of the ones that customers chose. Sure enough, they picked the ones that were more distant.[15]

Shifting the focus to see events and happenings from other points of view can involve changing the focus of observation from one person to another, or from one event or activity to another. Janet Beavin Bavelas's team members spent time observing the narrator before switching their focus to the listener. They went back and forth until they recognized a pattern in which listeners were acting out specific roles in assisting the narrator.

Researchers at the Tavistock Institute in London, England, were continually involved with psychoanalysis as an attempt to assist their exploration and so they could begin to see the problems and issues more objectivity. They also worked in research teams, and constantly questioned their observations.

Verifying Interpretations

In the management field, Henry Mintzberg's *The Nature of Managerial Work* illustrates the use of careful, methodical records in identifying an anomaly and exploding a conventional wisdom about management.[16] He was following a question that emerged for him as a child as he wondered what his father did as a manager of a small manufacturing firm. He returned to that question later on in graduate school, when he realized that very little was said about the job of the manager, even though hundreds of programs were designed to train managers.

Background Note 8.2: Mintzerg's Observational Method

Ask managers what they do and you are likely to be told, in Henri Fayol's words of 1916, that managers plan, organize, coordinate, and control. If you bury yourself in the library and read hundreds of books and articles, you will be able to cite literature and textbooks to illustrate this.

Mintzberg put these preconceptions aside and carried out a systematic observation of five managers, letting the concepts emerge as his observations and interviews took place. He collected a body of preliminary data, including a diary of scheduled appointments for one month and information about each organization and manager. During the one-week observation of each manager, Mintzberg collected two types of data. Anecdotal evidence, comprising critical or otherwise interesting incidents, were described in considerable detail. Structured data was collected on the pattern of activity throughout every minute of the workday and on all mail and verbal contacts. Three records were used to record the data: a chronological record, a mail record, and a contact record.

His analysis revealed a picture of managerial work that was very different than what managers themselves believed they did. The facts suggest the following:

- Managers perform a great quantity of work at an unrelenting pace.
- The work is characterized by brevity, variety, and fragmentation.
- The manager actually appears to prefer brevity and interruptions in work.
- The manager gravitates to more active elements of work—the current.
- Verbal and written contacts are the manager's work.
- Mail receives cursory treatment.
- The informal media (telephone and unscheduled meeting) are common.
- The scheduled meeting consumes most of the manager's time.
- Tours provide managers the opportunity to observe without prearrangement.
- External contacts consume one-third of the manager's time.
- Subordinates consume one-third to one-half of the manager's contact time.
- Managers spend little time with superiors.
- The manager's duties suggest he or she has little control of what he or she does.

In fact, managers do not plan, organize, coordinate, or control, as is conventionally described in textbooks. Instead, managerial work might be described by three roles:

Interpersonal Roles	Informational Roles	Decisional Roles
Figurehead	Monitor	Entrepreneur
Leader	Disseminator	Disturbance Handler
Liaison	Spokesperson	Resource Allocator
		Negotiator

Henry Mintzberg observed only five managers and verified his idea by carefully cataloguing their daily activities. He used his empirical work and the studies of others to illustrate an anomaly: Managerial work is very different from how we have conventionally described it. Other studies by others verified his results in other settings. Over the years, M.B.A. programs have changed their curricula to respond and emphasize new skills and competencies.

Mintzberg's sample was small and selective, and it is possible that five cases might not be representative. He was able to deal with this limitation by his careful record keeping and analysis. More generally, the representativeness of any small sample can be enhanced by (1) checking the accuracy of the findings with people in the field setting, (2) increasing the number of cases and encouraging other perspectives, (3) carrying out other studies in similar settings, (4) looking purposefully for contrasting cases that are extremely negative, positive, or otherwise different, and (5) sorting the cases systematically to look for differences. Each of these methods offers a different perspective in enhancing the data's representativeness.

Using information to illustrate a variety of perspectives and viewpoints is a developing tradition in the social sciences and has been described using terms such as "convergent," "multimethod/multitrait methods," or "triangulation."[17] It was the basis of Kurt Lewin's calling for a Galeliean science to illustrate how a single object or case can be studied in its totality. These ideas share the goal of trying to use qualitative and quantitative data together, and use multiple levels of information and perspectives to provide different viewpoints on a research issue.

Triangulation can be something more than the amalgamation of quantitative and qualitative viewpoints. It also encourages the use of different scales and indicators to improve reliability and validity, and can involve multiple frameworks or measures and multiple researchers. A multiple framework approach might be a combination of quantitative and qualitative data, experimental and survey evidence, or economic and sociological analysis. A multiple research approach often calls for different observers or groups who seek to analyze the same phenomena.[18]

Background Note 8.3: Triangulation

Triangulation is a nautical method used by sailors to ascertain their position at sea. A sailor will take a compass reading on three different positions in different directions. By drawing lines on a chart marking each different position a, b, and c (lighthouse, buoys, or landmarks), the sailor can determine his or her exact position (see Figure 8.1).

In the social sciences, the word triangulation has been defined as "a combination of methodologies in the study of the same phenomenon," and has been associated with practices in navigation and military strategy where multiple reference points are used to determine a ship's location.[19] The word has been associated with the use of multiple methods to improve validation so that the variation reflected the trait rather than the method.[20]

Figure 8.1
Triangulation

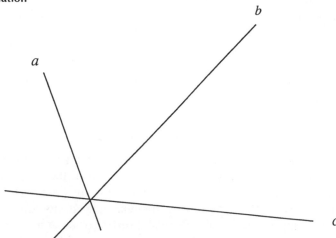

There are different types of triangulation: between methods and within methods. Between-methods comparisons involve the use of different and distinct research methods.[21] Interviews would be combined with observations, psychological testing, or a review of records. If multiple and independent methods reach the same conclusion, there is a higher level of confidence. Within-methods triangulation is the use of multiple techniques within a given method to collect and interpret data. This would involve multiple scales or indices focused on the same concepts. Different scales may not produce as wide a variety of perspectives as might be gained from combining other methods reflecting diverse observations or different levels of data (i.e., feelings, perceptions, behaviors).

All triangulation designs share the assumption that the weaknesses of one metaphor, perspective, method, or design can be strengthened by the counterbalancing strength of another. Triangulation designs recognize that much can be gained from methods that seek to understand nonempirical data. It also requires information that can be obtained nonempirically.

THE POWER OF OBSERVATIONAL STUDIES

Like the wine tasters who know how to judge great wines, we know a great idea when we see it, but it is often very difficult to define the steps and

processes that explain how it developed (the factors). It is even more difficult to understand how these concepts or factors are related, why they are
related (what are the underlying assumptions), and the conditions under
which any relationships might occur (who, where, and when).

In our attempt to discover new ideas and fruitful research directions, we
soon learn that an idea must have relevance when it illustrates an anomaly.
Observational studies allow us to see anomalies that are illustrated through
everyday life experiences or those challenging our ideas or beliefs.

Anomalies From Observing Everyday Experiences

Important problems might first be approached through observing behavior in everyday life. This was illustrated during one of the informal seminars with Lewin and his students. The sessions usually went on for two or
three hours and were characterized by freewheeling discussions in which
people would come and go and people would order coffee or a piece of cake
at various times. On one such occasion, somebody called for the bill and the
waiter knew exactly what people had ordered, even though he hadn't written anything down. One-half hour later, Lewin asked him to the write the
bill again. The waiter was indignant, saying that he couldn't remember:
"You already paid your bill." In psychological terms, this indicated that a
tension system had been building up in the waiter as they were ordering and
than upon payment of the bill the tension system was discharged. This life
experience gave rise to future research, Zeigarnick's famous study of tension systems. It is an obvious example of how the observations of real-life
experiences can pose new questions.[22]

Anomalies That Challenge Our Beliefs

Observational studies assist in challenging some of our conceptions. That
is, evidence-based observations of what we do may be very different from
what we say we do. For example, when we ask a person to identify when
they were absent from work, his or her perceptions often do not tally with
the records. Self-reports, in this case, may have been invalid because of an
inability to recall, an unwillingness to provide accurate data, or a tendency
to let one's beliefs structure one's thinking.[23]

EXAMPLE: AN OBSERVATIONAL GUIDE

The observation can be structured with explicit guidelines and instruments. Some observers might want to answer general questions about the
participants, their tasks, the setting, the behavior and outputs, timing, and
unique causes and consequences.

1. *The Participants*. Who are the participants? How many are there? How can they be characterized (age, sex, roles, occupations)? Where are they situated in relationship to each other? Is there any key groupings or relationships?

2. *The Tasks*. What are the functions of the various groups of people? How are they relating in this setting? What are they doing during the key events or observations? Are these functions formally defined? Do individuals and groups have a variety of purposes for being there? Are there conflicting goals of various groups or individuals? What are these conflicting goals?

3. *The Setting*. Each setting has unique features that are described by the technology: the equipment, facilities, and resources. As a result, a nursery school may be very different than a clothing factory. An airplane disaster is different than a burned building. How can I preserve the data or information that describes the equipment, facilities, and resources by sampling the records, taking pictures, or reconstructing the facilities elsewhere?

4. *The Behavior and the Outputs*. How do people actually behave during the event? Describe this behavior in descriptive terms. What are the specific movements made and activities that they carried out.

5. *Timing*. The time it occurred, the time it takes, and the frequency describe the timing of the behavior. What time did the behavior, output, or event occur? How long did it occur? How often did it occur?

6. *Unique Causes and Consequences*. What unique occurrences affected the people, tasks, setting, behaviors and outputs, and timing? What unique consequences affected the people, tasks, setting, behaviors and outputs, and timing?

PART III

RESEARCH

9

Focusing Research Using the Echo Sorting and Content Analysis Procedures

A hunch is creativity trying to tell you something.

Frank Capra

William James, a nineteenth-century psychologist, made the observation that when children enter the world they view what resembles a "great big buzzing confusion" or what his student John Dewey called "an indeterminate situation." It is a world of confusing and conflicting noises and sights. As adults, we learn to understand the reasons for many of the sights and sounds we see, but we still face a world where the information we receive is conceptless and messy, and many of the problems and issues we confront are not amenable to any conventional analysis. Many of the problems and issues we confront each day resemble what Russell Ackoff called a "mess"; what we confront are messes and not problems.[1]

Imagine the work of a group of police detectives who are trying to unravel a messy, complex crime. When there are no known clues, they will begin by amassing a variety of information, collecting photographs, interviews, and titbits of details. The volumes of information can be overwhelming, and detectives can easily lose sight of the overall picture and important themes or threads. The term "can't see the forest for the trees" might describe detectives who have lost sight of the central themes after months of painful investigation. The key element in understanding, in this case, is the ability to sort and make sense of conflicting data, and conceptualize the messy and conflicting information.

For Lewin and his group, the sorting process was very important, although he constantly stressed the importance of going beyond the compiling of facts. Facts alone will not give us answers to practical questions, such as "what must one do to obtain a desired effect in a specific situation?" To answer this question it is necessary to develop a theory that is empirical and not speculative. It is necessary to develop themes, categories, or trends that might help to describe the problems, challenges, or needs of a group of people we are studying.

SORTING AS A WAY OF DEVELOPING CONCEPTS OR CATEGORIES

How can we understand the themes within pages and pages of messy data from observations, interviews, Echo sessions, and documents? The ideas, comments, and suggestions generated are the source of hypotheses, theories, or possible topics for experimentation.

Sorting is an inductive process, somewhat of a *parenthetical encounter* in which researchers try to categorize the information they encounter, trying to suspend their normative judgment or preconceptions of what they might find.[2] Researchers let themes or categories emerge from the data rather than being led by hypotheses, previously defined categories, or expectations. The analysts are encouraged to suspend their preconceptions, to bracket them out or put them in parentheses.

The Echo approach encourages volunteers from the population to sort ideas and comments into categories to develop a framework for understanding. They are most familiar with the phrases and values of people who are in the population studied, and should be able to "read between the lines" in understanding what people might have meant in their ideas or comments. The process includes the following steps:

1. Initial preparations and pilot testing.
2. Sorting and classifying the notecards.
3. Assessing the reliability and validity.

Preparations and Pilot Testing

Open-ended data from interviews, observations, or Echo question sessions are messy, and we need some way to order them if we want to develop themes or avenues for further research or experimentation. One of the researcher's first tasks is to summarize the data so that they are easily read and understood in the words and phrases that people use to describe their values and experiences.

It is usually necessary to transcribe tapes or notes, as handwritten notes are cumbersome to deal with and may influence the judgments of those who will be sorting and content analyzing. The way that the interviews are transcribed or summarized should reflect, as closely as possible, the manners and nuances of communication and thoughts of the people interviewed. A literal transcription is desired, making sure not to lose the context of the response. While spelling mistakes might be corrected, grammar or wording should never be altered. The statements and the style reflect the ways people communicate and think, and they represent what makes one group distinguishable from another. The raw data are the basis for forming the categories or concepts defining the issue or problem to be studied.

Sorters begin by reading the transcribed notes to develop an understanding of the concepts or ideas that are being presented, perhaps making marginal notes. They can highlight possible concepts and general biographical information, such as person number, group, question asked, and so forth. Photocopy any notes or save the original computer files as a way of preserving the raw data, as subsequent steps require altering these data or cutting them up so that they can be sorted. An important preliminary step is to find a room with tables so that volunteer sorters can sort and arrange data into different piles. The process works best when they can arrange categories in different ways, while being able to see the full set of emerging categories in one overview.[3]

Cut up the interview or summarized notes so that each idea and comment is identified on a separate card or piece of paper. Each message, statement, idea, or concept should be separated from the rest so it can be sorted and displayed in relationship to other categories. You will be left with a large pile of pieces of paper, where each piece represents an idea, statement, or concept. A word processor can help you format your data summary so that when you cut them up, each slip of paper has a uniform size, like a notecard.

Each card might have identification codes reflecting the respondent and group (i.e., age group, level of management). These should be located peripherally so that they are not visible as part of the question or format. Although each respondent may be completely anonymous, the coding makes it possible to understand if differences might be attributed to certain individuals or groups. The numbers are a way of identifying question numbers but are also important for later analysis. Some Echo studies have employed supplemental psychological measures to be used in the classification process.[4]

Coding and indexing involves developing some system to preserve the uniqueness of the data, should you want to tally frequencies or analyze them later in different ways. Classical coding formats involve defining your sample by gender, age, or some other biographical variable. In qualitative data management, especially when computers are not used, the goal of the coding is to allow you to identify the origin of the comment or statement.

Background Note 9.1: Preparing for Sorting

One data gathering session produced 700 concepts related to problems in an environment, skills of effectiveness managers, strengths and weaknesses, opportunities, and threats. These concepts came from seventy participants, consisting of faculty, managers, and students.

In preparing for the analysis, we wanted to be able to develop a coding scheme to preserve certain information. Each concept was typed on a four-by-six-inch notecard and each card had a number, such as 0100110 or 5421515. The first two digits represented the subject number, the next three identified the card number, and the final two digits distinguished the question number. These numbers might be hidden in such a way that they do not affect the judgments of those classifying the cards.

We recruited twelve sorters who were involved in the organization and had experience with the issues. A large room with several tables was chosen as an appropriate room for conducting the sorting. We felt that teams of three sorters allowed for the appropriate amount of diversity. Each team was given a stack of notecards relating to a specific question area.

Each message, statement, idea, or phrase that might identify a concept should be labeled with a code. A concept might be the label for the category of ideas, statements, or phrases. It might define feelings or perceptions that are illustrated in a set of messages.

After all cards have been transcribed and marked with the desired identification codes, they should be thoroughly shuffled to ensure that sorters are working with a representative sample of the compete set of questions.

Questions are often raised about why one would use such a manual intuitive process when computers can be programmed to easily classify large data sets. The purpose of the sorting process is to help generate categories that form the concepts for the framework or theory. Many of the notes and messages in an interview may be vague and unclear to an objective computer because they reflect unique aspects of what is occurring in a particular group or organization. Sorters who are volunteers in an organization understand these fine distinctions and nuances and can easily make judgments about the communication. In other words, they can "read between the lines." The researcher might decide to use computers to collaborate the frequencies later on.

Pilot Testing

A pilot test can answer a number of questions related to the number of sorters needed, the number of cards they can handle, the clarity of the directions, the length of time the sorting will take, and how sorters can quickly become familiar with the procedure.

Select two or three volunteers from the population studied to act as sorters in the pilot sort. Take a sample of cards that you feel they might be able to sort in an hour's time. Sort a sample of these cards yourself to get an idea of some of the problems and questions they might ask. After the volunteers complete their sorting, make sure to ask them questions about the clarity of directions and the difficulties they had. Their suggestions will be valuable in developing the procedures for sorting.

Sorting and Classifying Notecards

The Echo classification technique is a means of sorting items, statements, or comments in categorizing almost any type of data, ranging from titbits of gossip to newspaper clippings and historical information. Sorting was used during World War II by Eric Trist, one of the cofounders of the Tavistock Institute, as a method of selecting officers. Candidates would be faced with a complex "field," and they would have to make choices in providing some meaning through a process of grouping and categorization. Alex Bavelas used the sorting process in arranging statements that might be used in developing a questionnaire, while others have used it for defining the values that illustrated a range of cultures.

Usually, groups of sorters are selected from the same population as those interviewed. They should have an understanding of the organizational issues, and, ideally, should be representative of different perspectives offered in the culture. Outsiders usually have their own preconceptions and may not be the best sorters, as they may not understand the nuances, values, and phrases of the culture studied. Distortions emerge when sorters are not familiar with the culture, such as if students are used to classify the responses of people in an organization. Since researchers often want to pick staff classifiers because they work more quickly, it is probably important to guard against distortions that might emerge when outsiders carry out the sorting.[5]

Normally, two or three people can be involved in the sorting process, although other groups might be used to verify the process. In preparation for sorting, the interview statements should be summarized on file cards. Groups of sorters are each given an identical set of cards and asked to sort them into homogeneous groups of cards that say the same thing.

The sorting process usually begins with a general summary of the previous and future research steps, and a general orientation of how the data in this session will be used. A history of the technique might be appropriate. Although questions should be encouraged at this stage, it is often helpful to remind people that many questions will be answered during the discussion that occurs during each step. Background Note 9.2 outlines some of the instructions that might be used to orient people to a sorting session. Questions most asked at this stage are "What do we mean by classifying 'similar' items together?" and "What is a category?" The most appropriate response is to suggest that comments are considered to be in a similar category if you have the intuitive feeling that they say the same thing or describe a general direction. A category might be a grouping of cards with similar content. All efforts should be made to encourage the sorter to rely on his or her intuition in sorting the cards.

The sorting process encourages creativity in defining and rearranging categories to define common themes in the data. The process usually consists of the following steps: (1) individually sorting the items on the cards in categories, (2) working as a team to develop common categories, (3) checking the categories to be sure they are homogeneous, and (4) deciding on representative statements to represent the category.

Background Note 9.2: Instructions for Sorting

The following set of procedures was used for sorting six hundred items from six question areas.[6]

The concepts you have before you come from general questions where alumni, faculty, students, and managers were asked a range of questions about this organization. Their responses were typed onto the cards you have in front of you. You are asked to sort these cards into groups of similar items. The categories will be used to help define how we might change our university program. Your sorting task consists of five steps:

1. Work individually and sort the items into separate categories.
2. Make a record of which cards you placed in which categories.
3. Work as a team to develop sets of agreed-upon categories.
4. Check the categories to ensure they are homogeneous.
5. Select representative or typical cards to represent the category.

Step 1. To begin, take a dozen or so cards at random and read them to get a sense of the range of responses. Replace them in the pile. Take cards one at a time and place them in piles in front of you, putting similar cards together in a category. If you run across any cards that don't seem to fit in any category, put them aside in a "extra" pile and try to categorize them after. Try to use your intuition and sense of what you believe to be the needs and values of people in this organization. Use the whole table to work on if this makes your job easier.

Step 2. On the coding sheet given to you, make a record of your individual decisions. Start with the category you feel is most clear-cut and well-defined. Call this Category 1 and give it a descriptive name. Write the category name and number at the top of the first column on the record sheet.

Step 3. In the third step, work as a team in developing a common set of items. We are asking you *not* to refer to your individual categorization, but to start anew and begin to recategorize one person's pile of notecards. You might identify a category that has the most obvious agreement. One person might read aloud the items in this category to begin a discussion on whether or not they fit. Move items in or out of this category based on the discussion. Then proceed with another category, moving items in and out to form new categories. Continue this process until you have agreement on all the categories.

Step 4. Each category will be refined to ensure it is homogeneous. Take the items in each category and read them aloud, and put aside items that you feel do not belong. If no category exists for a card, you should create another one. The goal of this step is to make sure that no card has been categorized by accident.

Step 5. You are asked to pick the most representative card or cards to represent the category. The cards that are chosen will define the category and might be used as items or measures should you wish to develop a questionnaire.

Sorters within each team might initially work independently and then as a team of classifiers. Individuals can begin to sort the cards into piles and begin to label the piles. Individuals are first asked to group cards together so that they have the same meaning. They are asked to take one card at a time and place it in a category by responding to the statement, "This generally describes . . ." They would then place the card in a separate area on the table. Some individuals might attach a general label (a sticker) to a group of cards.

The most useful sorting process is to let the categories emerge rather naturally. In some cases the researcher might decide to sort on the basis of predefined questions, such as "What are the challenges?" "What are examples of the decisions you make?" or "What were the types of concerns (either positive or negative) that people raised?"

The decision on card placement and interpretation is intuitive rather than logical. Sorting is a trial-and-error, iterative process of trying to understand how various items fit together. The sorters are not limited in the number of categories they are to develop and are simply given the information to arrange and asked to label the various interview statements into general categories. At some point it is appropriate to begin arranging the various observations and ideas and to develop classes or categories. The concepts become the substance for devising a questionnaire or theory, or for ordering and tallying a mass of interview or observational data.

Background Note 9.3: Results from a Sorting Session

In one example, 1,671 cards were divided among nine volunteers drawn at random from a pool of subjects.[7] Each classifier was instructed to read the statements and group them together, each constituting a separate category. After completing their tasks, the classifiers were grouped into three teams and, each team was asked to agree on categories. One team member was asked to read the cards aloud in each of her categories, and other members of the team would add their cards to the reader's pile. The same procedure was used to develop commonality among the three teams.

Untrained classifiers might be able to handle between 250 to 300 cards in one session.[8] Larger numbers of cards might be handled over two or more periods.

During the second stage of the process, the results of this initial sorting should be recorded so that comparisons can be made with other sorters' responses. This guards against errors resulting from different groups or individuals.

In the third step, the group or team sort, creativity and freethinking is encouraged in developing categories. The facilitator should guard against sorters trying to use analytical, tallying, or voting procedures. Decisions should be intuitive, and the facilitator should encourage participants to empathize with the feelings and values in the culture. When a disagreement occurs over the placement of an item, it should be put aside and dealt with later.

When the group has finished categorizing the cards, all the responses have been arranged in categories and each category represents a similar set of items. By reducing redundancy and overlap, the individual items within each category can be collapsed into more general definitions based on a common or similar intent of meaning. Some of the items might be edited to clarify the meaning and develop a definition for this category of items.

During the next step, each category is checked to ensure that its contents are homogeneous. The facilitator, researcher, or group spokesperson might take turns reading each card in each category to check for errors in classification. The goal is to make sure that cards have not been accidentally categorized and to agree on the labels for each category. For some purposes it may be appropriate to tally or record the frequency of responses within each category.[9]

The classification process assures that respondent issues, needs, and values, and the intensity by which they are stated, will emerge from the respondents rather than from the preconceptions of the investigators. Some needs and issues may be described more frequently and with more intensity, although the less frequently identified categories are also important, as they might help explain the results later on. While some categories might be more frequently identified, reflecting comments of a large number of people, less important categories also reflect possible trends and issues.

In verifying the sorting, two groups might be asked to sort the same items. After the categories and items within each of the categories are recorded, each group of sorters is asked to discuss their results. Categories that are immediately similar can be identified, and those that are not can be collapsed. The sorters can be asked to eliminate those statements that are redundant and to refine those that are unclear. Each group might then articulate why it had chosen to refine or eliminate a statement; other groups should either modify their statements according to the suggestion or defend the position of why it should not. With the knowledge of the initial sort, each group can conduct a second sort. This process may be repeated several times, until all groups agree upon a common list of categories.

The fifth step involves picking representative statements that illustrate each category in subsequent reports or tables, or developing a glossary of terms that would be used for content analysis or narratives. In some cases the items from the categories are used to develop measures for a questionnaire.

The categories and items underlying them should parallel, as closely as possible, the manner in which the individuals in the organization articulate the issues. They should summarize key phrases and ways of working in the same words and manners of the organization's participants. This is the terminology and logic that individuals in organizations find most relevant, and if accurately summarized will be a useful reflection of the individual's impressions of the organization or problem situation—an expression of manifest and latent values.

SUMMARIZING THE CATEGORIES

Developing a Glossary of Terms

A glossary of terms illustrates the words used to describe each category of items or statements. In one example, interview statements were sorted into categories illustrating behavioral skills important to the group studied.

- Organizational communications skills.
- Organizing and priority setting.
- Problem sensing and solving.
- Coaching.

Each category, with the edited statement of the actual words and phrases used, is operationally defined in the glossary. The list of categories and sample statements is like a glossary of terms, which can be used for writing narratives, verifying the sorting process, or content analyzing the data. Others who are asked to verify the sorting process can also use it. Here are some examples of these categories and sample statements.

Organizational Communication Skills. Keeping people informed so that they can understand what is happening in the organization. Ability to organize and present data in a way that is understood by the listener. Communicating to the right people. Keeping people informed but not overloaded with irrelevant information. Ability to understand the type of information needed by people for their work and for a sense of purpose in the organization.

Organizing and Priority Setting. Ability to establish priorities. Ability to manage competing demands for one's time. Ability to organize job duties. Ability to delegate tasks to others.

Problem Sensing and Solving. Ability to identify and define a problem. Ability to differentiate between real and apparent problems. Ability to assess the impact of a problem throughout the organization. Ability to develop appropriate solutions. Ability to implement solutions.

Coaching. Guiding, motivating, and helping staff. Encouraging and assisting others to perform well in their jobs. Providing feedback on performance in a constructive manner. Helping staff to set achievable goals. Making resources available to assist staff in developing their skills and achieving their goals. Assisting staff to make their own decisions and solve their own problems.

Picking Sample Statements to Represent the Categories

Sorters might select sample statements to illustrate each category. In describing some of the trends that will make public-sector management more difficult, sorters picked representative statements to illustrate what people were saying.

Downsizing

"Diminishing resources, especially personnel relative to political, public expectations of performance and programs."

"Achieving results with limited funds and time."

"Keeping staff motivated in the face of decreasing resources (constant pressure to justify programs/services)."

"Downsizing—20%–40% budget cuts over 5–10 years."

More with Less

"The voters' demands for less government and more value."

"Performing better, doing more with less."

"High expectations from taxpayers who want access 24 hours, 7 days per week."

Public Involvement

"Greater public involvement in decision-making—every move and decision will be open to view and attack from vested interests."

"Working cooperatively with unions to achieve efficiencies and share benefits/gains."

"More expectation of public input into decision-making process, precedents have now been set whereby the public is essentially held hostage to interest groups."

"Managing the interaction of government with outside groups in joint policy development."

VERFYING TRENDS THROUGH CONTENT ANALYSIS

The best-selling book *Megatrends 2000* provides an example of what one can do in content analyzing 6,000 local newspapers on a monthly basis.[10] Its authors, John Naisbitt and Patricia Aburdene, monitored local events throughout the United States. The book illustrates social trends, such as a booming global economy, privatization of the welfare state, and the triumph of the individual. Underlying this report is the metaphorical and spiritual significance of the millennium. As we look at the list today, most of us would agree that this analysis did point to trends we are living today.

The Booming Global Economy of the 1990s. Economic considerations almost always transcend political considerations.

The Renaissance of the Arts. The affluent information society has laid the economic groundwork for a modern renaissance in the visual arts, poetry, dance, theatre, and music throughout the world.

The Emergence of Free-Market Socialism. As we globalize our economies, individuals are becoming more powerful and more important. The welfare state and centralized systems are becoming too expensive.

Global Lifestyles and Cultural Nationalism. Travel, trade, and television lay the groundwork for the global lifestyle. Even as lifestyles grow more similar, there are unmistaken signs of a powerful countertrend: a backlash against uniformity, a desire to assert the uniqueness of one's culture and language, a repudiation of foreign influence.

The Privatization of the Welfare State. Globally the key to transforming socialism and the welfare state is the same approach that succeeded in Great Britain, privatization of state enterprise and private stock ownership.

The Rise of the Pacific Rim. The Pacific Rim is undergoing the fastest period of economic expansion in history, growing at five times the growth rate during the Industrial Revolution.

The Decade of Women in Leadership. To be a leader in business and government, it is no longer an advantage to be socialized as a male.

The Age of Biology. Animals will produce valuable biological products for humans almost like factories—which some people think very wrong, but they will thereby save many human lives.

The Religious Revival of the New Millennium. An array of new religions outside the Judeo-Christian framework is taking root.

The Triumph of the Individual. New technologies have changed the importance of scale and location and extended the power of individuals.

Content analysis is a way of observing, analyzing, and characterizing the meanings of communication in a systematic and quantitative fashion. In offering a description of the content of communication, the technique analyzes the extent of emphasis, or omission of emphasis, on any category. It requires a system of analysis and a method to form the concepts or categories to be used in the analysis. For example, the content of newspaper articles about a company might be investigated with regard to the frequency or appearance of certain words, themes, or characters.[11] Content analysis can be used for analyzing letters, autobiographies, diaries, ethnographic materials, newspaper articles, minutes of meetings, and so on. It can be used for verifying the categories used to describe values, beliefs, attitudes, feelings, and so forth.[12]

Background Note 9.4: Content Analysis

Content analysis was first used by students of journalism (and later by sociologists) to study the content of American newspapers on domestic affairs, politics, labor, crime, and so forth. The field of English also illustrates some early applications in the analysis of various stylistic features in English poetry and prose. During the late 1930s, content analysis was given an important boost because of the growing interest in analyzing propaganda and public opinion and the emergence of public radio. During World War II content analysis was employed by several government departments charged with the responsibilities in analyzing public and radio communications of adversaries.[13]

A study comparing the literature given to the Hitler Youth and the Boy Scouts of America is an illustration of the content analysis approach.[14] The study's findings illustrated that the German material stressed national loyalty and identification more than altruism and creativity. The literature consumed by the Hitler Youth encouraged membership in the national community, while the Boy Scouts highlighted individual satisfaction.

Sampling

Content analysis is only as good as the sample of data represented. Ideally, this involves the selection of a sample of dialogue or communications to analyze, whether it is interview statements from managers or prewar literature read by the youth and leaders of Boy Scout groups.

Picking the Unit of Analysis

The unit of analysis in content analysis studies might be the word, theme, time, or item.[15]

- *Word.* The content of words, including single words and phrases, might be used to study the dialogues of people, who might use words like "freedom," "liberty," "government," "communism," and so forth. The content might also be analyzed for a text's style or readability.
- *Theme.* The theme, an assertion or statement, is a single sentence including both subject and predicate. The statements of leaders might be analyzed to detect the themes, such as "managers who encourage employees to take charge" and "the organization's need to utilize new communication's technologies." Themes are often combined into sets of themes.
- *Character and space and time measures.* Use of the fictional or historical character is appropriate in analyses of stories, dramas, and biographical sketches. Space and time measures have classified content by such physical divisions as the column inch, the page, the line, the paragraph, or the minutes of time on a radio or television program. These units are less useful in the behavioral sciences.
- *Item.* Like the theme, the item unit is an indication of the whole communication or production: the essay, news story, television program, or discussion.

The selection of the unit of analysis depends on the problem and the content under investigation. For example, in the analysis of the interviews on the challenges faced by leaders, the theme was most important. In an analysis of magazine stories, both the characters and items are used.

Developing Categories for Coding

Since content analysis relies on the categories that are used for coding, great importance is attached to being clear on the problem being addressed and the purpose of the study. The categories used will depend on the problem under investigation. Some categories deal with what is said, while others deal with how it is said.[16]

"What Is Said" Categories

Subject matter. This describes what the communication is about, and the relative emphases given to different topics in a body of communications. Leaders might talk about their strategies, while workers might relate stories of frustrations working in an organization.

Directions. These categories relate to the way—the pros and cons—in which a subject is talked about. The categories seek to determine whether the communication is for or against the subject matter.

Standard. This category, also called grounds, refers to the basis on which the classification is made. Standards like strength and weakness and morality and immorality are used to judge whether the subject matter is approved because it is strong or moral.

Values. What people want and are focused on describes what they are after, whether it is money, love, social position, health, or advancement.

Methods. Values deal with the ends or reasons for actions. Methods deal with the means employed to realize the ends. The analysis of political matters has illustrated a number of methods, such as propaganda, violence, negotiations, and so forth.

Traits. This category illustrates abilities and competencies. In management research, this category might reveal skills such as communicating, listening, building teams, and implementing organizational changes.

Actor. Persons, groups, or other objects might be identified as the initiators of the actions.

Authority. The authority or source refers to the person, group, or object in whose name a statement is made. Specific managers might often be identified as the source of their frustration.

Origin. The place of origin of the communication is sometimes relevant in indicating how widely or narrowly the audience's attention is being directed. For example, in analyzing the trends of newspapers, it might be possible to identify sharp shifts in attention given to specific candidates because of something that happened in the community.

Target. Who is the communication directed at? The analysis might reveal which specific groups are being targeted in the communications.

"How It Is Said" Categories

Form or type of communication. The form of communication—speeches, interviews, informal discussions, observed actions—illustrates the mode of communication.

Form of statement. People might communicate as if something is a statement of fact (e.g., all good leaders communicate clearly), preference (e.g., they should decentralize the decision making), or identification statements (I am a conservative decision maker).

Intensity. People express their emotions, sentiments, or excitement by how they communicate.

Device. This category has been used in propaganda research to analyze the basis by which people communicate. Such propaganda "tricks" might be name calling, glittering generality, card stacking, and bandwagon.

The categories used for coding are more relevant when they emerge directly from the data. This allows the researcher to get a "feel for the data" because he or she sees the data in their rawest form and sorts them into categories. However, the researcher must focus the categories so that they answer relevant questions relating to what and how the communication occurs.

Often, the categories for coding might be developed after an initial sorting of a sample of data. Selected examples of statements or quotes to represent the categories can be included in a glossary of terms to illustrate the categories used for coding. These descriptions reveal the actual statements and words that people use to describe the way that people speak.

Background Note 9.5: Exploratory Content Analysis

In exploratory applications of a content analysis procedure, the categories might emerge after reviewing each of the interviews or observation notes. For example, a coder was only interested in understanding the crises experienced by entrepreneurs and the "subject matter they expressed." As the coder reviewed each interview, she developed categories illustrating the type of crisis experienced.

	1	*2*	*3*	. . .
	Finances	Partner Quit	Divorce	
Entrepreneur 1	✓	✓	✓	
Entrepreneur 2		✓	✓	
Entrepreneur 3			✓	

Eighteen categories emerged describing financial, job difficulties, competition, economic downturns, death in family, partner dropped out, staff problems, and so forth. For each of these categories, she began to develop a glossary of terms, two of which were as follows:

1. Finances. Undercapitalized, trouble with banks, pressures from banks, going into bankruptcy, and overbought on a product.
2. Partners Quit. Partner dropped out, partner died, partner wanted to split the business.

The eighteen categories were combined in four categories describing financial crises, personal and interpersonal crises, economic downturn, and other environmental crises.[17]

Checking Reliability and Validity

A central problem with sorting and content analysis evolves from the data reduction problems by which the words and phrases are classified into much fewer categories. The categories may seem valid to the extent that they describe what seems obvious, but this is always open to question because of the ambiguity of words used and the way that people categorize them.

Many of the procedures for checking the reliability and validity of the categories generated encourage the use of other groups or individuals to offer a second opinion on the categories that evolved or the items in the categories. Those who are part of any verification process should be as representative of that culture as those doing the initial sorting.

Reliability is the tendency of a measuring instrument or observation technique to give consistent readings under equivalent conditions. This is a measure of the consistency with which an individual or group sorts the questions into common categories.[18] Test–retest reliability might be calculated on the basis of the accuracy by which items are classified by two independent groups.

Reliability is sometimes calculated by allowing the sorters to develop their own categories. Thus, two teams of classifiers might come up with slightly different categories, although the categories might reflect a similar meaning. A *structured sort* is a procedure where the categories of one group might be used by the second team. That is, the second group would sort the cards used by the first group. Reliability, in this case, is an assessment of the ability of one group to duplicate the sorting of the other group. The categories can be refined until the teams are in agreement.

Three types of reliability are important in content analysis: *stability, reproducibility*, and *accuracy*. Stability, or the extent that a content classification varies over time, can be ascertained when the same content is coded more than once by the same coder. It may be the weakest form of reliability, because only one person is coding. Reproducibility, or the extent that more than one coder can produce the same results with the same text, offers a stronger indication of reliability. Stability measures the consistency of shared understanding, while reproducibility is an indication of personal interpretations. Accuracy is the extent a classification of text corresponds to a standard or norm. It can be used to test the performance of human coders.[19]

Validity is a statement of whether we are measuring what we think we are measuring. Do our categories represent what they are supposed to or are expected to represent? The emphasis in these questions is on what is being measured. For example, questions about a manager's educational background and experience may not be a valid statement of his or her abilities, just as questions on employee satisfaction may not describe what people feel is important in their work and lives.

Content validity is guided by the question, "Is the substance or content of this measure representative of the content being measured?" The validation is a matter of judgment. Alone or with others, one judges the representativeness of the items. Do the items or statements really represent the content of the items in that category? This means that each item or statement must be judged for its presumed relevance to the property being measured. Usually, other competent or representative judges should judge the content of the items.

Criterion-related validity is studied by comparing test or scale results with one or more external variables or criteria that are known in the present or future. When one predicts success or failure of managers on the basis of their responses to specific interview questions, one is concerned with criterion-related validity. Within criterion validity, there are two kinds: concurrent and predictive validity. The criterion exists in the present (e.g., another test) with concurrent validity and in the future with predictive validity.

The single greatest difficulty with criterion-related validity is the choice of the criterion to validate the categories. Aptitude tests predict future achievement, achievement tests predict present and future achievement, and the categories developed should describe the setting. The Echo findings might be presented to persons who are expert in that culture or who represent that culture. This provides an opportunity for others to offer another perspective on the values describing a culture. Alternatively, researchers might compare the Echo evidence with questions or constructs from alternative known instruments.

Construct validity is a way of testing hypotheses of a construct being measured. This is obtained when evidence from different sources gathered in different ways all indicates the same or similar meaning. In this regard, construct validity is the extent to which the category is compared with other measures of the same construct. The evidence yielded by administering the measuring instrument to different groups in different places should yield similar meanings. A measure of the satisfaction of people, for instance, should be capable of similar interpretations in different places.

Construct validity seeks to establish whether a measure discriminates in the sense of measuring something unique and not picking up artifacts. One tactic might be to try to compare the results of one set of constructs with others generated in different studies, although these results depend on the inherent differences in groups studied. For example, it is probably more valid to compare schoolchildren in Canada with those in the United States than it is to make comparisons between Singapore and the United States.

The Echo message technique is a way of checking on the reliability and concurrent validity of the categories.[20] In this case, a short list of messages or interview responses from a group of respondents is presented to members of a second group. Booklets are often used in the message sessions, where each page of the booklet contains a pair of messages, one of which is selected by the respondent. The second group is asked to judge the importance or acceptability of the items against a similar list from some other group or against a manufactured list. Echo validity is confirmed if the respondents picked the list or individual items coming from their own group over the alternative message.

DIFFERENT USES

The sorting and content analysis process for generating categories or concepts has different uses. The researcher may wish to understand the salient values and beliefs of a group and provide some interpretation of why they are important or unimportant, or develop a theory or set of constructs for further research. The categories might be used for structuring a qualitative description of a group or issue, or for developing a questionnaire or experiment for further research. The ideas, themes, or categories emerge from what participants perceive, value, or describe as relevant.

The many studies illustrating sorting and content analysis illustrate a wide variety of procedures, depending on their objectives. One might use procedures to test for reliability and validity. Or it is just as appropriate to use sorting and content analysis procedures in a less systematic way for developing ideas and hypotheses for further research.

10

Developing Echo Surveys or Questionnaires

A few observations and much reasoning lead to error; many observations and a little reasoning to truth.

Alexis Carrel

An Echo survey or questionnaire is designed from an inductive process in which people in the field are involved in defining the measures to use. The questions asked, words used, or concepts illustrated reflect or "echo" the specific nuances, values, and experiences of people in a group or organization. For this reason, standardized instruments are usually less appropriate.

DEVELOPING AN ECHO QUESTIONNAIRE

The words and concepts used in the Echo survey or questionnaire reflect those from Echo question sessions, interviews, on-site observations, and other explorations. They are intended to echo the phrases and words used by the people being researched. The concepts, which emerge from a sorting process, are "grounded" to those of the people in the culture being researched.

The process of developing questions also increases commitment and collaboration from the people being researched. The questions should also be more relevant, reliable, and useful in understanding a problem or in focusing organizational change. This should assist in designing theories or hypotheses, as well as in developing change initiatives.

Clarifying the Design Process

The initial stages of the process for developing an Echo questionnaire are nicely illustrated by a project to develop a student questionnaire for evaluating teaching.[1] Typically, faculty and administrators define teaching performance criteria and proceed to ask questions they believe illustrate that performance.

In Echo projects, researchers ask students to define what they care about and wish to evaluate in faculty performance. Based on interviews and Echo question sessions, they are able to develop a list of values, examples, and behaviors of what illustrates good and bad teaching. After sorting these statements into categories, they can develop a list of statements for defining teaching performance.

Background Note 10.1: Guidelines for the Questionnaire Project

It is often the case that students receive questionnaires that don't ask the questions students would like to evaluate their professors on. That is, the concerns outlined in the questionnaires are not necessarily the concerns of the students. In an attempt to alleviate this problem, we would like you to identify what you value and do not value in the way the class is delivered. The following general questions might serve as a guideline to structure your thoughts:

- What are some behaviors you would like professors to do in facilitating learning?
- What are some behaviors you do not want professors to do in facilitating learning?
- What types of learning activities do you find most valuable to your learning?
- What types of learning activities do you find least valuable to your learning?
- Give us examples of a learning activity in which you felt you learned a great deal.
- Give us examples of a learning activity in which you felt you learned the least.
- What things do you find dissatisfying about classroom experiences?
- What things do you find satisfying about classroom experiences?
- What are things the school can do to assist with your learning?
- What are things the school should not do to assist with your learning?
- You are free to write questions or statements that we might use to evaluate teaching. When writing a question, think about the behaviors that exemplify good teaching. The questions you write should be written in such a way that you and other students can easily understand what is being asked. Try to include response formats (e.g., true–false, five-point scale, multiple choice, etc.)

for each item. It will help us to understand the question if we know how it should be answered.

- Don't be academic or psychometric. The questions shouldn't sound like they came from a textbook or journal article. Just give your feelings about the important questions that reflect what you want to evaluate professors on.

Adapted from B. Cunningham, J. MacGregor, and J. McDavid, *Questionnaire to Evaluate Teaching Performance* (Victoria, B.C.: School of Public Administration, 1997).

To carry out the objective of designing a student-generated questionnaire of faculty teaching, Bavelas, Bavelas, and Schaefer randomly selected forty students from a class list for all third- and fourth-year psychology students. All participating students were entered in a lottery that made them eligible for a \$50 prize. Researchers informed the students that their aim was to develop a questionnaire that reflected the concerns of students, and that it was important to write statements that they felt were important.[2]

The questions and response formats were typed on ten-by-fifteen-cards, one question per card. Spelling mistakes were corrected, although no grammatical changes were made. This process resulted in 318 cards that were then used in the sorting procedure.

Sorting

In developing a student-generated questionnaire, six sorters were chosen from a pool of twelve third- and fourth-year psychology students who had previous sorting experience. Each sorter was given one-sixth of the cards based on pilot tests that revealed that each of the sorters could work with between fifty and sixty-five cards without any difficulty. The researcher read an overview of the instructions for the project.

During the initial steps the goal is to produce a number of homogeneous categories that ask the same question. If the categories meet this criterion in the sorters' opinion, the sort is successful regardless of the number of categories or how specific or general they are.

These steps encourage a great deal of discussion among sorters. While the experimenter might begin the process, sometimes carrying cards between the tables, the sorters soon take charge. The sorters are reminded that if there is any disagreement they can form a category of unclassified cards that they can deal with later. The steps proceeded smoothly, taking about an hour.

Picking Questions or Statements to Reflect the Categories

The choice of the statements or questions results after refining the categories and picking statements to best represent them. The experimenter read through the first couple of categories and the sorters refined them. Although a majority rule approach was adopted, most of the decisions on labeling categories and picking sample statements were consensual. Throughout, the experimenter's assistant recorded both the labels given to each category and the contents, using the identifying numbers on each card. The contents of each category (the cards) were spread out on a table where they were visible to all sorters. Using a process of elimination, the sorters were able to choose cards for the questionnaire while eliminating others.

Sorters picked nineteen cards for their student-evaluation questionnaire, each card representing a category. While they tried to prioritize the statements they felt were most important, they ended up agreeing that they should all be used in the questionnaire. After grouping these cards, the sorters recommended that certain cards follow others on the questionnaire and labeled these cards accordingly. They also recommended that additional space beneath each question allow for comments specific to the question. The sorters also endorsed the idea of a "not applicable" or "don't know" option for each question. These steps took approximately three-and-a-half hours.

The final questionnaire might require some changes to make it more consistent and professional. When changes are made, the wording of the questions or statements should reflect, as closely as possible, the actual statements illustrated in the categories. Normal rules of editing are appropriate to guard against vagueness, multiple indicators within one question, and so forth. Echo surveys and questionnaires include a range of question types. Some of the questions are rather open ended in nature and are generally oriented to a process of discovery.

Communicating the Project's Purpose

The final questionnaire needs a statement of the project purpose and the way that data will be used. Figure 10.1 illustrates how the purpose was articulated to respondents in a "360-Degree Feedback Project" that gave supervisors feedback from their employees and upper-level managers.[3] Note how the initial statement highlights issues relating to purpose, the role of the respondent, how the data will be used, and how confidentiality will be maintained.

Choosing a Recording Format

Sorters can review a number of possible questionnaire formats and choose the ones that are most suited to their purpose. Different formats are useful to record the importance of or agreement on what people value and believe in, or how or why they act in certain ways.

Figures 10.2 and 10.3 illustrate two different teaching-evaluation instruments developed from an Echo process. The examples use different scales, as sorters felt that each of these statements of teaching performance was unique and should be measured differently. They also did not want admin-

Figure 10.1
Title Page Communicating the Project's Purpose

Team Member Questionnaire

The purpose of this questionnaire is to examine the quality of relationships between front-line staff and their first-level supervisors within the division as a whole. You will also be asked to comment on how well you feel your team is functioning as a unit and to describe your job. Your feedback will be used to highlight organizational strengths as well as areas of concern in an attempt to create a better working environment for all staff. Your responses are therefore very important to the outcome of the study.

> This survey is anonymous, confidential, and voluntary. You can refuse to answer any questions you are uncomfortable with. Whether you participate or choose not to participate will have no bearing on your employment status. Please be assured that all information provided by you will be kept STRICTLY CONFIDENTIAL. You are not required to identify yourself by name anywhere in the questionnaire.

Only my academic supervisor and I will have access to the data. Your employer will not have access to the raw data. Code numbers will be used to identify results obtained from each team.

Move through it at your own speed, but do not dwell on any one question. You can complete the questionnaire during work hours. You do not have to complete it all at once. If you would prefer to work on it at home, you are welcome to do so. After you have completed the questionnaire, please seal it in the attached, preaddressed envelope and drop it into the internal mail system. I would really appreciate it if all questionnaires could be completed by August 16.

For the purposes of this questionnaire, SUPERVISOR is defined as your "first-level reporting relationship." (For the majority of you, this will be your Team Leader. If you are a Team Leader, you will complete a questionnaire for your Supervisor.) TEAM is defined as including front-line staff, team leaders, and supervisors.
Please check the coding sheet (included with this questionnaire) and write the number that corresponds to your <u>direct</u> supervisor defined in this box:

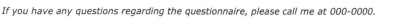

If you have any questions regarding the questionnaire, please call me at 000-0000.

Source: Adapted from M. Mayhew, *Supervisor–Employee Relations in a Team Setting: Case Study of the Financial Services Division* (Victoria, B.C.: School of Public Administration, University of Victoria, 1997).

istrators to calculate a total score, but wanted to give faculty members feedback of each of the statements of performance.

Another format is illustrated in Figure 10.4, a questionnaire developed to give staff and supervisors feedback. The items reflected what people desired in a supervisor and originated from questions like, "What are some examples of things your supervisor does to help you?" Figure 10.5 gives respondents an opportunity to rank a number of strategies that might be useful in motivating employees. Figure 10.6 illustrates a format for gathering demographic information.

Figure 10.2
Using Different Scales

> **Please circle the number that best represents how you feel about the instructor and the class.**

1 The course outline was closely followed throughout the course.

1	2	3	4	5
Disagree Completely	Disagree Somewhat	Neutral	Agree Somewhat	Agree Completely

☐   **Nonapplicable or don't know**

2 Does the professor encourage class discussion?

1	2	3	4
Never	Sometimes	Often	Always

☐   **Nonapplicable or don't know**

3 How was the workload of the course?
_____ **too heavy**
_____ **just right**
_____ **not enough**

☐   **Nonapplicable or don't know**

4 When answering my questions, both in and out of class, this instructor makes me feel the questions were:

Silly and   1   2   3   4   5   **reasonable**
Mundane

☐   **Nonapplicable or don't know**

Source: Adapted from J. B. Bavelas, A. Bavelas, and B. A. Schaefer, *A Method for Constructing Student-Generated Faculty-Evaluation Questionnaires* (Victoria, B.C.: University of Victoria Press, 1978).

Questions with Open-Ended Responses

Open-ended questions allow respondents to add examples or illustrations of their feelings on a topic. A questionnaire that seeks to gather information on motivation and job design might seek responses to general questions like, "Can you describe a time when you were extremely motivated?" "Can you describe a time when you were extremely unmotivated?" "What are some aspects of the job that you find increase your motivation?" or "What are some aspects of the job that you find decrease your motivation?"

Figure 10.3
Individualized Scales

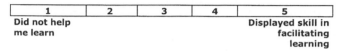

Please circle the number that best represents your opinion about what occurred in the course.

A. Instructor behaviours

A1 *The instructor displayed competence in facilitating learning (e.g., by use of appropriate instructional techniques, being attentive to needs of class, etc.):*

1	2	3	4	5
Did not help me learn				Displayed skill in facilitating learning

Comment_____

B. Learning activities and outcomes

B1 *How useful were the learning activities (projects, assignments, labs, exams, presentations, group work) in facilitating learning?*

1	2	3	4	5
Need to be rethought				Very effective in facilitating learning

Comment_____

B2 and B3 *How would you rate your knowledge of the course material (a) before entering the class (upper scale), and (b) after completing the class (lower scale)?*

	1	2	3	4	5
B2 On entry	1	2	3	4	5
	None	Slight	Some	Moderate	*Substantial*
B3 On completion	1	2	3	4	5

Comment_____

Source: Adapted from B. Cunningham, J. MacGregor, and J. McDavid, *Questionnaire to Evaluate Teaching Performance* (Victoria, B.C.: School of Public Administration, 1997).

Open-ended questions probe for details on events or behaviors. Newspaper reporters often use probes—like the five W's (what, who, where, when, and why)—to encourage a person's own interpretation rather than attitudes and feelings of others: "What did you do during the crisis?" "What do you think happened during the crisis?" "Who were some of the people involved?"[4] Such questions indicate when the events occurred, the time period, and what occurred during various days, weeks, months, or years. They can also suggest why the event occurred.

Open-ended questions allow respondents to recall a range of activities: "What managerial activities do you use to motivate people (involvement, incentives, interesting work, and the like)?" Although such lists encourage

Figure 10.4
General Scale for All Questions

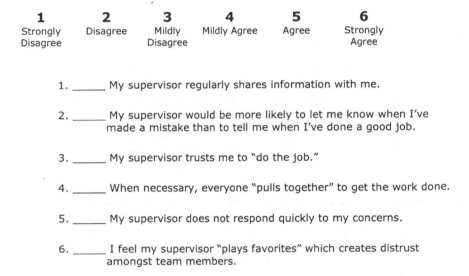

| 1 | 2 | 3 | 4 | 5 | 6 |

Relationships within the Team

Below are some statements that you might agree or disagree with. Please write a number in the blank beside each statement, based on the scale given. There is no right or wrong answer, only how you feel personally about the statement. This information cannot be used to identify you.

1	**2**	**3**	**4**	**5**	**6**
Strongly Disagree	Disagree	Mildly Disagree	Mildly Agree	Agree	Strongly Agree

1. _____ My supervisor regularly shares information with me.

2. _____ My supervisor would be more likely to let me know when I've made a mistake than to tell me when I've done a good job.

3. _____ My supervisor trusts me to "do the job."

4. _____ When necessary, everyone "pulls together" to get the work done.

5. _____ My supervisor does not respond quickly to my concerns.

6. _____ I feel my supervisor "plays favorites" which creates distrust amongst team members.

Source: Adapted from M. Mayhew, *Supervisor–Employee Relations in a Team Setting: Case Study of the Financial Services Division* (Victoria, B.C.: School of Public Administration, University of Victoria, 1997).

people to think of the range of possibilities, they might discourage further exploration. Very few items not on the list are likely to be reported.

Open-ended questions that are too general may be difficult to answer and interpret. For instance, the general question, "What is your general impression of your manager?" is an example of a question that can be answered differently by different individuals. One person's response might be based on a friendship, while another's might reflect the manager's ability to motivate people. The open-ended questions in Figure 10.7 ask for ideas and suggestions for change.

Finalizing the Questionnaire or Interview Schedule

There are several questions that must be answered in finalizing the schedule.

Figure 10.5
Ranking Different Values and Needs

Please rank order the following items in motivating your employees, giving 1 to the strategies which are most important and 15 to the items which are least important.

1. _____Learning new tasks
2. _____Being rewarded for what I do
3. _____A boss who is fair
4. _____Teamwork and harmony
5. _____Positive and helpful coworkers
6. _____Freedom to decide how to do his or her work
7. _____Good job security
8. _____Good pay
9. _____Chances for advancement
10. _____Interesting work
11. _____Chance to excel
12. _____Recognition
13. _____Higher level responsibilities
14. _____Time for outside interests
15. _____Participation in decisions regarding job

- How can the presentation be enhanced so that the questionnaire is professionally presented?
- Should questions be arranged in sections corresponding to different concepts?
- Should emotionally neutral and easy-to-answer questions be answered in the first section, or should the most central and important questions appear first? Should easy questions or those of different orders of magnitude precede the more important ones?
- How long should the questionnaire be?

How Can the Presentation Be Enhanced?

The format of the questionnaire should, in principle, recognize the respondents' needs as more important than the researcher's style or coding requirements. Failing to recognize these needs leads to erroneous responses and lower cooperation and reliability. The best way to improve the appearance of a questionnaire is to use a format that the sorters feel looks professional.

Should Questions Be Arranged in Different Sections?

Once the respondent is thinking about a topic, it may be sensible to ask other questions related to it. While some researchers argue that it is appropriate to switch back and forth between topics to check on reliability, re-

Figure 10.6
Demographic Information

Demographic Information

Please answer the following questions by placing an "x" in the box beside the appropriate answer.

This information will not be used to identify you. It is being collected for statistical purposes only.

E1

What is your age?

Less than 20 years of age

20-29

30-39

40-49

50 years of age or older

E2

What is your gender?

Male

Female

E3

What is your status in the organization?

Regular status

Auxiliary status

E4

How long have you been reporting to your current supervisor?

Less than 1 year

1-2 years

2-3 years

More than 3 years

---

spondents sometimes resent these changes. Logically grouping questions may encourage the respondent to continue thinking within the specific content area. Section changes might follow introductory phrases.

Instead of asking the same question in different sections, it may be useful to ask the same question in a different way (varying from closed to open-ended, for example).[5] Many questionnaires are constructed to make sure that a response set is not constructed, and this may be important for certain types of questionnaires (indexes or scales). That is, positive and negative

Figure 10.7
Open-Ended Questions

> Please use the space provided to answer the following questions.

A5 Please write one word that describes your current work atmosphere:

_____

A6 The single most important change that my supervisor could make to improve my satisfaction at work is.....

_____

_____

_____

_____

A7 The single most important change that my team members could make to improve my satisfaction at work is.....

_____

_____

_____

_____

_____

questions might be interspersed so that the interview does not develop a response set.

Sorters might assist in developing measurement scales where a concept is measured by adding a number of responses of individual statements. It may also be useful to encourage the sorters to arrange the questions on the questionnaire, while emphasizing the importance of reliability checks and so forth. To eliminate some problems of negativity, it may be more advisable to word all questions or statements in the affirmative; for example, satisfaction with the job as opposed to dissatisfaction with the job. Additional comment space might be available for "nonapplicable" and "don't know" options.

Should Emotionally Neutral Be Answered First?

The funnel principle, most used in interviews, suggests that more general questions might be followed by more specific probing ones.[6] One might ask questions that are really a series of more in-depth probes:

"Describe what it means to be challenged in your career."

"Describe how it might feel to be challenged."

"Are there periods in your career when you felt especially challenged?"

"Are you challenged in what you do now?"

"What do you find challenging now?"

"What do you find not challenging?"

The inverted funnel principle is often found in questionnaires. The goal is to ask specific questions and then ask for more general, summarizing questions, or even open-ended questions.

Researchers have to consider where they might ask for responses to biographical questions. Biographical questions about age, income, or employment status may be considered threatening to some. Thus, they might just as well be placed at the end of the questionnaire.[7]

How Long Should the Questionnaire Be?

Many researchers have conducted three-hour interviews and asked respondents to complete one-hour surveys. The length seems to be determined more by the salience of the topic to the respondent than anything else. However, rather than justifying a longer questionnaire, one important factor is to seek only information that is crucially important. When there is doubt about the salience of an issue, researchers might use the adage, "When in doubt, leave it out."

The best guide to salience is to use questions important to the respondents. On highly salient topics it is possible to construct questionnaires of as many as twelve to sixteen pages, without a loss in cooperation. Beyond that point, noticeable drops in cooperation occur.[8] The final sections of the questionnaire might ask for comments about what the respondent found important and not important in the questionnaire and how it might be improved. A note of thanks is always an appropriate ending to a questionnaire, and details on how and when respondents can expect feedback can also be provided.

The Pilot Test

No amount of thinking, editing, and foresight will take the place of a pilot test, which is a means of catching and solving unforeseen problems with the phrasing and sequence of questions and the length of the questionnaire. It is a way to question the appropriateness and wording of questions and the data-collection methods, as well as providing data for preanalysis.

A qualitative pilot study is a way to field test the instrument as if it were an interview schedule. The researcher directly asks respondents to answer questions normally to be answered in written form. The interviewer tries to make note of questions that are interpreted differently than intended, while being alert to respondent reactions.

The research pilot test is the actual "dress rehearsal" of the study. The procedure is laid out exactly as it would be in the actual study, including specific instructions, form letters, and the like. The researcher will ask respondents to complete the questionnaire in the same type of setting as they would normally be expected to complete it. This can provide information on the time the questionnaire takes and whether respondents actually follow instructions. Coding and analyzing the data can illustrate where questions are needed or not needed.

The process of designing Echo-type questionnaires based on open-ended interviews and Echo question sessions usually reduces the need for substantial changes as a result of the pilot test. However, if the pilot test produces a need for major changes, something might have gone awry in the instrument-development process. A careful and sensitive interviewing process is the most appropriate way to improve wording. Usually, the pilot test is a way of "polishing" the edges of the instrument.

Validation

To validate a questionnaire, we must ask whether the questionnaire does what it purports to do. In the project to develop a student-generated questionnaire measuring faculty performance, the question was, "Is this questionnaire more acceptable to students than other questionnaires currently in use?" Respondents were asked to compare the appropriateness of five questionnaires to test this question.

Background Note 10.2: Instructions for Validation

This folder contains five questionnaires for student evaluation of professors' teaching. We feel that it is often the case that students receive questionnaires that don't ask the questions the students would like to be evaluating their professors on. That is, the concerns outlined in the questionnaire are not necessarily the concerns of students. To enable us to determine which questionnaire is the most suitable for students to use, we'd like you to rank order them for us.

Read each questionnaire carefully and then rank order them by writing a number at the top of each questionnaire. Use number 1 to be the best choice . . . 5 to be your least choice. If you can't decide between two of them, you may tie them; just give the same rank order to each one. When ranking these questionnaires, it would be better to rank them on a pure gut-feeling level rather than trying to use some academic analysis

of them. In other words, we want your initial reactions to these questionnaires.

Assume that each of these questionnaires is used for evaluating psychology professors teaching third- and fourth-year courses; that each
would be anonymous and completed for each professor in each class.
Remember that the content, that is, the actual items, are the important
things to base your judgments on.

You can write anything else (relevant) on each sheet, while you are
reading or after your ranking. We would be especially interested in comments about why you ranked the questionnaire high or low—for example,
many items are on irrelevant topics, not clear, etc.[9]

This method of assessing validity, while not useful for all situations, is
more appropriate for the general question of whether the new questionnaire
was more suitable as an evaluation instrument. The method was not intended to assess the construct of teaching effectiveness, nor does it assess
the reliability of the measures.

The instruments developed from an Echo process, although appropriate
for a specific setting, are less useful in others. "No test is valid for all
purposes or in all situations or for all groups of individuals."[10] The goal of
the Echo process is to help design questionnaires for specific purposes.

Administering Questionnaires

Good questionnaires may still get poor responses if they are not administered properly. The administration of the research requires some system for
assuring that the questions are answered appropriately. This involves developing mechanisms for (1) distributing the questionnaire to the respondent,
(2) assuring the questionnaires are received and that the respondent does not
need assistance, (3) receiving and picking up questionnaires, (4) assuring
that late people are reminded, (5) checking the form, (6) filing and number-
ing questionnaires, (7) coding, (8) checking the coding, (9) creating mechanisms for computation or analysis, and (10) displaying the results so that
they can be communicated.[11] In most cases, the Echo steering committee
can offer valuable assistance in administering the questionnaire when members have the commitment and interest in the project.

RELEVANCE OF AN ECHO QUESTIONNAIRE

How does one develop a survey or questionnaire that is specifically relevant to the organizational or societal problems studied? Does a researcher
derive questions on the basis of an established framework or theory? Does

he or she search research articles to find what other people have asked, and borrow questions that seem to fit the purpose?

It might seem easier to take a standardized survey or questionnaire from the great variety of instruments for studying a whole range of topics, from productivity and efficiency, morale, organizational flexibility, and job satisfaction to values, attitudes, and beliefs. Such instruments also provide a basis for comparison with other settings.

An Echo questionnaire recognizes that the theoretical framework for the questionnaire must emerge from the setting being researched and include the perspectives of participants as well as researchers. The variables to gather information and the phrasing of the questions have been carefully worked out in pilot studies. Each statement or question provides information about a theory that sorters have developed inductively from the words and actions of respondents.

Other questionnaires are appropriate for other purposes. Hundreds, perhaps thousands of questionnaires, tests, and scales are commercially available. Scales are composite measures of attitudes and values and usually combine responses to several items measuring the same variable. Psychological tests are often considered in the measurement of a wide range of characteristics, including values, feelings, ability, aptitude, intelligence, and achievement tests.

Most such scales and tests would not be used in an Echo-type project because they are based on predefined constructs or theories and do not gather data inductively. However, such instruments need not be rejected just because they are based on a different paradigm of science. They might be used to add another perspective on the data gathered from an Echo-type questionnaire. The various concepts—self-esteem, confidence, intelligence, personality, attitude, and creativity—measured through standardized instruments are subject to many biases and are limited by specific time periods, populations, cultures, and the like. Such instruments lose their relevance and validity for particular local programs. Most such tests and scales can be divided into the following classes: intelligence and aptitude tests, achievement tests, personality measures, and attitude and value scales.[12] Lists of such instruments can be found in the *Psychological Bulletin,* the *Journal of Educational and Psychological Measurement*, and the *Encyclopedia of Education*. However, they represent only one perspective on the issues addressed.

11

Developing Experiments

There is nothing so practical as a good theory.

Kurt Lewin

This chapter illustrates how many experiments were developed from an inductive Echo-like process. Lewin's concern for social issues led him and others to intently listen and observe people in real settings, and to value knowledge that was relevant to resolving their problems. Research could resolve practical problems if it had a theory that was sensitive to these problems. Good theories were most practical. Real-world observations were the source of hypotheses. Experimental research was validated in the laboratory and in real-world settings.

Lewin's oft-quoted phrase, "There is nothing so practical as a good theory," has sometimes been misinterpreted as having an antitheoretical, practical emphasis. In fact, theory and experiments were an intrinsic part of the Lewinian tradition that sought to represent or echo the needs and sentiments of people. The theory evolved and became refined as the data unfolded, rather than being systematically detailed in advance. Lewin's experiments and research were led by both data and theory, each feeding the other.

LEWIN'S EXPERIMENTS

Lewin's interest in the study of social issues was spurred on by his experience in prewar Germany and wartime United States, times that illustrated conflict between nations and races, diminishing prosperity, and economic depression.

Background Note 11.1: The Original Experiments

The Practical Theorist, by Alfred Marrow, offers a review of several questions tested in the Berlin experiments.[1]

Question: How does the intention to carry out a task illustrate a psychological tension? How does the need to release this tension sustain a goal until the intended task is carried out? An unfulfilled goal continues to make its influence felt in thought and action (or both) as long as the tension is not yet discharged by completion of the activity. Bluma Zeigarnik illustrated that a desire to finish interrupted tasks illustrates the tendency to remember unfinished activities more readily than completed ones. The preferential recall of uncompleted tasks has become known as the Zeigarnik effect.

Question: How are tasks resumed after they are interrupted? The finding that interrupted tasks are often resumed illustrated that there is a direct correlation between the release of a tension and the satisfaction of a need.

Question: What are some of the factors that illustrate whether an intention, once formed, will either be carried out or forgotten? The strengths of these influences—among them, the nature of the intention itself, the connection between the intention, and other intentions in the subject's life—are part of a person's overall psychic activity.

Question: What are some of the factors that go into the decision to attempt a difficult goal or try for an easier success at a lower level? What are some of the reactions to success or failure in reaching the goal decided on? This study sought to investigate the factors that influence goal setting by measuring the effect of success or failure on the individual's decision to raise or lower the person's aspiration level.

Question: What are some of the factors that determine the level of aspiration? This study illustrates why people are not likely to attempt to seek even highly valued objectives when they see no way of attaining them. This study illustrated why social revolutions tend to occur only after there has been a slight improvement in the situation of the oppressed group; the improvement raises their level of aspiration, making goals which were once viewed as unattainable now perceived as realistic.

Question: What is the genesis of anger and why is it that frustrations in achieving one's aim or purpose cause anger in one setting and not in others? These studies showed that the emotional effect of felt need depended on the intensity (as opposed to the importance) of the need. Thus, a person engaged in a trivial task could react violently. Any barrier that frustrates a person can lead to anger.

Question: How does repetition of the same activity cause the subject to reach the point of refusing to continue (psychic satiation) irrespective of fatigue or other physical factors. These studies illustrate how mere repetition can have harmful effects on learning.

Lewin was interested in discovering how people change. This required experiments. He pointed out that for thousands of years people had everyday experiences with falling objects, but this did not provide them with the theory of gravity. Experiments were necessary in the systematic search for truth.

The original experiments at the Psychological Institute in Berlin consisted of a series of nearly twenty empirical studies. Under Lewin's direction, doctoral students used simple paper-and-pencil tests, tasks, or games to test ideas related to personality and the psychological environment. The experiments offered a new perspective in studying human behavior because they demonstrated the extent to which perception and memory depended on motivation. They tackled difficult questions relating to recalling unfinished tasks, goal definition, level of aspiration, satiation, and anger, issues that had been considered too difficult to study with experiments. They showed an interest in developing and testing theoretical concepts, instead of analyzing narrow propositions or ideas. He never produced a theory and then looked for facts to fit it. He would seek to ask, "What is the problem? Let's first look at the problem and see whether any of this is possible."[2]

Some of the Iowa experiments furthered the work that was begun at the Berlin Psychological Institute. Lewin and his students and colleagues pioneered the use of theory, using experiments to test hypotheses. These experiments illustrate bold research designs attempting to answer practical questions. Lewin believed that experiments were necessary to develop the principles that could be used in answering real-life problems.

Background Note 11.2: The Iowa Experiments

Here are examples of some of the Iowa experiments.[3]

In one study, experimenters wanted to find out what frustration did to intellectual and emotional development? These experiments induced frustration among children by restricting them from playing with toys that they had previously enjoyed playing with. Each child was encouraged to play with conventional toys for thirty minutes before the experimenter lifted a wire mesh that had closed off half of the room. There was a number of new, attractive, and exciting toys in this part of the room that the children were encouraged to play with. After the child had become thoroughly absorbed, the experimenter interrupted the play and led the child to the other side of the room, lowering the wire mesh and locking it. The exciting toys were still in view, but the child was not allowed to play with them. Not surprisingly, the child became frustrated and spent a considerable amount of time trying to penetrate the screen. The children tended to regress and become more babyish, illustrating increased unhappiness, restlessness, and destructiveness.[4] The higher the level of frustration induced, the less creativity and time given to constructive play.

In the autocracy–democracy study, the primary objective was to find out to what extent and in what ways the behavior of leaders shapes group behavior. To do this, two styles of leadership were considered. In the autocratic style, the leader would immediately tell the group (of eleven-year-old boys) what to do and how to do it, would dominate the group, and would make all judgments as to the progress of the work. In the second group, goals and the means for reaching them were left to the group to determine democratically. Although the groups behaved similarly at the outset, they rapidly became different, and were strikingly different by the last (eleventh) meeting. There was far more quarreling and hostility in the autocratically led group, and far more friendliness and group spirit in the one that was democratically led.[5]

The Food Habits study was directed at understanding and changing food habits during wartime shortages to increase the use of beef hearts, sweetbreads, and kidneys during a period of wartime shortage. In some of the groups a nutritionist presented an interesting lecture on the vitamin and mineral value and economics of the three meats. In other groups, Alex Bavelas facilitated a discussion that encouraged groups members to make a decision on the appropriate food to eat. The experiment illustrated the power of group decision making in encouraging change.[6]

DESIGNING EXPERIMENTS

If you were to design experiments within the Lewinian tradition, what process might you create?

Get Faculty, Colleagues, and Students to Collaborate on Projects

The assistance of others might be one of the critical components in developing and implementing insightful research designs. Many problems in organizations require creative solutions and are complexly intertwined with others; these problems are likely to be resolved through concerted effort rather than by the independent action of people who are unattached to the problems.[7] Rather than competing with others who are doing similar research, group members can be helpful in acting as observers, analyzing data, and acting as leaders in various experiments. More important, others can offer criticism, ideas, and support, seemingly crucial ingredients during the long hours of tedious work in trying to unravel a problem.

Lewin was famous for developing a cooperative environment where faculty and students worked together in helping others. Ideas often emerged from others, from brainstorming, questioning, discussion, and debate. In one experiment illustrating the effects of autocratic and democratic leadership, Alex Bavelas suggested that people could be trained to be quite democratic. Lewin asked, "How would you do it?" Bavelas indicated that he was not sure how to do it, but he was sure it could be done. Lewin persisted and asked again, "How would you do it?" Bavelas reluctantly outlined some ideas that he was later asked to try out. These ideas became the basis for further experiments that extended the autocracy–democracy studies to the field of industrial relations. This interaction illustrates how faculty and students teamed up to carry out the experiments.[8]

An elementary principle that they followed was "Keep questioning." They asked others for ideas, discussed, critiqued, and brainstormed. They used metaphors, topological diagrams, and other methods for encouraging creativity and insight. They explored their own thoughts, trying to follow their hunches. They had faith that one of their hunches would lead to an idea, an interpretation, or a way of finding a solution.

Use Echo Questions in Developing Hypotheses

The Echo process and Echo questions encourage researchers to try to develop sensitive hypotheses that are ultimately useful to people. The most creative and insightful ideas are of little value unless people have a need or use for them. The goals of practical field research may be very different from those in a more basic science where it is not clear how an idea will ultimately be used. In practical science, the ultimate goal is make useful discoveries, to find out what people need, to solve problems, or to conceptualize something that people could not clearly understand.

Observe how an Echo-like process was used in designing the classic experiments on changing food habits during a time of wartime rationing. During that time, Margaret Mead was asked to serve as the secretary for the Committee on Food Habits of the National Research Council. The committee had been requested to advise governmental agencies on how to alter habits and tastes "so that they would embody the findings of the new science of nutrition and also, during the war-time emergency, maintain the health of the American people."[9] The project encouraged a collaboration between Mead's nutrition program in Washington and Kurt Lewin's graduate students in Iowa. They began the project by first seeking to find out what American food habits were, what was the cultural setting within which different groups of Americans selected, prepared, ate, and enjoyed foods that kept them well.

Using open-ended Echo questions, the research group obtained new information about customs and finer differentiation of maternal and paternal moral roles in the local Iowa culture. They learned about the details, showing that the "Father presided over meat and butter, Mother over green vegetables and fruit juices, while desserts and soft drinks were wholly delightful and approved by no parent at all."[10]

The experiments revealed that the housewife was key in determining what the husband and family ate. The family ate what the wives themselves liked. To change food habits, then, all one had to do was promote and convince the housewives that a wider variety of meats was appropriate.

These studies revealed that groups of people "can do a thing better when they themselves decide upon it, and also how they themselves can elect to reduce the gap between their attitudes and actions."[11] Active participation was a more effective change tactic than passive participation (e.g., lecture).[12]

Using Experiments to Encourage Action

Lewin was very interested in what was going on in the world around him. His prewar and wartime experiences had left him with many questions about prejudices, anger, conflict, and change. Many of the experiments were clearly linked to an action research project, and many were used for discovering as well as testing hypotheses that have an identity in the real world. The real-world focus encourages a practical experimentation, one that helps people solve their real-world problems.

Focus on Complex, Important Issues

Lewin's experiments were not only concerned with finding things out, but were concerned with exploring the underlying reasons for them. They sought to investigate complex and important social issues. Lewin insisted that even the most complex human problems could be put in some kind of experimental framework. He was critical of those researchers who carried out experiments that were more or less unrelated to one another or those who collected facts that were further analyzed into their smaller components. Without theory, it was impossible for any science to progress. Experiments should therefore be constructed to test theoretical ideas rather than for merely collecting facts or classifying behavior.

Lewin was searching for theoretical concepts broad enough to encompass all the various psychological processes and all branches of psychology in the fields of needs, will, and emotion. While some basic concepts had already been developed in the realm of perception and memory, he felt that little progress had been made in understanding motivation, aspiration, and intention. This called for a better understanding of why people are energized to act in certain ways, beyond the traditional concepts of "association," "instinct," and "libido."

Background Note 11.3: Psychic Tension

Lewin illustrated his idea of psychic tension with an example of a child at play who suddenly discovers a ball at the bottom of a deep hole. Because the ball is too deep to reach, the child feels a tension with a positive valence. After making numerous attempts to reach it, he calls upon an adult to help him. When the ball is recovered, the child's goal is reached and his tension is released. When he perceives another toy, the process starts over again.[13]

The "release of tension" is similar to a "satisfaction of a need" and the "setting up of tension" is equivalent to "intention." Tensions result from a person's genuine needs and quasi-needs. Genuine needs are generally physiological, such as hunger and thirst. Quasi-needs involve a purpose or intention, such as going out for a drink, completing a task, or wanting to own something.

These ideas became the basis for a field theory that illustrated that a person's behavior is a function of the person and the environment, the "life space." For each individual, the life space embraces needs, goals, unconscious influences, memories, beliefs, and other events. The various factors in a given life space are to some degree interdependent.

The life space was a gestalt, a patterned whole, something more than an aggregate of distinct parts. The gestalt holism was important in Kurt Lewin's work. The Gestaltist suggested that the whole was more than the sum of individual parts, but takes on an added characteristic or quality as entities with distinctive structures. Any change in any one part will change the whole. To those who worked within the Lewinian tradition, all mental processes are patterned in some way and can take on new aspects by the way they are organized. The broad implications of this gestalt principle of perceiving and thinking held immense importance for modeling and understanding.[14]

Over the years, Lewin evolved the concepts underlying his theory to illustrate how a person is part of a complex energy field. Tensions experienced are not stresses or strains, as much as they are desirable states for increasing a person's efforts toward a goal. Tensions arise from needs or wants. They illustrate a state of readiness for action. It is this striving for discharge that supplies the energy for, and is consequently the cause of, all mental activity. Thus, to understand and predict behavior, one must deal with the psychic tensions operating in a psychic field.

Field theory was probably more important as a device of communication by means of drawings than it was in defining a theory of human behavior. The drawings encouraged people to develop and communicate ideas that were new, while suggesting the need to explore forces beyond those that were most obvious and observable. Other researchers have used similar displays, such as mapping and influence diagrams, to articulate the relationships between a number of important variables that might define an issue.[15] These illustrations summarize the interdependence of variables, or the influence that one event might have on another.

Whether a display illustrates a model about nuclear physics, complex social phenomena, or the feelings of angry people in an organizational setting, it provides a way to picture the many strands of data that you have worked with. The display is something akin to an artist's task of shaping a drawing from how people interact in their many environments.

Verify Findings

Lewin was convinced that the significance of an experimental finding lay in the contribution it made toward defining a general principle that was universally applicable. He was interested in illustrating its validity by showing the relationship to the whole situation.

Many of the people associated with Kurt Lewin were known to get their ideas from common observations and soaking up stimuli from the environment, including the verbal ideas of others, but also acting simultaneously on those ideas with their creative imagination. The ideas that people find useful and insightful depend on whether they are valid and insightful within their eyes. It must be "right" as they see it. If ideas are to be right, they must be situationally valid for solving organizational problems. They must represent the culture, and are ultimately verified by people in that culture.[16]

If an idea is truly insightful, it needs to be useful to those who are going to use it. This requires a process of verification, in which clients, customers, or organizational members are able to ground the ideas and concepts so that they respond to problems and issues. They are also better able to offer suggestions and solutions that are useful if they are provoked or challenged to think in new ways.

Verification of ideas can be accomplished by (1) checking the accuracy of the findings with people in the field setting, (2) increasing the number of cases and encouraging other perspectives, (3) carrying out other studies in similar settings, (4) looking purposefully for contrasting cases that are extremely negative, positive, or otherwise different, and (5) sorting the cases systematically to look for differences.[17] Each method offers a different perspective in enhancing the ideas or the representativeness of the data.

THE WORST PATH TO FOLLOW

The following statement by Janet Beavin Bavelas offers a perspective on, possibly, the worst path for any researcher in developing experiments:

Of all the criticisms leveled at Milgram's "obedience" research, there is one I have not seen, the most important to me. We knew that. The world had seen genocide on a very wide scale, in the Ukraine, in the Holocaust, and the dropping of two atomic bombs on civilian populations. We did not need a replica in the lab; we needed, and still need, to know why—to understand the process, not to repeat it. Milgram's experiment belittled and trivalized the phenomenon rather than leading us closer to its nature.[18]

That is, building experiments to imitate something is much less useful than seeking to understand it more fully or explain its cause, in a Lewinian sense.

PART **IV** ──────────────────────

TAKING ACTION

12

Communicating

The voice of the people needs a whole art of harmonic transcription to
be understood.

Woodrow Wilson

The heart of communicating is a style that demonstrates that we can "connect" with the people we research. We connect when we understand and
can echo what people expect, value, and know. This chapter offers principles and examples of how we might do this.

Psychologists often use an experiment where subjects are given glimpses
of playing cards and asked to name them, one at a time. At high speed, the
subjects felt their answers were perfect, but when the experimenter slowed
the sequence down, many subjects began to see certain anomalies. When
they were shown a "red" six of spades, they would yell out either six of
spades or six of hearts. When they saw such cards at longer intervals, some
of the subjects began to hesitate. Some recognized that there was a problem,
but were not sure what. It was odd, like a red border. When the pace of the
cards was slowed even more, most subjects caught on. They made the mental
shift and began playing without error. This experiment illustrates that when
we provide people with a glimpse of something that is different from what is
conventionally defined, there is bound to be confusion and dissonance.

A message is best understood when it is communicated in a way that recognizes how people think and what they expect to see. A message is more likely to be acted upon when it reflects the way that people in the setting articulate these issues.

A STRUCTURE FOR COMMUNICATING

All written communications follow some kind of structure. Strunk and White, in *The Elements of Style,* offer the following comment on structure:

A sonnet is built on a fourteen-line frame, each line containing five feet. Hence, the sonneteer knows exactly where he [she] is headed, although he [she] may not know how to get there. Most forms of composition are less clearly defined, more flexible, but all have skeletons to which the writer will bring the flesh and the blood. The more clearly he [she] perceives the shape, the better are his [her] chances of success.[1]

Beethoven, Handel, and Mozart had very different styles, but they structured their operas in the same way. Their structure begins with an overture, in which they introduce their mood, followed by three acts. The final scene is designed to provide one lasting statement of the theme illustrated during the composition.

A novel has a catchy opening and usually has a general theme or moral principle that follows throughout (something like a conceptual framework in a report). The novelist then defines the characters, the setting, and the history of events leading to an anticlimax and climax. The conclusion in a novel may not be so explicit, but the reader is often left with some powerful lessons, interpretations, moral principles, ironies of life, or principles of success.

In report writing, the writer structures the material so that it can be easily read and understood. Reports begin by demonstrating a need or problem and then illustrating ways to resolve it. The report-writing structure illustrates basic issues or problems, as the reader wants to know at the outset what the report is about. The structure asks you to first introduce the main issues, their importance, and the need for the study.

Following a structure—including an introduction, conceptual framework, methods section, results and observations, discussion, and conclusion—saves time and encourages you to make sure the appropriate information is included. Even more, the structure is familiar to other people. The normal structure for reporting of Echo reports includes sections such as the following:

Abstract or Executive Summary

Introduction

Review of the Literature and/or Conceptual Framework

Method or Procedure

Results or Observations

Discussion of Results

Conclusions, Recommendations, or Implications

A structure for reporting is like a road map, encouraging the author to make certain decisions in moving from one point to another. Writers alter this writing structure for many different reporting purposes, recognizing that for some audiences having a thorough literature review (writing a thesis) might be more important than displaying the results (a managerial report). Some managerial reports will highlight the executive summary, an introduction that summarizes the methods, results, and recommendations, leaving other information in the appendices.

DEVELOPING A STYLE THAT ECHOES
THE PEOPLE RESEARCHED

Style is often dictated by professional or organizational norms. As writers, we pick up the style of those who are writing organizational memos, reports, or procedure statements. If we go to the military or government organizations, we will find a completely different style than at a company like IBM.

Some writers assume that style comes from expressing things uniquely, as if it were some separate entity that can be learned by rules, mannerism, or other tricks. Henry Miller offers a critique of this point of view: "Observing the growth of a book under his/her hands, the author swells with delusions of grandeur. I too am a conqueror—perhaps the greatest conqueror of all! My day is coming. I will enslave the world—by the magic of words. . . . Et cetera ad nauseam."[2]

For Miller, style is more an attitude of mind than principles of composition. If one is to write about a subject, one has to truly believe in it and immerse oneself in it. Immersion means getting beyond one's ego and avoiding a patronizing attitude. A careful and honest writer does not consciously worry about style, but in the process of working on the use of language he or she begins to see a style emerging from the people being researched.

How might we develop a style of writing where the words and phrases "echo" the values and manners in a culture? Such a style develops from experience and being able to communicate about others in terms that are respectful of their culture. Style develops from a person's ability to understand others. Henry Miller seems to imply that it is best to take on the style and intonations of those we are studying. That is, we should echo their values, beliefs, intonations, and expectations.

Background Note 12.1: Communicating Naturally

For some writers, style not only reveals the spirit of a group of people we are talking about, but also reveals an identity, something like a finger-print. The words and phrases echo the values and manners in a culture. Henry Miller offers this statement of how he grew to understand the naturalness of his style:

I sank slowly into a chair by the table and with a pencil I began to write. I described in simple words how it felt to take my mother's hand and walk across the sun-lit fields, how it felt to see Joey and Tony rushing towards me with arms open, their faces beaming with joy. I put one brick upon another like an honest brick layer. Something of a vertical nature was happening—not blades of grass shooting up but something structural, something planned. I didn't strain myself to finish it; I stopped when I had said all I could. I read it over quietly, what I had written, I was so moved that the tears came to my eyes. It wasn't something to show to an editor; it was something to put away in a drawer, to keep as a re-minder of natural process, as a promise of fulfillment.

Every day we slaughter our finest impulses. That is why we get a heart-ache when we read those lines written by the hand of a master and recognize them as our own, as the tender shoots which we stifled because we lacked the faith to believe in our own powers, own criterion of truth and beauty. Every man, when he gets quiet, when he becomes desperately honest with himself is capable of uttering profound truths. We all derive from the same source. There is no mys-tery about the origin of things. We are all parts of creation, all kings, all poets, all musicians, we have only to open up, only to discover what is already there.[3]

COMMUNICATION STYLES THAT ECHO VALUES, EXPECTATIONS, AND NUANCES

Reports that echo the nuances, values, and beliefs of a culture are able to connect with those being researched. Imagine that you observed a culture in the mountains in Nepal, or the stories of mine workers in Cape Breton who had just experienced a mining disaster. Or you might have interviewed a number of leaders and have the general desire to define their skills and abilities. Alternatively, you might have tallied the results of a questionnaire that profile the needs of street people. Your job is to tell a story so that other people can empathize with this experience in the same way you did. You are the eyes and ears of participants in illustrating central trends or themes.

After analyzing interviews, observation notes, or numerical data, the first major problem is to develop and prioritize what needs to be communicated and how it should be communicated. Thus, the report is not simply a listing of quotes and statements. Qualitative statements might illustrate central themes by highlighting information about a quantitative analysis of the findings. They offer different perspectives in triangulating quantitative and qualitative information.

Reports that echo a social experience usually offer examples of what people said, central themes, statements, or conversations. They highlight real experiences using the words and nuances that people use in their everyday conversation. They might illustrate real examples, tell a story, or relate a conversation that describes the central issues. In the following sections, I offer a number of examples of people in various fields that might illustrate Echo principles in communicating.

Begin with Real Examples

If we want to understand some of the feelings and stresses that people are experiencing, we might start by illustrating examples. In introducing her topic, Kathleen Eisenhardt illustrates an example of an incident that is typical of the turmoil in fast-paced settings like the microcomputer industry:

In October, 1984, Gavilan Computer filed for bankruptcy protection under Chapter 11. Despite a $31 million stake from venture capitalists, Gavilan experienced delays and indecision that ultimately cost the firm its early technical and market advantages. The firm's leading-edge technology became a "me too" one and competitors flooded its empty market niche. As the firm died, one executive mourned: "We missed the window."

This story is not unusual.[4]

Another example, from David McLain, demonstrates the problems of managing a safe and healthy work environment:

Managing safe and healthy work environments is one of the most important challenges facing organizations. Each day, millions of individuals enter work environments that threaten their health and safety. Biological, chemical, physical, radiological, and other hazards pose dangers to members of many occupations. The dollar costs of the on-the-job accidents, already at record levels, continue to rise (*Wall Street Journal*, 1993), as does public awareness regarding workplace risks.[5]

Both introductions illustrate real examples of problems or issues that echo those faced in real organizations. They highlight typical examples of the turmoil of changing environments and safety and health issues in the workplace.

Telling a Story Using Dialogue

Readers who read about the experiences of social workers are very likely to empathize with stories of their feelings and frustrations as they try to do their jobs. William Kahn's study, *Caring for the Caregivers: Patterns of*

Organizational Caregiving, illustrates the frustrations and exhaustion that caregivers experience in their work as they give of themselves until they have nothing more to offer.[6] Kahn's analysis provides an extensive account of the recurring acts of caregiving, and illustrates various patterns of emotional giving—flow, reverse flow, fragmented, self-contained, and barren—in a meeting:

> The image here is of the social workers, as primary caregivers, wading out into a river of painful emotional emotions to help rescue homeless youths, and the other parts of the agency, instead of pulling taut on the lifeline connection and anchoring the social workers to the organization, unconsciously dropping the rope and abandoning the social workers to the force of the waves so as not be pulled in themselves.[7]

Each of Kahn's five patterns reflects the influence of superior–suborinate relationships. Examples of the dialogues within three of these patterns are illustrated below.

Flow

This pattern is characterized by caregiving flowing from agency superiors to subordinates during role-related interactions. This is the classic pattern of organizational caregiving that researchers note when discussing effective considerate leaders and supervisors. In this pattern, those charged with directing, coaching, managing, and supervising others exhibit caregiving behavior; they minister to others in the context of performing their tasks.

The flow pattern is illustrated in the interchange during a regularly scheduled meeting between the board of directors' executive committee and the executive director. The board president began exploring the implications of the report for staff members and the executive director. Throughout, he showed warmth and affection for the executive director by smiling, joking, and speaking gently. The conversation included the following interchange:

President: I have this fear of tying goals to revenues because then money gets confused with productivity. We should tie goals to staff positions and hook revenues to staff positions. Otherwise what message are we sending to the staff? How can we help them feel they've accomplished something at the end of the year?

Director: We need more staff if we want to grow and serve more kids. But we've determined not to do that until we see what happens with the economy.

President: But it sounds like your people are overworked. Look, it's your call. We're with you on whatever you decide.

Director: I need help. I drive people pretty hard.

President: That's okay. You're doing great. You're in charge and we're here to support you. This is your operation and I'm here to work with you but you're the one who has to live with it. What do you need from me?

This interchange shows the key dimensions of caregiving flows. The board president seeks to empower the executive director, making it clear that it is the latter's prerogative to making operating decisions ("This is your operation"). At the same time, the board president clarifies his own role as supporting the executive director's decision ("We're here to support you").[8]

Reverse Flow

This pattern is characterized by reverse caregiving in hierarchical relationships, with agency subordinates giving unreciprocated care to superiors.

Social worker 1: How are you feeling?

Supervisor: Tired. All the time, I'm going to have to cut back on my schedule. I'm talking to the doctors and to the Executive Director and after that I'll let you know. We're going to have to do the best we can.

Self-Contained

This pattern is characterized by the temporary retreat of subsystem members into mutual caregiving that occurs outside the hierarchical structure. This pattern resembles peer groups that caregivers form to offset job burnout and provide social and emotional support to one another that cannot be found elsewhere.

Social worker 1 (Facilitator): What else?

Social worker 2: It's been hard to get ahold of the volunteers; they don't seem to get their messages saying exactly when they can call you, so they don't think they have to waste their time trying.

Social worker 1: When you reach them, how do you find the conversations?

Social worker 4: Sometimes people don't offer much. I'm afraid to put words in their mouths. I don't want to feed them when we talk, I want them to talk on their own.

Social worker 2: I know, it can get like pulling teeth. Sometimes it's important just to stay on the phone with them, just to build the relationship. After a time, it gets easier.

These dialogues illustrate examples of conversations in three of the five patterns of caregiving identified by the author. While they do not convey the total story, they illustrate select conversations that illustrate the Echo principle of respectfully reporting on the feelings, needs, and values that people have.

Narrating a Story

Narratives take many forms and are told about many things, including the history of a culture or people, the profile of an individual's disease as told by a physician, or a description of an organizational crisis. The narrator's goal is to illustrate the story in a way that illustrates values, moral dilemmas, expectations, and behaviors.

Karl Weick, in *The Collapse of Sensemaking in Organizations: The Mann Gulch Disaster*, offers an analysis of a disaster in Montana where thirteen smokejumpers died trying to fight a forest fire.[9] His structure illustrates how data and theory are woven together to support the proposition that this disaster illustrates the collapse of organizational structure and sensemaking. Weick offers an extensive description of why the structure of the Mann Gulch crew illustrates some of the dynamics of an organization, and then suggests that the tragedy at Mann Gulch alerts us to some of the vulnerabilities in organizations when they lose their sense of meaning and common purpose.

One way to shift the focus from decision making to meaning is to look more closely at sensemaking in organizations. The basic idea of sensemaking is that reality is an ongoing accomplishment that emerges from efforts to create order and make retrospective sense of what occurs." Recognition-primed decision making, a model based in part on command decisions made by firefighters, has features of sensemaking in its reliance on past experience, although it remains grounded in decision making.[10] Sensemaking emphasizes that people try to make things rationally accountable to themselves and others. Thus, in the words of Morgan, Frost, and Pondy, "Individuals are not seen as living in, and acting out their lives in relation to, a wider reality, so much as creating and sustaining images of a wider reality, in part to rationalize what they are doing. They realize their reality, by reading into their situation patterns of significant meaning."[11]

When the smokejumpers landed at Mann Gulch, they expected to find what they had come to call a 10:00 fire. A 10:00 fire is one that can be surrounded completely and isolated by 10:00 the next morning. The spotters on the aircraft that carried the smokejumpers "figured the crew would have it under control by 10:00 the next morning."[12] People rationalized this image until it was too late. And because they did, less and less of what they saw made sense:

1. The crew expects a 10:00 fire but grows uneasy when this fire does not act like one.

2. Crewmembers wonder how this fire can be all that serious if Dodge and Harrison eat supper while they hike toward the river.

3. People are often unclear who is in charge of the crew (p. 65).

4. The flames on the south side of the gulch look intense, yet one of the smokejumpers, David Navon, is taking pictures, so people conclude the fire can't be that serious, even though their senses tell them otherwise.

5. Crewmembers know they are moving toward the river where they will be safe from the fire, only to see Dodge inexplicably turn them around, away from the river, and start angling upslope, but not running straight for the top. Why? (Dodge is the only one who sees the fire jump the bulge ahead of them.)

6. As the fire gains on them, Dodge says, "Drop your tools," but if the people in the crew do that, then who are they? Firefighters? With no tools?

7. The foreman lights a fire that seems right in the middle of the escape route people can see.

8. The foreman points to the fire he has started and yells "Join me," whatever that means. But his second in command sounds like he's saying, "To hell with that, I'm getting out of here" (p. 95).

9. Each individual faces a dilemma, I must be my own boss yet follow orders unhesitatingly, but I can't comprehend what the orders mean, and I'm losing my race with the advancing fire (pp. 219–220).

As Mann Gulch loses its resemblance to a 10:00 fire, it does so in ways that make it increasingly hard to socially construe reality. When the noise created by wind, flames, and exploding trees is deafening; when people are strung out in a line and relative strangers to begin with; when they are people who "love the universe but are not intimidated by it" (p. 28); and when the temperature is approaching 140 degrees (p. 220), people can neither validate their impressions with a trusted neighbor nor pay close attention to a boss who is also unknown and whose commands make no sense whatsoever. As if these were not obstacles enough, it is hard to make common sense when each person sees something different or nothing at all because of the smoke.

The crew's stubborn belief that it faced a 10:00 fire is a powerful reminder that positive illusions can kill people.[13] But the more general point is that organizations can be good at decision making and still falter. They falter because of deficient sensemaking.

Weick's description of events illustrates the weaving of theory and practice and a style of reporting that uses qualitative data to illustrate a point of view, much like a defense lawyer might weave the logic for the defense around a central theory. The author uses data that assist in respectfully illustrating different points of view.

Presenting Tabulations

After analyzing quantitative results, the researcher faces a formidable task of presenting and condensing a mass amount of data so that people empathize with the values, beliefs, and expectations of people. Most tabulations of survey responses, although concise, do not display such values.

One partial solution is to combine quantitative survey information with examples of statements and expressions that illustrate the central theme. The major quantitative findings can be presented within tables, frequency distributions, or pie charts. It is then possible to select quotes, details, or examples that triangulate the major finding.

Van Velsor and Leslie, in a study entitled *Why Executives Derail: Perspectives Across Time and Culture*, illustrate four enduring themes to describe why executives derail: problems with interpersonal relations, failure to meet objectives, inability to build a team, and inability to change or adapt during a transition.[14] The following excerpt describes problems with interpersonal relations:

On the whole, problems with interpersonal relations were mentioned in two-thirds of the cases in Europe, as compared to one-third of the cases among derailed American managers. Manager who have problems with interpersonal relationships are those who are successful early in their careers generally because they are good at what is often referred to as task-based leadership. When presented with a higher level job that requires a more relationship-oriented leadership style, however, they have a difficult time. Among other things, such managers are often described as insensitive and manipulative.

> He was a bad people manager. . . . A manipulator of people. He started creating a poor climate in the office, making the work life not productive. After several warnings, he was fired (1993, Europe).

> He is a great strategic thinker and he has high ethical standards, but he lashes out at people, he can't build trusting relationships. He is very smart, but he achieves superiority through demeaning others. He is abusive, he hits people with intellectual lightning. He instinctively goes after people. Many people have tried to work on this flaw because he has extraordinary skills, but it seems hopeless (1994, United States).

Being overly critical and using others to further one's own ambitions are two other characteristics of managers with interpersonal relationship problems. A European senior executive described what this looked like in terms of the behavior of one country manager.

> He was always criticizing others, he felt free to do so without taking any responsibility for himself. . . . His relationships with subordinates were not sound; he could be over-friendly but not over-concerned. His behavior was arrogant. In fact he used other people for his ambition. When he hired people he looked for people like himself, mirror images. Always a mistake. He left the company two years ago and I think that he is still looking for a job.

In their presentation of results, the authors offer examples of interviews to illustrate the four categories that describe why managers derail. They do not present us with frequency distributions or statistical analysis, but this information is certainly available in other reports.

THE MEDIUM IS THE MESSAGE

Marshall MacLuhan introduced the phrase "the medium is the message" to indicate that the structure, style, and method of communication may be more important than its content.[15] Similarly, when understanding social settings, the medium (the structure or style for understanding) may be as important as the variables describing the settings. All individuals and social phenomeon cannot be separated from the structures by which they are defined or understood. We often try to describe individuals and social settings as if this was the sole message to be communicated. However, just as important to any communication is the medium in which it is described.

EXAMPLE: THE REPORT STRUCTURE

Abstract or Executive Summary

The abstract or executive summary is a review of the study; its purpose, method, key results or findings; and the conclusions and implications.

Introduction

An introduction includes examples of problems, a description of the need for the study, and the purpose. It offers a road map telling the reader where he or she is going and what to expect along the way. Possibly, the writer might illustrate the history or background of why this problem is now important to investigate.

The Conceptual Framework

In most research papers or reports there is a section called Theory, Model, or Conceptual Framework. The conceptual framework illustrates the concepts or criteria that guide how the problem might be researched and how the results will be presented.

Procedure or Method

This section illustrates the research design (evaluative, interview, survey, qualitative), the sample (number, characteristics, representativeness), data-gathering methods that articulate the conceptual framework (questionnaire, interview, library search), controls (triangulation, how "good" data was assured), methods used to analyze the data (type of statistics used, content analysis), and limitations.

Results or Observations

This section uses the conceptual framework to guide the presentation of results. Many of the results can be presented in tables and figures that are explained in the paragraphs making up each subsection. Tables and figures are only illustrations and do not substitute for your description of them.

Discussion

The most important question in the results section is, "What happened?" The crucial question for the discussion section is, "Why did it happen?" or "Is there a better way to think of this issue?" The discussion section is often an interpretation of the results, perhaps in relation to previous theory or other findings. This section might offer propositions to help explain the findings or story. It might illustrate a new framework to guide others.

Conclusions, Recommendations, and Implications

Conclusions, recommendations, and implications are interrelated. Conclusions highlight the results, pull them together, and respond to questions. What have we learned from this? What would we tell others we found out?

Recommendations illustrate actions that might be taken. Justifications for these recommendations might highlight key findings that support the recommendations. The implications subsection provides an opportunity to answer additional questions. What do the findings really mean? What do they mean in relation to each other as well as separately? What do they mean for future hypothesizing and hypothesis testing, as well as for existing states of knowledge? What do the findings mean for improving current practices? What steps do we have to take to implement these recommendations?

13

Learning and Change

> To question all things,—never to turn away from any difficulty; to ac-
> cept no doctrine either from ourselves or from other people without a
> right scrutiny by negative criticism; letting no fallacy or incoherence,
> or confusion of thought, step by unperceived; above all, to insist upon
> having the meaning of a word clearly understood before using it, and
> the meaning of a proposition before assenting to it;—these are the les-
> sons we learn from ancient dialecticians.
>
> John Stuart Mill

Kurt Lewin's ideas in learning and change provide several examples of
Echo principles. When I was trying to characterize a Lewinian process of
learning, Janet Bavelas reminded me of a set of seminars by Max Wertheimer,
one of the leading scholars at the Psychological Institute in Berlin, where
Kurt Lewin was a junior faculty member.[1] Lewin had expressed his appreciation of the teaching of Kurt Wertheimer and the fundamental principles
of gestalt theory.[2]

For Max Wertheimer, it was possible to teach an appreciation and genuine understanding of some concepts, even in physics, without teaching mathematical laws. Learning the form of the concepts in physics—such as the

concept of gravity—did not guarantee that one would understand or even remember them, as students who had learned the laws of physics did not, sometimes, understand them and often forgot them after the final examination. If they really understood the concepts, they would still be able to explain them in a sensible way even though they might have forgotten the mathematical expression. They might even be able to derive the mathematical form of the law.

The gestalt tradition is alive throughout Wertheimer's seminars and his book *Productive Thinking*.[3] The distinction is made throughout between a blind solution, in which the learner applies a formula, and a sensible solution, in which the learner understands what he or she is doing in relation to the essential structure of the situation. The blind solution is often an unsuccessful application of the formula to the situation not seen to be inappropriate.[4] It is always better to proceed in a manner that favors discovery of the essential nature of the problematic situation, of the gaps that require filling in, so that, even at the cost of elegance or brevity, the proof is "organic" rather than "mechanical."[5]

ASSUMPTIONS OF LEARNING AND CHANGE

The Lewinian style of learning and change relies on questioning, engaging participants in groups, and taking responsibility in solving here-and-now, real problems. Many of these ideas illustrate the spirit of the Echo approach.

Asking Questions

Max Wertheimer began a seminar on problem solving with the following questions: "Why is it that some people, when they are faced with problems, get clever ideas, make inventions and discoveries? What happens, what are the processes that lead to such solutions? What can be done to help people to be creative when faced with problems?"[6]

No one responded. He continued by highlighting that these are age-old questions that needed both theoretical and practical solutions, trying to elicit responses by asking other questions, such as, "How should we proceed in this seminar? How would you go about studying productive thinking?" Again, no response.

He queried them on whether they should begin by first deciding what methods should be used, just as some psychologists clearly decide on the procedures and rules they will use in carrying out their research. When one student agreed, he asked how this might interfere with the solution. Could this lead to overlooking crucial aspects of a problem and ignoring features of the results? It might even lead to a reformulation of the problem so that it fitted the methods. "Might it not be better, therefore, to allow the problem confronting us to suggest the methods to be used in solving it? Even after one had decided on the method, one must be ready to change it, or even drop it, if it was required."

Wertheimer proceeded to tell the class what he proposed to do during the seminar: "We will concentrate on concrete cases of problem solving in order to see what happens in such situations." Like a physicists or physician who does not decide in advance on the methods of investigating a phenomenon or treating a new disease, a problem solver should look at the problem and let it suggest what was to be done. Even if there were a universally accepted theory of thinking, it might still not be advisable to start with it because the theory might blind us to certain nuances of creative thinking.

Background Note 13.1: Wertheimer's Style of Questioning

In one of his seminars Wertheimer gave an example of the way the concept of gravity had been discovered by elementary students.[7] He asked a group of students, "If you dropped at the same time from the same place a heavy object and a light object, which will fall down quicker?" One student had said, "I don't know." An older student had said, "Of course the heavier one will fall down quicker." Wertheimer asked him to explain this. "If you fall down from a tree, you fall quickly." A third student said that he was not certain which one would fall faster, but that he disagreed with the second student's explanation. The second student suggested an experiment and proceeded to go upstairs and threw two objects—a key and a piece of paper—from the window. Predictably, the key landed first.

One student said he was wrong: "The wind did it. It blew the paper around so that it could not land." They repeated the experiment in the house but got the same results.

The third student who had refused to agree that heavier objects fall faster came up with an experiment of her own. She put the key and the piece of paper in two separate boxes of the same size and weight. The two other students, who observed, had to agree that both boxes landed at the same time. One student commented, "This is unbelievable."

Wertheimer asked his seminar participants whether the three students had discovered the so-called law of gravity. A great deal of discussion ensued, after which he asked, "What are the dynamics of this problem solving situation; what are the determining factors that made the discovery possible? What factors interfered and what factors would have made the solution impossible? What methods of teaching may lead to the correct answer but to little understanding of what is involved?"

The discussion took various directions, some students pointing out that it illustrated how a student's curiosity might be aroused. Others said that students might learn more this way, while others said that it was not feasible to wait until each student discovered all the necessary knowledge and skills. It would be impractical and it was important to develop a general curriculum of studies to learn what was necessary in life.

In the discussion, Wertheimer suggested that the question might not be whether or not we have the teachers who had such a grasp of the material so that it could be taught properly. Several students protested, objecting that it was necessary for a person to learn certain knowledge and skills. For Wertheimer, if one wanted to make students appreciate certain structures, one had to structure the situation in a certain way. Good teaching revealed the structure by creating the proper learning situation and by developing clear and starkly simple exemplars of the concept.

Learning in Groups

Within the Berlin Institute, Lewin's students formed close-knit, freewheeling groups, one of which was called the *Quasselstrippe*. Many of Lewin's students met together with Wertheimer's and Köhler's students, talking about one another's projects and offering suggestions.

The group experience was as important for Lewin's Iowa students as it was in Berlin. Discussions were sparked by a general or casual question or notion, changing in one part of the group and evolving and flowing dynamically. It might emerge as something remotely connected to the original conversation. They held regular meetings every Saturday morning, and soon were the talk of the institute, partially because of the meetings' highly interactive and stimulating nature. "The interactions between Lewin and this group of students was so free, and the disagreements so intense that I remember them as the most stimulating experiences I have ever had. . . . There were creative discussions during which ideas and theories were generated, explored, and controverted."[8] Lewin sometimes brought students home with him in the afternoon, keeping them busy past midnight.

These group experiences allowed people to learn with and from each other. While the members in such a learning group are often a source of ideas and support on a project, they do challenge and question others. Group members gain the experience of others in gathering, collating, and analyzing information from several sources, in developing and testing hypotheses, and in weighing and selecting alternate solutions. Group participants learn from the experience of working with others, an experience that can possibly produce some positive changes in behaviors and beliefs.

Group meetings serve as an external source of pressure upon members to keep working on a project. Apart from the encouragement to meet timely project deadlines, the group might assist in supporting participants to undertake more difficult tasks. The groups also provide a regular opportunity to review and adjust plans.

Group members worked closely with their peers, sharpening their ideas on other criticisms. The conversation always moved in a constructive direction. Members were loyal to each other, although there was no conformity of views, as Lewin never saw himself as a proponent of a set doctrine. However, he was known to not be helpful to students who were trying to work in other areas. He was a close friend to his students and assistants, often calling on them in their homes, chatting about personal matters, and treating people as if they were part of the family.

Focusing on Real Problems

Lewin, like Sigmund Freud, was interested in problems of personality and motivation, problems that had been largely ignored by academics in universities. Such problems were the concern of practicing psychoanalysts. Many students who joined Lewin in Iowa came with a practical interest in the social uses of psychological research. They were interested in real-life problems. Real-life problems were the source of ideas for learning and research. They used a bottom-up process of letting examples of behavior or problems provoke them.

Lewin quite naturally focused on everyday human problems in his experiments to respond to real-life social problems during and after World War II. Many projects involved assisting a client in industry or the community. In many of these situations, such as those involving industrial production problems or gang violence, clients wanted immediate solutions. Researchers also felt pressure to make their work immediately useful in solving a problem or changing something.

Experiential Learning

In the summer of 1946 Lewin and his colleagues set out to design a new approach to leadership and group-dynamics training for the Connecticut State Interracial Commission.[9] The two-week training program began with an experimental emphasis encouraging group discussion and decision making in an atmosphere where staff and participants acted as peers. They discovered that learning is best facilitated in an environment where there is a dialectic tension and conflict between immediate concrete experience and analytic detachment. Participants used their experience in challenging the conceptual idea of the observers.

Although Lewin was to die in 1947, the discovery was not lost. Colleagues continued to develop his ideas when they held a three-week program for change agents in the summer of 1947 in Bethel, Maine. Here, the outline for T-group theory and the laboratory method began to take shape, a movement that had a profound influence on the practice of laboratory education, training, and organizational development.

Background Note 13.2: People Should Participate in Their Own Learning

At the leadership and group dynamics training program for the Connecticut State Interracial Commission, it was common practice for research staff to meet and discuss the data collected during the day. While most staff members preferred a confidential meeting, Lewin was receptive when a small group of participants asked to join in. Ronald Lippitt, one of the researchers, describes a discussion when three trainees attended.

During the evening, an observer made some remarks about the behavior of one of the three persons who was sitting in—a woman trainee. She broke in to disagree with the observation and described it from her point of view. For a while there was quite an active dialogue between the research observer, the trainer, and the trainee about the interpretation of the event, with Kurt an active prober, obviously enjoying this different source of data that had to be coped with and integrated.

At the end of the evening the trainees asked if they could come back for the next meeting at which their behavior would be evaluated. Kurt, feeling that it had been a valuable contribution rather than an intrusion, enthusiastically agreed to their return. The next night at least half of the 50 or 60 participants were there as a result of the grapevine reporting of the activity by the three delegates.

The evening session from then on became the significant learning experience of the day, with the focus on actual behavioral events and with active dialogue about differences of interpretation and observation of the events by those who had participated in them.

T-groups highlighted the value of subjective personal experience in learning, and an emphasis on personal involvement, responsibility, and humanistic values. These core values stimulated ideas of participative management philosophies and organizational development activities. The emergence of a number of experiential exercises—structured experiences, simulations, cases, games, observation tools, and role plays—illustrated how to create such personal experiences in simulated situations.

Experiential learning encourages a continuous cycle of experience through self-awareness, an understanding of one's feelings and those of others, observation and reflection, the development of abstract concepts and generalizations, and application and integration with real-life practices.[10] The experiential learning process structures activities so that participants can do the following:

1. Develop the need to understand the concepts, either by the recognition of problems that need to be resolved or by personal awareness of needs.
2. Experience the problems or issues in real or simulated settings.

3. Observe problems or issues.

4. Reflect on the concepts, principles, or practices that are derived from the experience and observations; develop hypotheses to be tested and methods for applying concepts, principles, and practices.

5. Analyze and evaluate the implementation of these principles, and develop new principles, plans, and ways to test and apply this learning.

DEVELOPING LEARNING EXPERIENCES

Thomas Merton writes, "Mark would come into the room, and, without any fuss, would start talking about whatever was to be talked about. Most of the time he asked questions. His questions were very good, and if you tried to answer them intelligently, you found yourself saying excellent things that you did not know you knew, and that you had not, in fact, known before. He had 'educed' them from you by his questions."[11] How do we develop a Lewianian-like environment for encouraging students to learn? Some of this might depend on the style of the teacher, although there are some practical steps in beginning.

Involving Groups in Solving Real-Life Problems or Tasks

Class assignments, organizational problems, community projects, counselling, or tasks where colleagues want to work together in solving a problem are natural projects for any learning group to experience. Similar learning groups have been used for providing support and counselling for problems related to alcohol, drugs, smoking, weight, and mental health. Groups have been used to provide support for men, women, immigrants, people who have been abused, and other related issues. These group experiences offer an environment where people can share their experience on an issue with experts and people who have similar experiences. The groups are based on the assumption that people need to take responsibility for their learning and change.

Background Note 13.3: Learning Groups in Other Settings

Learning groups have been used in a variety of settings in organizations and universities, and are illustrated by Professor R. W. Revans after World War II in Britain's newly nationalized coal industry.[12] He used the term "action learning" to describe a training program that encouraged colleagues to meet and work together in groups for the purpose of solving organizational problems within the British coal industry.[13] These action learning groups or "sets" are described as "the heart of the action learning process." Revans later became frustrated with what he considered a very slow rate of change and left management to work with the miners.

The model was successfully used in resolving problems in hospital and community environments.[14] In the early 1960s he tried to start an experienced-based management development program with the Management Business School, only to become frustrated with traditional university education. He moved to the Foundation Industrie-Université of Belgium, which was connected with the University of Brussels. In 1967 he set up the first action learning program, which was applied to management education. In the program, a score of enterprises were invited to nominate a senior manager to spend a period in some enterprise other than his or her own, working upon a strategic problem of concern.

Action learning is a strand of training that is philosophically connected to the action research tradition. It is based on a training process that is experience based, and highlights a process of learning by doing. It includes learning by posing fresh questions rather than by copying what others have already shown to be useful—perhaps in conditions that are unlikely to recur. Participants become aware of their own values and beliefs. They have to confront failure and their ability to take action. In explaining this, Revans quotes George Bernard's statement, "It is not enough to know what is good; you must be able to do it."[15]

In university classes, groups can be organized to take on specific projects. In one class project we asked learning groups to act as consultants and report on the challenges and skills needed for middle managers in various government departments. They had to interview managers and develop a report to an audience of fellow students, professors, and senior public-sector managers. The following is a list of projects that various learning groups were asked to report on in various stages of their general management curriculum of studies:

1. How can we develop and implement a strategic plan?
2. How can we learn how to perform a cost–benefit analysis of some of services?
3. How can we evaluate a program?
4. How can we assess our training needs?
5. How can we establish benchmarks for our performance?
6. How do we develop a plan for negotiating and administering a collective agreement that is positive for management and union members?
7. How can we carry out a performance audit of some of our operations?

Note that these questions do not encourage a definition of skills and abilities. Rather, each question focused a class experience. By carrying out projects to respond to important questions, participants are able to develop problem-solving skills and abilities.

I have also observed learning groups with Janet Bavelas. One of Janet's colleagues called himself a Janet "junkie" because of his attachment to the group that often meets with Janet and others. The colleagues and students meet on a monthly basis, often spending hours discussing an idea, project, or way to investigate problems. In her meetings, no one seems to have an agenda. Discussions spin off in completely different directions from where they started. This is where most of Janet's students find their dissertation topics. These learning groups are also vibrant in the community, where colleagues meet and work with others who have been involved in the counselling and psychotherapeutic experience.[16]

Learning groups can be used for colleagues who want to work together to further their needs, such as developing an idea for a business, improving one's knowledge in an area (such as training or research), or offering feedback to others on ideas (writers' groups or think tanks). The group learning experience encourages a culture of problem solving on topics that participants—professors and students or managers and employees—feel are important to work on. Interesting questions, commitment to working with others, and interests in learning are the criteria that guide the projects.

Membership in a group learning experience could include a range of individuals who have a diversity of experience and interest. In practice, the best people are those who are interested in an idea or who want to be involved in solving a problem. Personal qualities such as having a "future outlook," a risk-taking attitude, and a general curiosity and desire to learn are encouraged. However, interest in a problem and commitment to the group are the important determinants in selecting people. Once a group has begun to meet, it is important to stress the value of the group relationship and its importance to participants' growth and learning.

The facilitator can be a person who is the project or group leader, the professor in charge of a class, or an external consultant who has taken on the responsibility to help the group develop. In normal circumstances he or she intervenes only to ask questions or encourage the discussion. However, the facilitator is often given responsibility to make sure that team members develop the expertise related to the problems to be solved or the research and training skills for carrying out the process. As the work proceeds, participants take on more responsibilities in interviewing, developing questionnaires, making presentations, and writing proposals or reports. The facilitator's role becomes less important.

Questioning

Since the time of Socrates, the idea of using questions to get students to think and learn has been at the forefront of educational theory. To question well is to encourage others to learn. In the skillful use of the question lies the fine art of helping people learn to think. It is a "way of evoking stimulating responses or stultifying inquiry."[17] Questions are a guide to clear and vivid ideas. They assist our learning and are the stimulus to thought and an incentive to action.

Take a moment and respond to the following questions and, perhaps, discuss them with someone you know:

- Describe what happens (what you actually observe) with respect to a discussion or seminar you have participated in when you were frustrated with the way the person led the conversation.
- For example, do you feel they talked too much? Were certain participants dominating the discussion? Did the leader listen attentively?
- For now, focus less on why these things happen and more on what it is that happens that is troublesome. What things troubled you?

In some discussions of these questions we may find that the key to an interesting seminar was the instructor's ability to ask interesting questions that steered the learning. Questions beginning with "what," "why," "where," and "how," might be more facilitative, while those beginning with "are you," "when are," and "where is," might lead to simpler, yes/no responses.

Being Too Open-Ended Is Likely to Get a Poor Response

Consider questions like, "How are things going?" "What are some of your concerns?" or "How do you feel about working in this organization?" Such questions are likely to be as unprovocative as closed-ended questions in getting insightful responses. They may yield responses, but there may be a higher degree of variation from different questions. Respondents might appropriately ask, "Concerns about what?" and "Feelings about what?"[18]

The structure of the question can encourage or discourage discussion and problem solving. Questions should encourage high-level thinking, have a number of possible correct answers, be structured in providing background information, and follow a single direction of inquiry.[19]

Background Note 13.4: The Lady in the Flour Predicament

Here is an example of the questioning that Max Wertheimer used in his seminars, taken from the story of the lady in the flour predicament.

A woman was once kneading dough in front of the center pole of her tent. She needed more flour. Since the bag of flour was behind the pole, she bent down, encircling the pole with her arms as she cupped her hands, and scooped out some flour from the bag. When she tried to get the flour to the dough that she had been kneading, she found that the tent pole obstructed her cupped hands. She did not want to drop the flour back into the bag for fear of wasting it. Not knowing what to do, she began to cry.

A Mullah came along and he gave her a suggestion that solved the problem. What did he suggest? What would you suggest that she do?

No one in the seminar ventured a guess as to what the Mullah had said. After a pause, Wertheimer continued with the story. The Mullah had told the lady to walk around the tent pole until her cupped hands were directly over the dough she had been kneading, and then to drop the flour on the dough. Why had the woman herself not thought of this solution?[20]

High-Level (Thinking) versus Low-Level (Rote) Questions

High-level questions require individuals to think rather than simply recall, paraphrase, or summarize (e.g., What are some ways we might make it easier for you to complete these jobs more quickly?). Low-level questions are those asking for a person to recall, repeat, summarize, or paraphrase what has already been stated or written down. These questions simply ask people to recall what has been recorded elsewhere. Such questions are important sometimes, but should be followed by high-level questions to encourage people to think about what they have done (e.g., How long did it take for you to cut the set of mirrors for the new house? or How many hours does it take to construct this window panel?).

Divergent (Many Answers) versus Convergent (Few Answers) Questions

The number of possible right answers indicates a question's divergence. *Divergent questions* are those for which there can be a number of "correct" or discussible answers (e.g., What do you think might be some of the reasons that our workload was very high during January, and yet our profits were only marginal?). Convergent questions imply that there is one right answer. Such questions are also important, but they, too, need to be supplemented with divergent questions (e.g., What do you think were the exact billable hours during the month of August?).

Structured versus Unstructured Questions

Certain questions are more structured that others. Structured questions provide background information, specify or narrow the focus, and otherwise orient the respondent to the question and its aims (e.g., One way to approach the problem is to examine the differences and similarities between organizations. Let's do this for the southern and northern divisions. What are some similarities or differences between the divisions?). Unstructured questions are wide open and amorphous. Such questions are too open-ended (e.g., What about the various divisions in the company? How do you see them?).

Single Direction versus Multiple Direction Questions

The number of answers to a question is another factor that affects the likelihood of responses. Single questions contain one main direction for exploration. They may also contain structured information to facilitate answers. Note that a single question does not necessarily require convergence or a single answer. (E.g., After I took over the organization, I tried to make changes gradually as I got to know the industry and the people I was working with. What might be some of the reasons why employees are reluctant to get involved in changing the organization to increase our profits and morale?). Multiple questions contain more than one direction in which people can respond. They may also contain asides, elaborate explanations, and elaborations. They are confusing. Which question do you answer? (E.g., After the take-over, did things change? I mean, to the extent that we haven't been able to respond to the market, can you explain why? Why did we have difficulty changing? What market factors might have affected our ability to change? Might it be that certain employees were quite resistant? What were they afraid of?).

The most promising questions are obviously high-level, divergent, unstructured, and single direction.

THE LEARNING PROCESS

The Lewinian process of learning emphasizes two dialectics: the conflict between concrete experience and abstract concepts and the conflict between observation and action. Learning, change, and growth are best facilitated by a process that encourages experiences followed by the collection of data and observations about the experience. People analyze these data and draw conclusions before taking action. This model is developed in David Kolb's *Experiential Learning* (Figure 13.1).[21]

Concrete experiences focus on a person's unique feelings and reactions to events. This phase of the learning cycle responds to the following questions:

1. What problem are you experiencing?
2. How do you feel about it?
3. How are you reacting to it?

Observations and feedback allow people to see and hear these events or issues. This phase responds to these questions:

1. How are others reacting to this problem?
2. What are you observing?
3. What are you learning from your observations?

Figure 13.1
Kolb's Experiential Learning Model

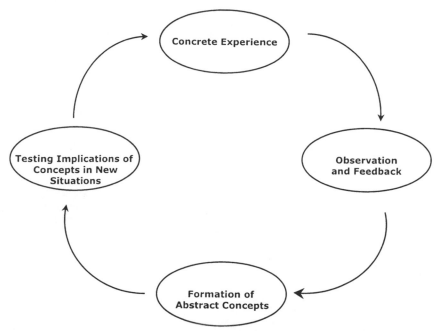

The processes of experiencing and observing go hand in hand, and it is sometimes difficult to separate them. For this reason, you may find it easier to describe your experiences before you try to understand your feelings and reactions, or you may have no trouble "getting in touch" with your feelings.

Our experiences and observations form the basis for developing some concepts or principles that generalize the experience. This learning phase emphasizes thinking rather than feeling and responds to these questions:

1. What concepts or principles can you use or develop to define a new future?
2. What concepts or principles are important for resolving the issue?

The concepts or principles provide a framework (or theory) for responding to the problem through active experimentation. Whether logical or not, this framework is the basis for acting. This action phase responds to these questions:

1. How can you implement this framework (the new concepts and principles)?
2. What is your plan?
3. How can you apply your framework to resolve the issue?
4. How can you apply the solution to the original situation?

14

Action Research

If I am not for myself, who will be for me?
If I am for myself alone, what am I?
And if not now, when?

Rabbi Hillel, first century B.C.E.

This chapter outlines the assumptions of the action research process relating to solving real-life problems, collaborating with practitioners, using groups, applying scientific principles in research, developing theory, and implementing changes. It illustrates how the Echo approach can be used within an action research process of becoming immersed in the research setting, research, and action.

The lines from Hillel that open this chapter had special significance for Kurt Lewin. The first two lines illustrate the need to investigate ourselves and our ideals just as we are ready to investigate others. The final line is a commitment to action, and action now.[1]

Lewin used the term "action research" to outline a type of social research in which scientists could assist in changing the world while simultaneously contributing to the advancement of scientific knowledge. The process of research assists in developing a commitment to change.

Lewin and colleagues outlined four varieties of action research: diagnostic, participant, empirical, and experimental. Diagnostic action research is "research designed to lead to action." Researchers could step into an existing problem—a race riot or industrial conflict—and diagnose the problem and need for change. They would seek solutions that are "feasible, effective, and acceptable to the people involved." Research is really a process of immersing oneself in a problem and offering solutions. Participant action research assumes the participants will help in effecting the solution and thereby be more keenly interested. This type of action research is more suited to community-related problems such as surveying community needs or encouraging action on crime prevention or environmental programs. It was useful in gathering and presenting data that are useful to a particular setting and less useful for illustrating general principles. Empirical action research is a way of record keeping and accumulating experiences in day-to-day work, ideally with a variety of similar groups, such as Boy Scouts or Girl Guides. When the results are drawn from more than a single case, the type of action research is useful in illustrating principles. Experimental action research calls for a controlled study of the relative effectiveness of various techniques in nearly identical situations. This type of research, although most difficult to carry out, has the most potential for the advancement of knowledge.[2]

ACTION RESEARCH EXPERIENCES

Alfred Marrow, in *The Practical Theorist*, describes how Lewin found a great deal of satisfaction in relating to people who offered a way of keeping in close touch with practical and social issues. Action research was an easy transition for Lewin and the majority of his colleagues, who wanted to investigate real-life problems during World War II. They were responding to questions like the following: What is the state of morale and its probable future course both in enemy countries and on the home front? What techniques of psychological warfare would most effectively weaken the enemy's will to resist? What kind of leadership in military units was likely to be the most successful? How could more such leaders be found and trained? How could home-front consumption of foods in short supply be cut back and the use of more available foods be encouraged? How did human relations in office and factory affect production in America's industries? What measures could be taken to care for and psychologically rehabilitate those injured in combat?[3]

While Lewin's interests in action research projects in industry were illustrated in his work with the Harwood Manufacturing Corporation in Virginia, other projects at the Commission of Community Interrelations focused on the community and society at large.[4] In one of the projects researchers were responding to an issue provoked when a gang of Italian Catholic teenagers interrupted the religious services on Yom Kippur at a synagogue in Coney Island. They involved citizens in a survey that illustrated that the real problem lay in the frustrations and disappointments that all people in the community experienced each day of their lives. These related to housing, recreation, and transportation, as well as activities bringing together racial and religious groups in a friendly atmosphere. Over the course of the project—involving surveys, interviews, and problem-solving discussion—the gang's relations with the adult world vastly improved, as the boys fundamentally wanted to please adults to whom they looked for recognition. Other community projects focused on racial integration, group loyalty, integrated housing, and sensitivity training (the origin of the T-group).

Background Note 14.1: Action Research in the Community

Over the years, Lewin's wartime travels produced several tensions among his Iowa colleagues, who seemed to resent his frequent absences and perceived that his consulting activities were forcing him to neglect duties such as attending faculty meetings. Some colleagues, in addition to criticizing his theory and emphasis on the philosophy of science, rejected his approach because it did not emphasize large-scale testing and statistical analysis. This, in addition to his inability to attain a new academic position in Washington, caused him a great deal of self-questioning.[5] He felt that he needed to find a new institute connected to a university where he could make further progress on action research and group dynamics projects.

The searching finally culminated in two new and parallel commitments: the Commission on Community Interrelations (CCI) for the American Jewish Congress (AJC) and the Research Center for Group Dynamics at the Massachusetts Institute of Technology in 1945. The funding by the American Jewish Congress offered the opportunity to do research on community and intercultural relations.[6] With the assistance of Douglas MacGregor, Lewin finally received an invitation to set up the Research Center at M.I.T. Its task was to educate research workers in theoretical and applied fields of group life and to train practitioners and persuade specialists in various fields—education, group psychotherapy, social group work, and industrial management—of the need for a more systematic and comprehensive review of group functioning.[7] The main methodology continued to be group experimentation in the laboratory and in the field.[8]

CCI's work complemented the experimental work carried out at the Research Center for Group Dynamics. CCI concentrated on responding to problems that people confronted in fighting prejudice, while the Research Center carried out studies on group productivity, communication, social perception, intergroup relations, group membership, and the training of leaders. There was hope that the research and actions would lead to learning: "Such action would lead to more reliable knowledge. Action would become research, and research action."[9]

Within CCI there was continual pressure to carry out a number of "fire-fighting projects" while deemphasizing long-range research. At the same time, frequent policy changes resulted because of the need for publicity arising from the dependence on public funds, competition with other Jewish agencies for funds, and criticism from activists with the AJC. Even so, during the next five years more than fifty separate projects were carried out.

Action Research in the United Kingdom

Researchers at the Tavistock Institute for Human Relations in the United Kingdom, under the directorship of Eric Trist, attached a fair degree of importance to Lewin's work. They were as committed to the development of an applied social science based on a psychoanalytical tradition. The Institute and the Research Center for Group Dynamics created a new international journal, *Human Relations*, to illustrate the connection between field theory and object relations psychoanalysis. It sought to further the integration of psychology and the social sciences and to relate theory to practice.

The Tavistock action research process is best known for projects in industrial organizations. In the Glacier Project, researchers sought to use a form of process consultation in observing and resolving conflicts. It was a very serious and practical attempt to explore the relationship between industrial efficiency and industrial democracy. In the experiments, researchers created a legislative system made up of committees representing all grades and skills, because they believed that relationships within the firm could be improved if rules were made in a fair way. Once the rules were made, managers were entirely responsible to the legislators for administering them effectively—the executive system.

Background Note 14.2: Action Research at the Tavistock Institute

Another stream of action research can be found in the experiences of a number of psychologists, social psychologists, and social anthropologists in Great Britain. These research efforts grew out of developments in the wartime army by a group, most of whom were at the prewar Tavistock Clinic. The original organization, the Tavistock Institute of Medical Psychology, was brought into existence in 1920 to respond to the suggestion that neurotic disabilities were not just a wartime phenomenon. It was composed of key doctors who were concerned with neurosis during World War I.[10]

The group that entered the Directorate of Army Psychiatry during World War II took a novel approach of going out into the field to find out from commanding officers what they saw as the pressing problems. They would listen to their troubled military clients as a psychoanalyst would to a patient, believing that constructive ideas for problem solving would emerge in these discussions. The concept of "command" psychiatrist arose to describe this approach. A psychiatrist with a roving commission was attached to each of the five army commanders in home forces.[11]

Toward the end of the war, a number of psychiatrists and social scientists undertook a large number of projects using an action-oriented philosophy of relating psychiatry and the social sciences to society. This was labelled Operation Phoenix and sought to define the new postwar role. The democratic tradition at the Tavistock Institute made possible the election of an interim planning committee made up of those who had led the work in the army.[12]

During and immediately following the war, this group of researchers conducted a number of successful action programs in personnel selection and treatment and rehabilitation of wartime neurosis casualties of returning prisoners of war.[13] The work in this period was the basis for the formation of the Tavistock Institute of Human Relations. The general approach was to use the collaboration of members of an organization while attempting to solve their problems.[14] Unlike the emphasis at the Research Center for Group Dynamics and CCI, the Tavistock research method or process for carrying out action research was not used for constructing a general theory of groups. Rather, it was intended as a type of social science not described in conventional academic journals.

The system allowed individuals to participate in matters affecting their work and learn the consequences of their decisions. It affirmed managerial authority and created an atmosphere where people felt free to express themselves. In all, it removed some of the inequalities and injustices generating tension, uneasiness, and distrust, making it possible for people to work effectively in roles that were clearly defined and equitably rewarded. Eliot Jacques's book, *The Changing Culture of the Factory*, illustrates this collaborative experience between social scientists and managers over the many years of the project.[15]

The most renowned illustration of the Tavistock action research process is the story of the discovery of self-regulating work groups in the coal mining industry and the developing of the concept of organizations as sociotechnical systems.[16] Their observations on organizing groups around task specialities and encouraging group management were put to the test on projects in the coal mining industry in the United Kingdom and later in textile mills in Ahmedabad, India. Absenteeism and productivity were much improved under the new work arrangements. In spite of the general difference in cultures between India and Western societies, the action research process produced similar findings.

The Tavistock action research process was characterized by the creation of a steering committee (made up of key actors who had some knowledge and influence to bear on the problem) to develop and implement a strategy to carry out and implement the research.[17] The researchers obtain data from interviews and unobtrusive measures (e.g., of absenteeism, turnover, and other organizational records), and implement their findings in a test area of the organization under protected conditions. The steering committee is quite active from start to finish.

ASSUMPTIONS UNDERLYING THE
ACTION RESEARCH APPROACH

The early action research experiences in the United States and Great Britain have much in common. They illustrate a unique way of solving real-life problems, collaborating with practitioners, using groups, applying scientific principles in research, developing theory, and implementing changes.

Solving Real-Life Problems

These action research projects emerged as researchers attempted to provide solutions to real organizational or social problems. Researchers were committed to a practical problem-solving approach involving a great deal of collaborative consultation with people in the field. Eric Trist offered the following comment on how the field should provoke or prompt the field exploration:

If you don't have something in the field to prompt you, you may find you have nothing at all useful for practice. The field must provoke you. I never think rigorously when I first look at a problem or research opportunity. But once I begin to understand the field, I can begin rigorously to arrange the new conditions—the constituent problems and issues—into an overall configuration. New factors enter in from the most unsuspected places. Then, I look at the relations, and seek to investigate relations between system levels.[18]

Collaborating with Practitioners

The researchers in both the American and British settings sought ways to encourage collaboration with the "client." Both parties were jointly responsible for the research, change, and knowledge generated. The collaborative strategy involved people in defining the problem, research process, and change strategies.

The action researcher was like a physician trying to help a patient. The patient is more willing and committed to be scrutinized if he or she believes the physician is committed to helping. In organizations, the need for the client's collaboration is even greater, since much of the relevant data concern feelings and motives. Clients tend to guard much of this information. These feelings and motives are likely to be understood and communicated when a researcher is part of a collaborative process in which researcher and client have vested interests.

Using Groups and Teams

These action research experiences illustrate the importance of groups, teams, and semiautonomous work groups in encouraging change. The experiences illustrate the adage that one of the more successful ways to change people is to change groups. Individual change is slow and labor intensive, even in small organizations. When the focus is group change, there is a stronger compulsion for the new behavior to be reinforced by other group members.[19]

The findings of Lewin and his associates illustrate how powerfully social forces affect group decisions and actions. Group discussions generate pressures for action much more effectively than when the individuals make decisions alone. The group's impact can be felt in several ways:

- Findings can be examined in a broader perspective, because the group brings together a rich variety of experience.
- Groups provide a psychological situation in which superiors and subordinates can work together without wide role differences.
- Improved interpersonal relations in cohesive groups leads to more acceptance, trust, and confidence among members. Each member develops a sense of security and personal worth by being involved in a cohesive group.
- Groups, if trust is properly developed, are helpful for the open discussion of problems and frustrations.
- Group decisions put powerful pressure, in the form of reciprocal expectations, on each member to carry out what the group has agreed on.[20]

In several cases, these research projects illustrate an interdisciplinary approach in understanding real social problems.

Applying Scientific Principles in Research

It is often argued that a client's involvement will introduce a Hawthorne-type effect in which the research process affects the results as much as the change. This same effect, called the placebo effect, has been noted in the medical field, where people's expectations and attitudes affect the health of a patient.

Action researchers knew that organizations did not "hold still" while they negotiated entry, made their intervention, and waited for the appropriate time to collect the follow-up data. However, any organization that illustrated the controls of a laboratory would be rather static in nature, and unlike the vast majority of organizations that might be more normal.

They knew that they were studying cases that could not be generalized to other settings.[21] However, they searched for consolidating cases, comparison groups, in-depth explanations, and various types of data. The process is a continuous process of immersion, research and experimentation, action, and further immersion and research. This episodic nature of action research distinguishes it from other aspects of problem solving. Developing a continuous cycle of research involves getting legitimization, where the goal is to move from practice to theory and then to improve practice.

Developing Theory

Because of its practical base, action research is often thought to be something like consulting. However, these pioneers were committed to the development of theory in illustrating their experiences in changing behavior. They placed a premium on theory that was inductively derived, empirically based, and practically relevant.

Lewin's comment, "There is nothing so practical as a good theory," is used to guide action researchers. Action research aims to "contribute both to the practical concerns of people in an immediate problematic situation and to the goals of social science by joint collaboration within a mutually acceptable ethical framework."[22] As such, action research was a type of applied social research differing from other varieties in the immediacy of the researcher's involvement in the action process.

Implementing Change

For Lewin, change at its most basic level consists of events of unfreezing, moving, and freezing.[23] In encouraging change, action researchers recognized that participants needed to understand the need for change, either because of pressures such as a loss of competitiveness or internal pressures from high rates of turnover or absenteeism, high grievance rates, sabotage, complaints, and dissatisfactions. In some cases, the pressure was most apparent in a crisis or dispute. The key problem, then, was to carry out the research and build a momentum for change.

People were motivated because they perceived that the change would lead to a desirable outcome in the end. This included the desire for personal power, prestige, income, or security.[24] During the *moving* stage, people are actively reconstructing these self-interests. Movement is encouraged by several forces, including external influences (authority, peer influence, and external rewards), interactive influences (participation and competition), and internal factors (expectancy and internal rewards).[25]

Gaining commitment to a direction is no easy task. In a classic study of workers in a pajama factory, workers routinely showed lower productivity after products were changed and they had to perform with new standards and piece rates. The workers resisted, even though supervisors exercised their authority and used an incentive bonus system.[26] The researchers observed that workers felt they could not attain the new standards and banded together to restrict production. There seemed to be a lack of trust and support.

Steering groups, peer influence, and group facilitation are instruments used to encourage people to keep moving in the same direction. During this freezing stage, people are learning to accept the new direction and are learning new norms and behaviors. When people publicly understand the need for change and publicly announce their goals and directions, there is greater commitment and more persistence.[27]

STEPS IN THE ACTION RESEARCH PROCESS

Any change program usually involves sequences such as immersion, research to identify the need for change, and action and implementation. These sequences are illustrated in Figure 14.1.

Immersion

An action research process is highly inductive and participatory, involving people from various parts of the organization. It is a process in which practitioners become jointly responsible for managing the process of change through a steering committee or action research group. Participants or organizational members are involved in the definition of the need and have the opportunity to use their creativity in developing the idea and its proposal.

The action research steering group is made up of people who have access to individuals who support the research as well as those opposing it. Anyone in the organization can be part of the action research process, but the most successful projects usually include people who are keenly interested in examining organizational processes and taking action. Action research is suited for people who are interested in developing new programs or ideas or in resolving problems or issues that are of importance to them and others. Participants often illustrate strong feelings, passions, and interests.

The formation of the steering group is a mechanism to initiate research and action, as well as an opportunity to become clear on the issues or problems to be addressed. When the group meets together, members begin to develop a joint understanding of issues to be addressed, goals, principles

Figure 14.1
The Action Research Process

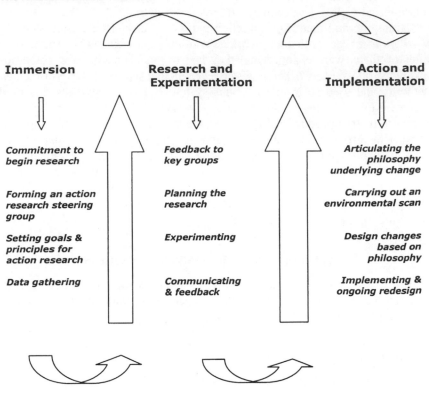

Immersion	Research and Experimentation	Action and Implementation
Commitment to begin research	*Feedback to key groups*	*Articulating the philosophy underlying change*
Forming an action research steering group	*Planning the research*	*Carrying out an environmental scan*
Setting goals & principles for action research	*Experimenting*	*Design changes based on philosophy*
Data gathering	*Communicating & feedback*	*Implementing & ongoing redesign*

for working together, expectations, and the methods for gathering data and taking action.

Successful problem or need identification is the crux of an action research effort. Problem identification provides a starting point for beginning the research, as well as serving as an initial and important diagnosis of organizational members and their skills, perceptions, attitudes toward work, and capacity to change. A well-defined problem meets a number of characteristics:

- It has significance for the group's, organization's, or community's functioning.
- It is manifested in real terms, such as dissatisfaction, low productivity, or conflict.
- It involves social, group, or organizational issues of working together or adapting to new technologies.
- It is clearly articulated.

Research and Experimentation

The temptation may be to proceed too casually, and to accept too quickly the initial views defining a problem and its resolution. Individual members bring with them their own personal motivations and views of what needs to be done in solving a group's or organization's problem.

Action research is based on the assumption that any solution depends on research—using experiments, surveys, interviews, and observations—for understanding the principles that are most useful for the setting. Lewin pointed out that for thousands of years our everyday experiences with falling objects did not suffice to illustrate the correct theory of gravity. In the same way, a sequence of designed experiences or experiments was necessary to bring about a change from less adequate to more adequate concepts. Systematic scientific experimentation was needed to study problems in small and large settings.

Several of the experiments at Harwood Manufacturing in Virginia illustrate this general approach. One such case involved the resistance of workers to changes in methods and job operations that were necessitated by new technologies, consumer demands, or needs to be more competitive. Models changed several times a year, making it necessary to transfer workers from old jobs to new jobs. Workers always resisted these transfers.

After interviewing, the research team learned that the resistance to change and the slow relearning were primarily motivational problems. Employees indicated they were frustrated and they had lost hope of ever gaining the former level of production, among other things. Between 1940 and 1946 researchers conducted a number of small-group studies to see if it was possible to transfer workers more smoothly without the usual hostility and falloff in production. These enquiries revealed that participation methods might provide a solution to the problem of overcoming resistance to change.

While the experiment was planned, an appropriate situation did not arise until the fall of 1947, after Lewin's death. In this experiment, carried out by John French and Lester Coch, three different groups were involved. Each group illustrated a different degree of employee collaboration in working out details of the proposed new job assignments:

- Group 1 members did not participate in any way. Workers were told of the changes and the production department explained the piecework.
- Representatives were appointed from Group 2 to meet with management to consider methods, piece rates, and other problems created by changes.
- Group 3 members took a more active role, all serving as representatives when they met with management. They had detailed discussions about all aspects of the change, made a number of recommendations, and even helped plan the best methods to do the new job.

The results were dramatic in illustrating how motivation, morale, and productivity are linked to the degree of participation in decision making. In Group 1, the nonparticipation group, production dropped off by 20 percent immediately and did not recover. Nine percent of the group quit, amidst low morale and marked hostility toward the supervisor. The group manifested slowdowns, complaints to the union, and aggressive behavior. In Group 2, in which workers participated through representatives, they required two weeks to recover their prechange output. Their attitude was cooperative and no one quit. Group 3, the total participation group, regained its prechange output after only two days. The output then climbed steadily until it reached a level about 14 percent above the earlier average. All members worked well with their supervisor and no one quit.

These and other studies illustrate how Lewinian methods helped shift the focus of management from mechanistic engineering approaches to social–psychological concepts. Any solution had to satisfy both technical requirements (efficiency) and social requirements (the need to respond to culture and values and acceptable practices).

Many action research projects used interviews, questionnaires, and observations, all of which emerged from a process of immersion. That is, the statements generated from the interviews or Echo question sessions—consisting of feelings and frustrations, examples of problems and incidents, and criteria for developing a survey—are the source of the survey. The statements are the basis for forming the concepts defining the issue or problem to be studied.

Action research group members develop the skills for designing experiments and questionnaires as well as analyzing data and making decisions based on the findings. They learn to use the information to enhance their decision making, and write up the findings so they are useful for others. They have to decide on how the information might be used in a program of research that seeks to identify problems and solutions. Part of their responsibility is to communicate the results to key groups before deciding on other research or whether to begin a larger-scale program of change.

Action and Implementation

Implementing new ideas or changing an organization's design relies on understanding what is realistic and possible as well as what has occurred previously. An architect has a similar problem in renovating an old heritage building. Implementation requires the adaptation of ideas gained from experience and past applications to the constraints of the present construction, needs of the tenant, and community norms.

Action planning is a useful strategy for assisting an organization's participants to define how they will go about implementing their ideas and research findings in a larger context. In action planning, an organization's membership is involved in identifying opportunities for change and implementing these results. It is based on the experiences of social scientists who have been instrumental in planning and implementing new technological designs in large-scale industrial organizations, as well as for focusing organizational change.[28] Such action planning groups influence decision making at other organizational levels and encourage commitment.

Action planning processes have been used in introducing work changes such as team management, industrial democracy, and quality of working life, which stem from the learning of Tavistock researchers in the United Kingdom and India. Another more famous example was the Norwegian Industrial Democracy Program, which developed and tested alternative organizational forms and their impacts on employee participation on different job levels. The program was seen as a large-scale collaborative effort between researchers and the researched. The Trade Union Council, the Employers' Association, and the government created the Joint Research Council, and worked together in implementing experiments to understand how to design work so that it responded to the major psychological needs of people. Others examples in Sweden, such as the Saab-Scania plant at Sodertalje and the Volvo plant at Kalmar, illustrated how teams could be used to eliminate the conventional assembly lines in manufacturing organizations.

Implementing a new organizational design, especially one that is based on new research evidence, is no easy task. New designs, such as team management structures, require new technologies and new work roles. They also require that people accept new norms for working together. Teams require that people perform new roles, and that they be involved in making decisions and solving problems that were always given to management.

When managers tried to introduce a team management design in the Shell chemical plant in Sarnia, Ontario, they knew that they could not simply ask people to accept the idea based on research evidence in other industries.[29] They implemented a long participative process that involved many discussions, workshops, conferences, and negotiations. Through these discussions, managers worked with Shell's general mission and philosophy statement, which articulated its unique purpose and set it apart from other companies. They were united by the general commitment not to perpetuate traditional methods of organizational and job design.

In June 1975 Shell established a task force to design the new chemical plant within this goal. The task force addressed itself to such questions as the following: Why do we want to change anything at all? What is wrong with the way we conduct ourselves today? If we could, would we wish to change? What are the reasons for the resulting practices? These questions led to a list of organizational practices that the task force considered from the standpoint of productivity and employees' needs, such as commitment, boredom, underutilization, and so forth. These discussions and others led to the development of a philosophy statement outlining the values underlying the new ideas, the way decisions would be made, and how staff and clients were treated. It outlined a general commitment to the joint optimization of social and technical systems, and expressed a belief that workers were responsible, trustworthy, capable of self-regulation, and interested in opportunities for decision making and growth.

Many organizations develop "credos" that are the public articulation of the mission statement or intent of existence. For example, the police credo is "To Protect and Serve," and Ford suggests that "Quality Is Job One." Some organizations have a vision statement to illustrate their mission, philosophy, and focus on clients and employees. The vision is like an architect's description or sketch before the plan is implemented. It is a public illustration of the ideas, concepts, and principles in designing a house. It provides enough detail so that people can understand the design, just as a vision statement sketches out what the organization will look like.

After the task force received top-management approval, it sought union participation and commitment. The union caucused after listening to management's proposal and, when they returned, they said they would agree to collaborate only if they could be "full partners and maintain a high profile."[30] This was certainly acceptable to the company, and the local union president was nominated to join the task force.

The task-force members carried out research and held several discussions to understand the economic and social environment affecting the new design. Some of the key obstacles identified were pressures from neighboring external plants for Shell employees to conform, the need to staff extensively with personnel experienced in traditional practices, the need for all levels of management to accommodate the new philosophy, the need to introduce a novel style of management while dealing with a technology that was totally new to Shell, and the willingness of the union to accept the new methods. In other cases involving community change, some of the initial discussion focused on understanding the community environment and the economic and social issues affecting the change.[31]

The philosophy statement was the instrument that guided the change at Shell in designing the challenging jobs and in deciding on the technologies to be used. The new design encouraged teamwork and greater worker responsibility in managing operations at the plant. As a result, it seemed desirable for every member of each team to be fully capable of operating all sections of the plant. Attention was then directed to specifying other team skills that would satisfy the objectives of greater self-regulation and improved response time to problems. To supplement these shift teams, a craft team was created, composed of fourteen tradespeople. While the social system was being designed in accordance with the philosophy statement, the technical system was constantly surveyed to assess its compatibility, and the need for several major changes in the engineering design became obvious.

An implementing plan is a list of actions to implement the new design.

The simplest form may be nothing more than a written agreement in the minds of key decision makers about their organization's mission and what it should do, given the circumstances. In this sense, the process of planning is as important as the actual plan. The formal action plan is most useful as a communication document, and is especially important if there is a need to coordinate with a range of people in a diversity of programs, and for keeping people "on track" with the plan's intentions. As people forget and new people are added on, a formal plan can provide an important set of targets to focus activities. In addition, a plan can serve as an important public-relations document for external and internal audiences.

A simple form of action plan might include the following sections:[32]

1. A statement of the mandate and mission.
2. A philosophy statement and vision.
3. An environmental scan that articulates the economic and social environment, as well as the obstacles, opportunities, strengths, and weaknesses to the new design.
4. The design, which articulates the way the philosophy statement is implemented in the job's design and the new technologies and ways of working.
5. A listing of responsibilities and roles.
6. A schedule for implementation and evaluation.

The plan is really a summary of the previous steps that have been undertaken. The major responsibility of the action researcher at this stage is to facilitate the transfer of information and decisions so that they evolve into a plan of action. Under normal circumstances, a program includes a list of projects that have identifiable tasks, target dates, and people responsible for undertaking various tasks. These targets can be defined so that they are likely to get commitments of time, effort, and logistical support.

At some point in most change efforts a number of questions are appropriate. These relate to assuring that the implementation is on track and that the change is having some of its expected impacts. These questions do not need to be asked in formal evaluations, but they can be posed at strategic times during the change effort.

Regardless of the specific action, the action research process remains the same. Every action is evaluated and the data fed back to the steering group to determine the validity of problem identification, general plan, action, and hypotheses. There are consecutive cycles of planning, execution, evaluation or fact finding, replanning, action, and reevaluation. Thus, action research has no terminus. The specific actions taken and the problems to which they are directed will, of course, change. But organizational improvement will always be an issue for the entire organization.

The times at which action plans are to be reviewed will differ. A plan will indicate when the checkpoints occur, and a schedule for review will be prepared for the organization as a whole as well as for individual departments. It will be necessary for the planning group to monitor this review to ensure that it is carried out and that a high level of involvement of staff is maintained. The phrase "summative evaluation" has been associated with many information-gathering efforts using traditional scientific procedures and analyses. Such evaluations take place at the final stage of a change effort and are often used to satisfy outside funding agencies.

An important purpose of formative evaluations is to solicit explanations for existing gaps and ideas on an ongoing basis. The evaluation can also address the framework that was established in the research phase. It can consider whether the problems identified have been addressed, the level of commitment, and the effectiveness of certain actions. It can assess whether interventions are contributing positively to the change.

Getting commitment to a plan of action is possibly the most important aspect of the implementation process. The most effective implementation plan has a number of ingredients: they are incremental and recognize immediate needs, they illustrate a grand design and steps that need to be carried out, and they illustrate that the grand design or map will be modified at each stage of the change process.

Action research encourages a participative approach to planning, with an emphasis on actions that are driven by the requirement of adjusting organizational decisions to the overall strategies. The steps are driven less by a rational, grand design. It is akin to a sports strategy of winning one point at a time or one game at a time. There may be a game plan and a strategy for "shadowing" certain players, but opportunities at certain moments are important to capitalize on. This idea of action planning is compatible with studies on technological innovation, which indicate that small, rather than large, organizational changes play a key role in reducing production costs.[33] Daily accomplishments form the basis for a consistent pattern that allows people to see instant gains. The strategy includes the following:

- Dividing tasks into smaller units, or problems into identifiable chunks.
- Avoiding overcommitting and underdelivering and practicing undercommitting and overdelivering.
- Being patient and politely persistent.
- Accepting the principle that the more the researcher does, the less responsibility people will take on.

The integral and most difficult element of getting commitment to projects is allowing individuals to articulate goals in relation to their roles and responsibilities. In conventional, top-down planning, goals or objectives are usually stated at the beginning of the process; it is the step on which all other steps are based, not the product of those steps. This is the crucial point of the whole process. Action research focuses on defining workable strategies and implementing them by creating opportunities and reducing restraints. It is a bottom-up process of developing goals and objectives based on participation and involvement.

Commitment not only involves the sequence of events for carrying out a project. It also involves understanding who in the organization must be committed to the change and to carrying it out. This is an understanding of the politics of the change. As a result, most change agents have suggested such ideas as "getting the executive's approval," "getting key people on board," "making sure the union is committed," and "having the membership understand it."

Successful implementations require a systematic analysis of who is committed to the idea, who is able and willing to provide resources, and who is willing to carry out and persevere with the new process. In any change process, a critical mass of people is necessary to assure implementation. This may mean five of nine participants, but it may also mean two of nine participants who are the strongest informal leaders. In this sense, the critical mass includes "those individuals or groups whose active support will ensure that the change will take place. Their number may be small, but it is the critical number."[34]

An implementation plan describes a series of action steps devised to secure the support of people vital to the change effort.[35] It outlines who is involved and how their commitment is assured.

THE IMPORTANCE OF THE LEWINIAN APPROACH

Alfred Marrow, in *The Practical Theorist*, illustrates that Lewin spoke often about the role of action research in responding to community and social problems. He became absorbed by critical questions:[36]

- Under what circumstances does a neighborhood which is open to Jews become all Jewish?
- When does it stay "mixed"?
- Which procedure in giving jobs to minority members serve to increase, and which to decrease, group tension?
- Under what circumstances and to what degree is the building of self-respect among minority members a prerequisite to improvement?
- How can one avoid the "shot-in-the-arm effect," which improves intergroup relations for a while, only to have them fall back again to earlier or even lower levels?
- What kind of training and education facilitates adjustment?
- What problems develop in a community with the arrival of minority group members?
- Which methods of dealing with these problems resolve them most readily?

His basic assumptions, hypothesis, and methodology could not be confined within the traditional boundaries of any specialized field, school of thought, or established system. His research undertakings were problem oriented, cutting across and mobilizing the knowledge of various disciplines.

As Lewin began the task of setting up the Commission on Community Inter-relations, he acknowledged the problems that they would have to confront:

I know that we will have to face an unknown number of obstacles, the most severe of which, I am sure, is hidden from us a present. The sailing for a while may be easier than I expect. But somewhere along the road, maybe in a half-year, maybe in two years, I am sure we will have to face major crises. I have observed this type of development in many research undertakings, and we will have to be unusually lucky if this time we avoid it. To my mind the difference between success and defeat in such undertakings depends mainly upon the willingness and the guts to pull through such periods. It seems to me decisive that one knows that such developments are the rule, that one is not afraid of this period, and that one holds up a team that is able to pull through.[37]

Lewin's comment illustrates that any action researcher is first and foremost a problem solver. Creativity and insight in problem solving is as important in understanding a problem, clarifying a research objective, or interpreting a maze of data, as it is in resolving the conflicts between researchers or clients or finding funds.

Notes

FOREWORD

1. For adults, the term "criticize" would be used instead of "scold."
2. A. Bavelas, A method for investigating individual and group ideology, *Sociometry* 5 (1942): 371.
3. K. Danziger, The origins of the psychological experiment as a social institution, *American Psychologist* 40 (1985): 133–140; K. Danziger, *Constructing the Subject: Historical Origins of Psychological Research* (Cambridge: Cambridge University Press, 1990).
4. Danziger, *Origins*, 134.
5. Ibid., 135.
6. B. Schaefer, J. B. Bavelas, and A. Bavelas, Using Echo technique to construct student-generated faculty evaluation questionnaires, *Teaching of Psychology* 7 (1980): 83–86.

CHAPTER 1: INTRODUCTION

1. P. Nutt, Surprising but true: Half the decisions in organizations fail, *Academy of Management Executive* 13 (1999): 75–90.
2 R. P. Barthol and R. de Mille, *Project ECHO Final Report*, contract no. DAHC04-69-C-0018 (Santa Barbara, Calif.: General Research Corporation, 1969), 4.
3. A. J. Marrow, *The Practical Theorist: The Life and Work of Kurt Lewin* (New York: Basic Books, 1969), 108.

4. Ibid.

5. K. Lewin, Psycho-sociological problems of a minority group, *Character and Personality* 3 (1935): 175–187.

6. The Iowa appointment was from 1935 to 1944. Marian Radke, Leon Festinger, Ronald Lippitt, and Dorwin Cartwright were the first staff members at the Center for Group Dynamics at M.I.T. All had worked for Lewin at the University of Iowa. Others joined after. See Marrow, *The Practical Theorist*, 180–190.

7. Ibid., 156.

8. D. Cartwright and A. Zander, eds., *Group Dynamics: Research and Theory*, 2d ed. (Evanston, Ill: Harper and Row, 1968), 3–32; see also K. Lewin, *Field Theory in Social Science: Selected Theoretical Papers*, ed. D. Cartwright (New York: Harper and Brothers, 1951).

9. A. Bavelas, A method for investigating individual and group ideology, *Sociometry* 5 (1942): 371–377.

10. J. Kalborn, Ideological difference among rural children. Master's thesis, State University of Iowa; J. Kalborn, Values and sources of authority among rural children, in *Authority and Frustration*, ed. K. Lewin, C. E. Meyers, J. Kalborn, M. L. Farber, and J.R.P. French (Iowa City: University of Iowa Press, 1944), 101–151; R. J. Havighurst and B. L. Neugarten, *American Indian and White Children: A Sociopsychological Investigation* (Chicago: University of Chicago Press, 1955), 84–151.

11. Kalborn, Ideological differences.

12. F. W. Osborn, The ethical contents of children's minds, *Educational Review* 8 (1894): 143–146.

13. Barthol and de Mille, *Project ECHO Final Report*. See also Bavelas, A method for investigating individual and group ideology; R. P. Barthol and R. G. Bridge, The Echo multi-response method for surveying value and influence patterns in groups, *Psychological Reports* 22 (1968): 1345–1354; R. de Mille, Logical and empirical oppositiveness in value responses, *Psychological Reports* 26 (1970): 143–154.

14. G. Morgan and L. Smircich, The case for qualitative research, *Academy of Management Review* 5 (1980): 491–500; G. Burrell and G. Morgan, *Sociological Paradigms and Organizational Analysis* (London: Heinemann, 1979).

15. Lewin describes a process of change as unfreezing, moving, and freezing, and a process of planning that includes planning, executing, and evaluating. The Lewinian research process characterized the way this group of researchers carried out their research.

CHAPTER 2: AN OVERVIEW OF THE ECHO APPROACH

1. J. B. Bavelas, Permitting creativity in science, in *Scientific Excellence*, ed. D. N. Jackson and P. Rushton (Beverly Hills, Calif.: Sage, 1987), 307–327. Many of the ideas in this chapter are based on this article and conversations with Janet Beavin Bavelas.

2. T. S. Kuhn, *The Structure of Scientific Revolutions*, 2d ed. (Chicago: University of Chicago Press, 1970).

3. The checklist of areas might result in a set of fourteen or fifteen pairs of questions, which are later reduced to seven or eight pairs after editing.

4. M. Mayhew, *Supervisor–Employee Relations in a Team Setting: Case Study of the Financial Services Division* (Victoria: School of Public Administration, University of Victoria, 1997).

5. K. Lewin, Action research and minority problems, *Journal of Social Issues* 2 (1946): 34–46.

6. R. N. Rapoport, Three dilemmas in action research, *Human Relations* 23 (1970): 499–513.

7. K. Lewin, The conflict between Aristotelian and Galileian modes of thought in contemporary psychology, *Journal of Genetic Psychology* 5 (1931): 141–177.

8. Ibid.; Marrow, *The Practical Theorist*, 57–59.

9. K. Lewin, *Principles of Topological Psychology*, trans. F. Keider and G. M. Heider (New York: McGraw-Hill, 1936), Chapter 2.

10. S. W. Hawking, *A Brief History of Time* (New York: Bantam Books, 1988).

11. J. Gleick, *Chaos: Making a New Science* (New York: Penguin Books, 1987), 3.

12. Ibid., 21.

13. Marrow, *The Practical Theorist*, 57–59.

CHAPTER 3: PRINCIPLES UNDERLYING THE ECHO APPROACH

1. K. Lewin, Formalization and progress in psychology, *University of Iowa Studies in Child Welfare* 16, no. 3 (1940).

2. Marrow, *The Practical Theorist*, 48–49.

3. Ibid., 10–14.

4. Bavelas, *A Method*, 371–377; R. P. Barthol and R. G. Bridge, The Echo multi-response method for surveying value and influence patterns in groups, *Psychological Reports* 22 (1968): 1345–1354.

5. Alex Bavelas was then at the University of Iowa (W. French joined Bavelas for some of the later experiments).

6. K. Lewin, Group decision and social change, in *Readings in Social Psychology*, ed. G. E. Swanson, T. M. Newcombe and E. L. Hartley (New York: Holt, 1947).

7. K. Lewin, *Focus Behind Food Habits and Methods of Change* (Washington, D.C.: National Research Council, 1943), 108; Lewin, Group decision and social change; K. Lewin, R. Lippitt, and R. White, Patterns of aggressive behavior in experimentally created "social climates," *Journal of Social Psychology* 10 (1939): 271–299; Lewin, Action research and minority problems; K. Lewin, *Dynamic Theory of Personality: Selected Papers by Kurt Lewin* (New York: McGraw-Hill, 1935); K. Lewin, *Field Theory in Social Science: Selected Papers* (New York: Harper and Row, 1951); K. Lewin, Frontiers in group dynamics: Part I, Concept, method and reality in social science; social equilibria and social change, *Human Relations* 11 (1947): 5–40; K. Lewin, Frontiers in group dynamics: Part II, Channels in group life, social planning, action research, *Human Relations* 12 (1947): 143–153.

8. Marrow, *The Practical Theorist*, 53–54.

9. J. B. Bavelas, A. Bavelas, and B. A. Schaefer, *A Method for Constructing Student-Generated Faculty-Evaluation Questionnaires* (Victoria: University of Victoria, 1978), 4.

10. Ibid., 5.

11. N.R.F. Maier, *The Appraisal Interview* (New York: Wiley, 1958).

12. J. Dewey, *Democracy and Education* (Toronto: Collier-MacMillan Canada, 1966), 240.

13. Ibid., 238–243.

14. Ibid.

15. M. Rokeach, *Beliefs, Attitudes, and Values* (San Francisco: Jossey-Bass, 1968).

16. Barthol and Bridge, The Echo multi-response method.

17. G. A. Kelly, *The Psychology of Personal Constructs* (New York: Norton, 1955).

18. C. E. Osgood, G. J. Suci, and H. Tannenbaum, *The Measurement of Meaning* (Urbana: University of Illinois Press, 1957).

19. de Mille, Logical and empirical oppositiveness.

20. G. Morgan, *Images of Organization* (Newbury Park, Calif.: Sage, 1997).

21. T. Jantz, L. Hellervik, and D. C. Gilmour, *Behaviour Description Interviewing: New, Accurate, Cost Effective* (Toronto: Allyn and Bacon, 1986).

22. Marrow, *The Practical Theorist*, 107. This slogan was quoted by Alfred Marrow from Alex Bavelas.

23. E. de Bono, *The Use of Lateral Thinking* (London: Jonathan Cape, 1967); E. de Bono, *Lateral Thinking: Creativity Step by Step* (New York: Harper and Row, 1970).

24. R. Fisher and W. Ury, *Getting to Yes: Negotiating Agreement Without Giving In* (New York: Penguin Books, 1981).

25. E. Kübler-Ross, *On Death and Dying* (New York: Macmillan, 1969), 37.

26. E. Kübler-Ross, *Death: The Final Stages of Growth* (London: Prentice Hall, 1975), 117.

27. Ibid., xiv–xxii.

28. Ibid., xvii–xviii.

CHAPTER 4: COLLABORATION:
A FIRST STEP IN THE ECHO APPROACH

1. Marrow, *The Practical Theorist*, 141–143.

2. Ibid.

3. S. Milgram, Behavioral study of obedience, *Journal of Abnormal Social Psychology* 67 (1963): 371–378.

4. Ibid.

5. Ibid., 371.

6. Ibid., 377.

7. Ibid., 374.

8. D. Baumrind, Some thoughts on ethics of research: After reading Milgram's "Behavioral study on obedience," *American Psychologist* 19 (1964): 421–423.

9. Statement by Margaret Mead. See Marrow, *The Practical Theorist*, 130.

10. J.F.O. McAllister, Dinner with George, *Time*, 29 November 1999, 26–27.

11. W. Bennis and P. Biederman, *Organizing Genius: The Secrets of Creative Collaboration* (Reading, Mass.: Addison-Wesley, 1997), 2.

12. Fisher and Ury, *Getting to Yes*.

13. C. R. Rogers, *Client-Centered Therapy* (New York: Houghton Mifflin, 1951).

14. As part of the PIC analysis, participants can be asked to rate the probability, impact, and capacity to control. Those actions that are rather high on the following dimensions are those where action is needed.

CHAPTER 5: DESIGNING A PROCESS
THAT ENCOURAGES INSIGHT AND CREATIVITY

1. C. A. Kaplan and H. A. Simon, In search of insight, *Cognitive Psychology* 22 (1990): 374–419.

2. M. Allais, An outline of my main contributions to economic science (1988), in *Economic Sciences: 1981–1990*, ed. Karl-Göran Mäler (Singapore: World Scientific, 1992), 236.

3. G. T. Stigler, The process of progress of economics (1982), in *Economic Sciences: 1981–1990*, ed. Karl-Göran Mäler (Singapore: World Scientific, 1992), 70.

4. J. B. Bavelas, Permitting creativity in science, in *Scientific Excellence*, ed. D. N. Jackson and J. P. Ruston (Beverly Hills, Calif.: Sage, 1987), 308.

5. This section and chapter have been stimulated by the works of Dr. Janet Beavin Bavelas. See ibid.

6. B. Zeigarnick, On finished and unfinished tasks, in *A Sourcebook of Gestalt Psychology*, ed. and trans. W. D. Ellis (London: Routledge and Kegan Paul, 1938).

7. J. B. Bavelas, Permitting creativity, 310.

8. de Bono, *Lateral Thinking*.

9. J. A. Barker, *Paradigms: The Business of Discovering the Future* (New York: Harper Business, 1993).

10. H. Mintzberg, *The Nature of Managerial Work* (New York: Harper and Row, 1973).

11. P. B. Medawar, *Advice to a Young Scientist* (New York: Harper and Row, 1979). This was referenced by J. B. Bavelas, Permitting creativity.

12. R. Fisch, J. H. Weakland, and L. Segal. *The Tactics of Change: Doing Therapy Briefly* (San Francisco: Jossey-Bass, 1982). Cited in J. B. Bavelas, Permitting creativity.

13. R. L. Daft and A. Y. Lewin, Can organization studies begin to break out of the normal science straitjacket? *Organizational Science* 1 (1990): 1–9; R. L. Daft, Learning the craft of organizational research, *Academy of Management Review* 8 (1983): 539–546; R. L. Daft and J. Wiginton, Language and organization, *Academy of Management Review* 4 (1979): 179–191; J. M. Bartunek, J. R. Gordon, and R. P. Weatherby, Developing "complicated" understanding in administrators, *Academy of Management Review* 8 (1983): 262–273.

14. The words describe how people feel and do not describe the process that occurred. See comments by Wertheimer in A. S. Luchins and E. H. Luchins, *Wertheimer's Seminars Revisited: Problem Solving and Thinking* (Albany: State University of New York Press, 1970), 137.

15. H. Simon, Rational decision-making in business organizations (1977), in *Nobel Lectures: Economic Sciences: 1969–1980*, ed. Assar Lindbeck (Singapore: World Scientific, 1992), 343–371.

16. M. Wertheimer, *Productive Thinking*, enl. ed. (New York: Harper and Row, 1959).

17. Luchins and Luchins, *Wertheimer's Seminars Revisited*, 246–247; W. Köhler, *Mentality of Apes* (London: Routledge and Kegan Paul, 1925).

18. Marrow, *The Practical Theorist*, 57–59.

19. L. Gundry, Critical incidents in communicating culture to newcomers: The meaning is the message, *Human Relations* 47 (1994): 1063; W. Darou, Training the people who help troubled kids, *Training and Development Journal* 4 (1990): 54; T. Daniel, Identifying critical leadership competencies of manufacturing supervisors in a major electronics corporation, *Group and Organizational Management* 17 (1992): 57.

20. J. B. Bavelas, Permitting creativity, 318.

21. Kübler-Ross, *On Death and Dying*.

22. Luchins and Luchins, *Wertheimer's Seminars Revisited*.

23. de Bono, *The Use of Lateral Thinking*; de Bono, *Lateral Thinking*.

24. S. Spender, The making of a poem, in *The Creative Process*, ed. Ghiselin, Brewster (New York: Mentor, 1952), 112–125.

25. Ibid.

26. Ibid., 1.

CHAPTER 6: INTERVIEWING INDIVIDUALS WITH DIFFERENT TYPES OF QUESTIONS

1. E. Mayo, Hawthorne and the Western Electric Company, in *The Social Problems of an Industrial Civilization* (New York: Routedge, 1949).

2. See Jantz, Hellervik, and Gilmour, *Behaviour Description Interviewing*.

3. Dewey, *Democracy and Education*, 16.

4. Barthol and de Mille, *Project Echo Final Report*.

5. H. Fayol, *Administration Industrielle et Générale* (Paris: Dunod, 1950).

6. Mintzberg, *The Nature of Managerial Work*.

7. J. C. Flanagan, Defining the requirements of the executive's job, *Personnel* 28 (1951): 28–35; J. C. Flanagan, The critical incident technique, *Psychological Bulletin* 51 (1954): 327–358.

8. Gundry, Critical incidents, 1063; Darou, Training the people, 54; Daniel, Identifying critical leadership competencies, 57.

9. Jantz, Hellervik, and Gilmour, *Behaviour Description Interviewing*.

10. Kelly, *The Psychology of Personal Constructs*, 1.

11. V. Fournier, Change in self construction during the transition from university to employment: A personal construct psychology approach, *Journal of Occupational and Organizational Psychology* 67 (1994): 297.

12. J. Crotts, Adding psychological value to visitor attractions, *Parks and Recreation* 29 (1994): 98.

13. D. Burnett, Exercising better management skills, *Personnel Management* 26 (1994): 42–46.

14. S. Brown, Cognitive mapping and repertory grids for qualitative survey research, *Journal of Management Studies* 29 (1992): 287.

15. S. R. Covey, *The 7 Habits of Highly Effective People* (New York: Simon and Schuster, 1989).

16. Schein, *Process Consultation*, 97.

17. N. Sanford, Whatever happened to action research, *Journal of Social Issues* 26 (1970): 12.

18. J. MacGregor, J. B. Cunningham, F. Safayeni, and R. Dumering, *Communications Involving the Control Room of a Nuclear Power Plant*, AECB project no. 2.212.1 (Ottawa, Canada: Atomic Energy Control Board, 1992).

CHAPTER 7: INTERVIEWING GROUPS

1. Marrow, *The Practical Theorist*, 170.

2. The term Echo question session evolved as a result of our experiences using Echo interview questions in groups.

3. R. K. Merton, M. Fiske, and P. L. Kendall, *The Focused Interview*, 2d ed. (New York: Free Press, 1990).

4. K. Lewin, Field theory and experiment in social psychology, *American Journal of Sociology* 44 (1939): 868–897.

5. Lewin, Group decision and social change, 330–344.

6. G. W. Allport, Catharsis and the reduction of prejudice, *Journal of Social Issues* 1 (1945): 3–10; N.R.F. Maier, *Psychology in Industry* (Boston: Houghton Mifflin, 1946).

CHAPTER 8: COMBINING INTERVIEWS AND OBSERVATIONS

1. W. F. Whyte, *Street Corner Society* (Chicago: University of Chicago Press, 1943). Although this study was undertaken before the Echo approach was invented, it illustrates the spirit of Echo research.

2. There are several terms that might illustrate an observational method of data collection, including the following: participant observation, naturalistic inquiry, case study, field study, ethnography, and so on. See L. Schatzman, and A. L. Strauss, *Field Research: Strategies for a Natural Sociology* (Englewood Cliffs, N.J.: Prentice Hall, 1973); J. Van Maanen, Making things visible, in *Varieties of Qualitative Research*, ed. J. Van Maanen, J. M. Dabbs, and R. R. Faulker (Beverly Hills, Calif.: Sage, 1982); P. Spradley, *Participant Observation* (New York: Holt, Rinehart and Winston, 1980); P. Spradley, *The Ethnographic Interview* (New York: Holt, Rinehart and Winston, 1979).

3. M. Q. Patton, *Qualitative Evaluation Methods* (Beverly Hills, Calif.: Sage, 1980).

4. In the observational studies of management, several limitations are apparent, such as small sample sizes, lack of reliability checks, activities that occur at the same time, and the inability to differentiate between groups. See M. J. Martinko and W. I. Gardner, Beyond structured observation: Methodological issues and new directions, *Academy of Management Review* 10 (1985): 676–695.

5. Control effects may be reduced by the observer assuming an incognito role, by which the observer can become completely immersed in the system being studied. One might also take care in choosing informants, and recognize or sample those who might be classified as good informants (knowledge, physical exposure, effective exposure, perceptual abilities, availability of information, motivation. See K. W. Back, The well-informed informant, in *Human Organization Research*, ed. R. N. Adams and J. J. Preiss (Homewood, Ill.: Dorsey Press, 1960), 179–187.

6. K. Lewin, R. Lippitt, and R. White, Patterns of aggressive behavior in experimentally created "social climates," *Journal of Social Psychology* 10 (1939): 271–299.

7. There are, or course, cases of more comprehensive data-collection efforts, as after the bomb explosion aboard Pam Am Airlines over Lockerbie, Scotland. The inspectors not only sampled the data after the disaster, they reconstructed it for further analysis.

8. It shares many goals with a pure description of a naturalistic qualitative assessment that derives its philosophical orientation from phenomenology. Phenomenology suggests that groups of people have different views of the reality and different ways of interpreting it. Thus, people take action based on ideas and beliefs about the world, regardless of what the world is objectively. In this sense, it would be important to "get inside" the organization and try to explain its consequences in terms of participants' realities and meanings. E. G. Guba, Criteria for assessing the trustworthiness of naturalistic inquiries, *Educational Communication and Technology Journal* 29 (1981): 75–92.

9. J. B. Bavelas, Personal communication, 2000.

10. J. B. Bavelas, L. Coates, and T. Johnson, Listeners as co-narrators, *Journal of Personality and Social Psychology* 79 (2000): 941–952.

11. J. B. Bavelas, Personal communication, 2000.

12. "Maps for action" is a term used by Chris Argyris to describe a way to help us understand and explain why human beings behave as they do. They are intended to represent the problems or causal scripts people use to inform their actions. See C. Argyris, Making knowledge more relevant to practice: Maps for action, in *Doing Research That Is Useful to Theory and Practice*, ed. E. E. Lawler III, A. M. Mohrman, Jr., S. A. Mohrman, G. E. Ledford, Jr., T. G. Cummings and Associates (San Francisco: Jossey-Bass, 1985). "Cognitive mapping" is a similar term that has been used to model a person's beliefs and assist clients in exploromg their thinking on a particular problem. There are two elements that describe cognitive mapping: a person's concepts of ideas in the form of descriptions of what is occurring, and beliefs or theories about the relationship, shown in the map by an arrow or line. The arrows indicate the positive relationships that exist between people. See C. Eden, S. Jones, and D. Sims, *Thinking in Organizations* (London: MacMillan, 1979).

13. R. W. Leeper, *Lewin's Topological and Vector Psychology: A Digest and a Critique* (Eugene: University of Oregon Press, 1943).

14. Marrow, *The Practical Theorist*, 95.

15. Ibid., 105.

16. H. Mintzberg, *The Nature of Managerial Work* (New York: Harper and Row, 1973).

17. E. J. Webb, D. T. Campbell, R. D. Schwartz, and L. Sechrest, *Unobtrusive Measures: Nonreactive Research in the Social Sciences* (Chicago: Rand McNally, 1966); R. K. Yin, *Case Study Research: Design and Methods* (Newbury Park, Calif.: Sage, 1989).

18. P. Reason, Issues of validity in new paradigm research. In *Human Inquiry: A Source-Book of New Paradigm Research*, ed. P. Reason and J. Rowan (Chichester: Wiley, 1981).

19. T. D. Jick, Mixing qualitative and quantitative methods: Triangulation in action, *Administrative Science Quarterly* 24 (1979): 602–611.

20. D. T. Campbell and D. W. Fiske, Convergent and discriminant validation by the multitrait–multimethod matrix, *Psychological Bulletin* 56 (1959): 81–105.

21. N. K. Denzin, *The Research Act*, 2d ed. (New York: McGraw-Hill, 1978).

22. Marrow, *The Practical Theorist*, 27–28.

23. See C. W. Mueller, D. S. Wakefield, J. L. Price, J. P. Curry, and J. C. McCloskey, A note on the validity of self-reports of absenteeism, *Human Relations* 40 (1987): 117–123.

CHAPTER 9: FOCUSING RESEARCH USING THE ECHO SORTING AND CONTENT ANALYSIS PROCEDURES

1. R. Ackoff, The art and science of mess management, *Interfaces* 11 (1981): 20–26.

2. A. G. Ramo, A parenthetical trip, working paper, University of Southern California, 1970. The idea is based on a phenomenological assumption that a social scientist needs to understand that reality is always perceived within a perspective.

3. A. M. Huberman and M. B. Miles, *Data Management and Analysis Methods* (Thousand Oaks, Calif.: Sage, 1994), 428–444.

4. Barthol and de Mille, *Project ECHO Final Report*.

5. Ibid.

6. These are based on the instructions used in Bavelas, Bavelas, and Schaefer, *A Method for Constructing*; B. A. Schaefer, J. B. Bavelas, and A. Bavelas, Using Echo technique to construct student-generated faculty evaluation questionnaires, *Teaching of Psychology* 7 (1980): 83–86.

7. Barthol and Bridge, The Echo multi-response method.

8. Ibid.

9. It is usually considered sound practice to calculate the correlation between groups of sorters before they discuss or adjust differences.

10. J. Naisbitt and P. Aburdene, *Megatrends 2000* (New York: William Morrow, 1990).

11. W. G. Zikmund, *Business Research Methods* (Forth Worth: Dryden Press, 1994), 234. Over the last twenty years, the field of discourse analysis has replaced content analysis in many disciplines. One difference is that it includes spoken as well as written material. The approach is explicitly inductive and is Echo compatible. For references on discourse analysis, see L. A. Wood and R. O. Kroger, *Doing Discourse Analysis: Methods for Studying Action in Talk and Text* (Thousand Oaks, Calif.: Sage, 2000); T. Van Kijk, The study of discourse, in *Discourse as Structure and Process*, vol. 1, ed. T. Van Keji (London: Sage, 1997), 1–34.

12. B. Berelson, Content analysis, in *Handbook of Social Psychology*, vol. 1, ed. G. Lindzey (Cambridge, Mass.: Addison-Wesley, 1960), 488–522; B. Berelson, *Content Analysis in Communication Research* (New York: Free Press, 1952); R. R. Jauch, R. N. Osborn, and R. N. Martin, Structured content analysis of cases: A complementary method of organizational research, *Academy of Management Review* 5 (1980): 517–525; F. N. Kerlinger, *Foundations of Behavioral Research* (New York: Holt, Rinehart and Winston, 1967), 479–485.

13. Some of the early organizational theorists that used content analysis include Eric Trist and Alex Bavelas. See E. L. Trist and V. Trist, Discussion on the quality of mental test performances on intellectual deterioration, *Proceedings of the Royal Society of Medicine* 36 (1943): 243–249; E. Weigl, On the psychology of so-called processes of abstraction, trans. M. J. Rioch, *Journal of Abnormal Psychology* 36 (1941): 3–31; see also A. Bavelas, A method.

14. H. S. Lewin, Hitler Youth and the Boy Scouts of America, *Human Relations* 1 (1947): 206–227.

15. Berelson, Content analysis.

16. Ibid.

17. Be careful not to double count when combining categories. For example, if we combine the categories of partners quitting and divorce into one category, then a person who experienced both of these should still only be counted once.

18. T. W. Milburn, R. P. Barthol, and R. de Mille, *The ECHO Method and the Study of Values* (Santa Barbara, Calif.: General Research Corporation, TM 951, December, 1968).

19. K. Krippendorf, *Content Analysis: An Introduction to Its Methodology* (Beverly Hills, Calif.: Sage, 1980). This monograph illustrates ways of calculating reliabilities. It also indicates the need to encourage practices of calculating reliabilities between raters before resolving the differences between them. Resolving the differences may produce judgments biased toward the opinion of the most verbal or senior spokesperson.

20. Barthol and Bridge, The Echo multi-response method.

CHAPTER 10: DEVELOPING ECHO
SURVEYS OR QUESTIONNAIRES

1. Bavelas, Bavelas, and Schaefer, *A Method for Constructing*; see also Schaefer, Bavelas, and Bavelas, Using the Echo technique.

2. Ibid., Bavelas, Bavelas, and Schaefer, *A Method for Constructing*, 10.

3. Mayhew, *Supervisor–Employee Relations*.

4. It may also be appropriate to indicate why these questions are being asked: "So that we can see how your opinions compare with those of other people, we'd like a few facts about you." See S. Sudman and S. S. Bradburn, *Asking Questions* (San Francisco: Jossey-Bass, 1982), 219.

5. Ibid., 222–223.

6. The term "funnel" refers to a procedure of asking the most general and unrestricted question in the area first, and following it with successively more restricted questions. In this way the content is gradually narrowed to the precise objectives. One of the main purposes of the funnel sequence is to prevent early questions from conditioning and biasing the responses to those that come later. The funnel sequence is especially useful when one wants to ascertain from the first open questions something about the respondent's frame of reference. See R. L. Kahn and C. F. Cannell, *The Dynamics of Interviewing: Theory, Technique, and Cases* (New York: Wiley, 1957), 159–160.

7. It may also be appropriate to indicate why these questions are being asked: "So that we can see how your opinions compare with those of other people, we'd like a few facts about you." See Sudman and Bradburn, *Asking Questions*, 219.

8. Ibid., 227.

9. Adapted from Bavelas, Bavelas, and Schaefer, A method for constructing, 17–18.

10. *Standards of Educational and Psychological Tests* (Washington, D.C.: American Psychological Association, 1974), 25 ff.

11. Sudman and Bradburn, *Asking Questions*, 252–258: S. L. Payne, *The Art of Asking Questions* (Princeton, N.J.: Princeton University Press, 1951); W. J. Goode and P. K. Hatt, The collection of data by questionnaire, in *Methods in Social Research* (New York: McGraw-Hill, 1951), 132–161.

12. A. Anastasi, *Psychological Testing* (New York: MacMillan, 1982). Many practical instruments and tests have appeared in publications like the *Annual Handbooks of Group Facilitators* (San Francisco: Jossey-Bass, Pfeiffer, 1998).

CHAPTER 11: DEVELOPING EXPERIMENTS

1. Marrow, *The Practical Theorist*, 40–47.

2. These comments were made by Tamara Dembo. Ibid., 40–41.

3. Ibid., 119–131.

4. Lewin, Lippitt, and White, Patterns of aggressive behavior.

5. R. Lippitt and R. White, *Autocracy and Democracy: An Experimental Inquiry* (New York: Harper and Row, 1960).

6. Lewin, Group decision and social change.

7. W. R. Torbert, Why educational research has been so uneducational: The case for a new model of social science based on collaborative inquiry, in *Human*

Inquiry: A Source-Book of New Paradigm Research, ed. P. Reason and J. Rowan (Chichester: Wiley, 1981).

8. Marrow, *The Practical Theorist*, 127.

9. Ibid., 129.

10. Ibid., 129–131.

11. Ibid.

12. K. Lewin, *Focus Behind Food Habits*; Marrow, *The Practical Theorist*, 129–131; Lewin, Lippitt, and White, Patterns of aggressive behavior; Lewin, Action research and minority problems; Lewin, *Dynamic Theory of Personality*; Lewin, *Field Theory and Social Science*; Lewin, Frontiers in Group Dynamics: Part I; Lewin, Frontiers in Group Dynamics: Part II.

13. Marrow, *The Practical Theorist*, 31–32.

14. Ibid., 13–14.

15. Argyris, Making knowledge more relevant to practice; F. Jensen, F. V. Jensen, and S. L. Dittmer, From influence diagrams to junction trees, in *Proceedings of the Tenth Conference on Uncertainty in Artificial Intelligence*, Seattle, Washington, 29–31 July 1994, ed. R. L. de Mantaras and D. Poole (San Mateo, Calif.: Morgan Kaufmann).

16. P. Shrivastava and I. Mitroff, Enhancing organizational research utilization: The role of decision makers' assumptions, *Academy of Management Review* 9 (1984): 18–26.

17. M. B. Miles and A. M. Huberman, *Qualitative Data Analysis* (Beverly Hills, Calif.: Sage, 1984).

18. J. B. Bavelas, Permitting Creativity, 314.

CHAPTER 12: COMMUNICATING

1. W. Strunk, Jr. and E. B. White, *The Elements of Style* (New York: MacMillan, 1959), 10.

2. H. Miller, Creation *(Sexus)*, in *Henry Miller on Writing*, selected by T. H. Moore (New York: New Directions, 1964), 21–22.

3. Ibid., 25.

4. K. M. Eisenhardt, Making fast strategic decisions in high-velocity environments, *Academy of Management Journal* 32 (1989): 543.

5. D. L. McLain, Responses to health and safety risk in the work environment, *Academy of Management Journal* 38 (1995): 1726.

6. W. A. Kahn, Caring for the caregivers: Patterns of organizational caregiving, *Administrative Science Quarterly* 38 (1993): 539–563.

7. Ibid., 560.

8. Ibid., 547–548.

9. K. E. Weick, The collapse of sensemaking in organizations: The Mann Gulch disaster, *Administrative Science Quarterly* 38 (1993): 628–652.

10. G. A. Klein, A recognition-primed decision (RPD) model of rapid decision making, in *Decision Making in Action: Models and Methods*, ed. G. A. Klein, J. Orasana, R. Calderwood, and C. E. Zsamok (Norwood, N.J.: Ablex, 1993).

11. G. Morgan, P. J. Frost, and L. R. Pondy, Organizational symbolism, in *Organizational Symbolism*, ed. L. R. Pondy, P. J. Frost, G. Morgan, and T. C. Dandridge (Greenwich, Conn.: JAI Press, 1983), 24.

12. N. Maclean, *Young Men and Fire* (Chicago: University of Chicago Press, 1992), 43.

13. S. E. Taylor, *Positive Illusions* (New York: Basic Books, 1989).

14. E. Van Velsor and J. B. Leslie, Why executives derail: Perspectives across time and cultures, *Academy of Management Executive* 9 (1995): 62–72.

15. M. MacLuhan, *Understanding Media: The Extensions of Man* (New York: McGraw-Hill, 1964).

CHAPTER 13: LEARNING AND CHANGE

1. Luchins and Luchins, *Wertheimer's Seminars Revisited*, 246–247; Marrow, *The Practical Theorist*, 22–24. At the Institute, Kohler and Wertheimer were breaking new ground in the formulation of gestalt theory. Lewin and Wertheimer's problem-solving styles had much in common, although Lewin was probably too independent in his thinking to be a disciple of anyone.

2. Lewin, *A Dynamic Theory of Personality*.

3. Luchins and Luchins, *Wertheimer's Seminars Revisited*, 246–247; Wertheimer, *Productive Thinking*.

4. E. R. Hilgard and G. H. Bower, *Theories of Learning*, 3d ed. (New York: Appleton Century Crofts, 1966), 229–263.

5. K. Duncker, On problem-solving, *Psychological Monographs* 58, no. 5 (1945): whole no. 270.

6. Luchins and Luchins, *Wertheimer's Seminars Revisited*, 1.

7. Ibid., 246–247.

8. Statement by Norman Maier, in Marrow, *The Practical Theorist*, 24

9. Colleagues included Ronald Lippitt, Leland Bradford, and Kenneth Benne. See R. Lippitt, *Training in Community Relations* (New York: Harper and Row, 1949).

10. D. A. Kolb, *Experiential Learning* (New York: Prentice Hall, 1984).

11. Thomas Merton, *The Seven Story Mountain* (New York: Doubleday, 1948), 139.

12. Revans worked with Sir Geoffrey Vickers and other team members, such as E. F. Schumacher, *Small Is Beautiful: Economics As If People Mattered* (New York: HarperCollins, 1989); and J. Bronowski, *The Ascent of Man* (New York: Little, Brown, 1976). Some of the history of this work is contained in N. G. McNulty, Management development by action learning, *Training and Development Journal* 33 (1979): 12–18.

13. H. McLaughlin and R. Thorpe, Action learning—A paradigm in emergence: The problems facing a challenge to traditional management education and development, *British Journal of Management* 4 (1993): 19–27; R. W. Revans, *Developing Effective Managers: A New Approach to Business Education* (London: Longman, 1971).

14. M. MacNamara and W. H. Weekes, The action learning model of experiential learning for developing managers, *Human Relations* 35 (1982): 879–901.

15. R. W. Revans, The nature of action learning, *Omega* 9 (1981): 9–24.

16. B. Stewart, *Echo Study of Open Door* (Duncan, British Columbia: Duncan Mental Health, 2000).

17. J. Dewey, *How We Think* (Boston: D. C. Heath, 1933).

18. The four categories are found in J.D.W. Andrews, The verbal structure of teacher questions: Its impact on discussion, *POD Quarterly* 3 (1980): 129–163.

19. Ibid.
20. Luchins and Luchins, *Wertheimer's Seminars Revisited*, 11.
21. Kolb, *Experiential Learning*.

CHAPTER 14: ACTION RESEARCH

1. Marrow, *The Practical Theorist*, 193.
2. I. Chein, S. W. Cook, and J. Harding, The field of action research, *American Psychologist* 3 (1948): 45. They wrote this article to illustrate how the Commission on Community Interrelations might carry out its objectives.
3. Marrow, *The Practical Theorist*, 154.
4. Ibid., 141–152. Projects involved group decision making and productivity, self-management, leadership training, changing attitudes toward hiring older workers, and overcoming resistance to change.
5. He had been proposed by Horace Kallen, then dean of the graduate faculty at the New School, as the successor to the late Max Wertheimer, who—together with Kohler—had been a colleague of Lewin's in Berlin.
6. Marrow, *The Practical Theorist*, 161–164.
7. As quoted in ibid., 171–172. See also K. Lewin, The Research Center for Group Dynamics at Massachusetts Institute of Technology, *Sociometry* 2 (1945): 126–136.
8. See Marrow, *The Practical Theorist*, 169. Lewin also planned to link some of the work of the Research Center for Group Dynamics with work at the Commission on Community Relations.
9. Ibid., 197.
10. H. Murray, B. Trist, E. Trist, and F. Emery, *The Social Engagement of Social Science: A Tavistock Anthology* (Philadelphia: University of Pennsylvania Press, 1997).
11. Ibid.
12. It consisted of J. R. Rees, Leonard Browne, Henry Dicks, Ronald Hargreaves, Mary Luff, and Tommy Wilson. They coopted two wartime associates to join this Tavistock group: Jock Sutherland and Eric Trist. Ibid.
13. W. R. Bion, *Experiences in Groups and Other Papers* (London: Routledge, 1991); W. R. Bion, *Learning From Experience* (London: Heinemann, 1962); W. R. Bion and J. Rickman, Intra-group Tensions in Therapy, *Lancet* 2 (1943): 678–681; H. Bridger, The Northfield Experiment, *Bulletin of the Menninger Clinic* 6 (1946): 71–76.
14. The Industrial Productivity Committee (I.P.C.) made a decision to create (1) a clinic to enter the National Health Service to focus on outpatient psychiatry, and (2) the Tavistock Institute of Human Relations to study wider societal problems. The decision to construct a clinic was made in anticipation of the Labour government's plans to construct a national health service. A Rockerfeller Foundation grant provided some financial support for the initial projects. The Tavistock Institute of Human Relations was formed in September 1947. See Trist and Murray, *The Social Engagement of Social Science*.
15. E. Jaques, *The Changing Culture of the Factory* (London: Tavistock, 1951).
16. E. L. Trist and K. W. Bamforth, Some social and psychological consequences of the longwall method of coal-getting, *Human Relations* 4 (1951): 1–38.

17. A. W. Clark, ed., *Experimenting With Organizational Life: The Action Research Approach* (New York: Plenum Press, 1976).

18. Eric Trist, Personal communication with author, 13 July 1988.

19. Lewin, Frontiers in group dynamics: Part I.

20. Lewin, *Field Theory*.

21. D. P. Schwab, Reviewing empirically based manuscripts: Perspectives on process, in *Publishing in the Organizational Sciences*, ed. L. L. Cummings and P. J. Frost (Englewood Cliffs, N.J.: Prentice Hall, 1985).

22. Rapoport, Three dilemmas.

23. Lewin, Frontiers in group dynamics: Part I.

24. V. H. Vroom, *Work and Motivation* (New York: John Wiley, 1946); E. E. Lawler, *Motivation in Work Organizations* (Monterey, Calif.: Brooks/Cole, 1973).

25. E. A. Locke, G. P. Latham, and M. Erez, The determinants of goal commitment, *Academy of Management Review* 13 (1988): 23–39.

26. L. Coch and J.R.P. French, Overcoming resistance to change, *Human Relations* 34 (1948): 555–566.

27. Locke, Latham, and Erez, The Determinants of Goal Commitment. See also K. Lewin, Group decision and social change, in *Readings in Social Psychology*, ed. T. Newcomb and E. Hartley (New York: Holt, Rinehart and Winston, 1952), 330–344.

28. M. Emery and F. Emery, Searching for new directions in new ways . . . for new times, in *Management Handbook for Public Administrators*, ed. J. W. Sutherland (Toronto: Van Nostrand, 1978); E. L. Trist, Action research and adaptive planning, in *Experimenting with Organizational Life*, ed. A. Clark (New York: Plenum, 1976); J. B. Cunningham, *Action Research and Organizational Development* (Westport, Conn.: Praeger, 1993).

29. N. Halpern, Sociotechnical systems design: The Shell Sarnia experience, in *Quality of Working Life*, ed. J. B. Cunningham and T. H. White (Ottawa: Labour Canada, 1984), 31–75.

30. Ibid.

31. B. Painter, Joint development of community and worklife, in *Quality of Working Life*, ed. J. B. Cunningham and T. H. White (Ottawa: Labour Canada, 1984), 329–355.

32. J. M. Bryson, *Strategic Planning for Public and Nonprofit Organizations* (San Francisco: Jossey-Bass, 1989), 174–175; See also B. W. Barry, *Strategic Planning Workbook for Nonprofit Organizations* (St. Paul, Minn.: Amherst H. Wilder Foundation, 1986).

33. S. Hollander, *The Success of Increased Efficiency: A Study of Du Pont Rayon Plants* (Cambridge: MIT Press, 1965).

34. R. Beckhard and R. T. Harris, *Organizational Transitions: Managing Complex Change* (Menlo Park, Calif: Addison-Wesley, 1977), 53.

35. Ibid., 54.

36. Marrow, *The Practical Theorist*, 175–176.

37. Ibid., 176–177.

Selected Bibliography

Argyris, C. 1970. *Intervention Theory and Method: A Behavioral Review*. Reading, Mass.: Addison-Wesley.

Argyris, C. 1985. Making knowledge more relevant to practice: Maps for action. In *Doing Research That Is Useful for Theory and Practice*, edited by E. E. Lawler III, A. M. Mohrman, Jr., S. A. Mohrman, T. A. Cummings, and Associates. San Francisco: Jossey-Bass.

Argyris, C., R. Putnam, and D. M. Smith. 1985. *Action Science*. San Francisco: Jossey-Bass.

Bacharach, S. B. 1989. Organizational theories: Some criteria for evaluation. *Academy of Management Review* 14: 496–515.

Bannister, D., and J.M.M. Mair. 1968. *The Evaluation of Personal Constructs*. New York: Academic Press.

Barthol, R. P., and R. de Mille. 1968. The Echo multi-response method for surveying value and influence patterns in groups. *Psychological Reports* 22: 1345–1354.

Barthol, R. P., and R. de Mille. 1969. *Project Echo Final Report*. Contract no. DaHC04-69-C-0018. Santa Barbara, Calif.: General Research Corporation.

Bartunek, J. M., J. R. Gordon, and R. P. Weatherby. 1983. Developing "complicated" understanding in administrators. *Academy of Management Review* 8: 262–273.

Baumrind, D. 1964. Some thoughts on ethics of research: After reading Milgram's "behavioral study on obedience." *American Psychologist* 19: 421–423.

Bavelas, A. 1942. A method for investigating individual and group ideology. *Sociometry* 5: 371–377.

Bavelas, A. 1950. Communication patterns in task-oriented groups. *Journal of Acoustical Society of America* 22: 725–730.

Bavelas, J. B. 1987. Permitting creativity in science. In *Scientific Excellence: Origins and Assessment*, edited by D. N. Jackson and J. P. Rushton. Beverly Hills, Calif.: Sage.

Bavelas J. B., A. Bavelas, and B. A. Schaefer. 1978. *A Method for Constructing Student-Generated Faculty-Evaluation Questionnaires*. Published internally by the University of Victoria, Victoria.

Bavelas, J. B., L. Coates, and T. Johnson. 1999. Listeners as co-narrators. Unpublished.

Berelson, B. 1952. *Content Analysis in Communication Research*. New York: Free Press.

Berelson, B. 1960. Content analysis. In *Handbook of Social Psychology*, edited by G. Lindzey. Vol. 1. Cambridge, Mass: Addison-Wesley.

Bion, W. R. 1991. *Experiences in Groups and Other Papers*. London: Routledge.

Burrell, G., and G. Morgan. 1979. *Sociological Paradigms and Organizational Analysis*. London: Heinemann.

Campbell, D. T. 1957. Factors relevant to the validity of experiments in social settings. *Psychological Bulletin* 54: 297–312.

Campbell, D. T., and D. W. Fiske. 1959. Convergent and discriminant validation by the multitrait–multimethod matrix. *Psychological Bulletin* 56: 81–105.

Campbell, D. T., and J. C. Stanley. 1966. *Experimental and Quasi-Experimental Design for Research*. Boston: Houghton Mifflin. Also published as Experimental and quasi-experimental design for research on teaching. In *Handbook of Research on Teaching*, edited by N. L. Gage. Chicago: Rand McNally, 1963.

Cartwright, D., and A. Zander, eds. 1960. *Group Dynamics: Research and Theory*. 2d ed. New York: Harper and Row.

Chein, I., S. W. Cook, and J. Harding. 1948. The field of action research. *American Psychologist* 3: 43–50.

Clark, A. W., ed. 1976. *Experimenting with Organizational Life: The Action Research Approach*. New York: Plenum Press.

Coch, C., and J.R.P. French. 1948. Overcoming resistance to change. *Human Relations* 34: 555–566.

Cook, T. D., and D. T. Campbell. 1979. *Quasi-Experimentation: Design and Analysis Issues for Field Settings*. Boston: Houghton Mifflin.

Corbin, J., and A. Strauss. 1990. Grounded theory method: Procedures, canons, and evaluative criteria. *Qualitative Sociology* 13: 3–21.

Cunningham, J. B. 1993. *Action Research and Organizational Development*. Westport, Conn.: Praeger.

Daft, R. L. 1983. Learning the craft of organizational research. *Academy of Management Review* 8: 539–546.

Daft, R. L., and J. Wiginton. 1979. Language and organization. *Academy of Management Review* 4: 179–191.

de Mille, R. 1970. Logical and empirical oppositiveness in value responses. *Psychological Reports* 26: 143–154.

Dewey, J. 1966. *Democracy and Education*. Toronto: Collier-MacMillan Canada.

Eisenstadt, K. M. 1991. Better stories and better constructs: The case for rigor and comparative logic. *Academy of Management Review* 16: 620–627.

Fisher, R., and W. Ury. 1981. *Getting to Yes: Negotiating Agreements Without Giving In*. New York: Penguin Books.

Glaser, B. G., and A. L. Strauss. 1967. *The Discovery of Grounded Theory: Strategies for Qualitative Research*. New York: Aldine.

Guba, E. G. 1981. Criteria for assessing the trustworthiness of naturalistic inquiries. *Educational Communication and Technology Journal* 29: 75–92.

Hall, C. S., and G. Lindzey. 1978. *Theories of Personality*. 3d ed. New York: John Wiley and Sons.

Hampden-Turner, C. 1981. *Maps of the Mind*. New York: Macmillan.

Hunter, M. G. 1992. The essence of "excellent" systems analysts: Perceptions of five key audiences. Ph.D. diss., University of Strathclyde.

Jantz, T., L. Hellervik, and D. C. Gilmour. 1986. *Behaviour Description Interviewing: New, Accurate, Cost Effective*. Toronto: Allyn and Bacon.

Jaques, E. 1951. *The Changing Culture of the Factory*. London: Tavistock.

Jauch, R. R., R. N. Osborn, and R. N. Martin. 1980. Structured content analysis of cases: A complementary method of organizational research. *Academy of Management Review* 5: 517–525.

Jick, T. D. 1979. Mixing qualitative and quantitative methods: Triangulation in action. *Administrative Science Quarterly* 24: 602–611.

Kalborn, J. 1941. Ideological differences among rural children. Master's thesis, State University of Iowa.

Kalborn, J. 1941. Values and sources of authority among rural children. In *Authority and Frustration*, edited by K. Lewin, C. E. Meyers, J. Kalborn, M. L. Farber, and J.R.P. French. Iowa City: University of Iowa Press.

Kelly, G. A. 1955. *The Psychology of Personal Constructs*. New York: Norton.

Krippendorf, K. 1980. *Content Analysis: An Introduction to Its Methodology*. Beverly Hills, Calif.: Sage.

Kübler-Ross, E. 1969. *On Death and Dying*. New York: Macmillan.

Kübler-Ross, E. 1975. *Death: The Final Stages of Growth*. London: Prentice Hall.

Kuhn, T. S. 1970. *The Structure of Scientific Revolutions*. 2d ed. Chicago: University of Chicago Press.

Leeper, R. W. 1943. *Lewin's Topological and Vector Psychology: A Digest and a Critique*. Eugene: University of Oregon Press.

Lewin, K. 1931. The conflict between Aristotelian and Galileian modes of thought in contemporary psychology. *Journal of Genetic Psychology* 5: 141–177.

Lewin, K. 1935. *A Dynamic Theory of Personality: Selected Papers by Kurt Lewin*. New York: McGraw-Hill.

Lewin, K. 1935. Psycho-sociological problems of a minority group. *Character and Personality* 3: 175–187.

Lewin, K. 1936. *Principles of Topological Psychology*. Translated by F. Keider and G. M. Heider. New York: McGraw-Hill.

Lewin, K. 1939. Group decision and social change. In K. Lewin, R. Lippitt, and R. White. Patterns of aggressive behavior in experimentally created "social climates." *Journal of Social Psychology* 10: 271–299.

Lewin, K. 1946. Action research and minority problems. *Journal of Social Issues* 2: 34–46.

Lewin, K. 1947. Frontiers in group dynamics: Part I. Concept, method and reality in social science; social equilibria and social change. *Human Relations* 1 (1): 5–40.

Lewin, K. 1947. Frontiers in group dynamics: Part II. Channels in group life, social planning, action research, *Human Relations* 1 (2): 143–153.

Lewin, K. 1947. Group decision and social change. In *Readings in Social Psychology*. 2d ed., edited by G. E. Swanson, T. M. Newcombe, and E. L. Hartley. New York: Holt.

Lewin, K. 1951. *Field Theory in Social Science: Selected Papers*. Edited by D. Cartwright. New York: Harper and Row.

Luchins, A. S., and E. H. Luchins. 1970. *Wertheimer's Seminars Revisited: Problem Solving and Thinking*. Albany: State University of New York Press.

Maier, N.R.F. 1958. *The Appraisal Interview*. New York: Wiley.

Marrow, A. J. 1969. *The Practical Theorist: the Life and Work of Kurt Lewin*. New York: Basic Books.

May, R. 1975. *The Courage to Create*. New York: Bantam Books.

Milburn, T. W., R. P. Barthol, and R. de Mille. 1968. The ECHO method and the study of values. Santa Monica: General Research Corporation TM 951, December.

Miles, M. B., and A. M. Huberman. 1984. *Qualitative Data Analysis*. Beverly Hills, Calif.: Sage.

Milgram, S. 1963. Behavioral study of obedience. *Journal of Abnormal Social Psychology* 67: 371–378.

Milgram, S. 1965. Some conditions of obedience and disobedience to authority. *Human Relations* 18: 57–76.

Miner, J. B. 1984. Validity and usefulness of theories in an emerging organizational science. *Academy of Management Review* 9: 299.

Mintzberg, H. 1973. *The Nature of Managerial Work*. New York: Harper and Row.

Mintzberg, H. 1979. An emerging strategy of "direct" research. *Administrative Science Quarterly* 24: 582–589.

Morgan, G. 1986. *Images of Organization*. Newbury Park, Calif.: Sage.

Morgan, G., and L. Smircich. 1980. The case for qualitative research. *Academy of Management Review* 5: 491–500.

Reason, P. 1981. Issues of validity in new paradigm research. In *Human Inquiry: A Source-Book of New Paradigm Research*, edited by P. Reason and J. Rowan. Chichester: Wiley.

Roberts, R. M. 1989. *Serendipity: Accidental Discoveries in Science*. New York: John Wiley and Sons.

Rokeach, M. 1968. *Beliefs, Attitudes, and Values*. San Francisco: Jossey-Bass.

Rothenberg, A. 1979. *The Emerging Goddess: The Creative Process in Art, Science, and Other Fields*. Chicago: University of Chicago Press.

Schaefer, B. A., J. B. Bavelas, and A. Bavelas. 1980. Using Echo technique to construct student-generated faculty-evaluation questionnaires. *Teaching of Psychology* 7: 83–86.

Simon, H. 1992. Rational decision-making in business organizations (1977). In *Nobel Lectures: Economic Sciences: 1969–1980*, edited by Assar Lindbeck. Singapore: World Scientific.

Strauss, A., and J. Corbin. 1990. *Basics of Qualitative Research: Grounded Theory Procedures and Techniques*. Newbury Park, Calif.: Sage.

Torbert, W. R. 1981. Why educational research has been so uneducational: The case for a new model of social science based on collaborative inquiry. In *Human Inquiry: A Source-Book of New Paradigm Research*, edited by P. Reason and J. Rowan. Chichester: Wiley.

Trist, E. L., and K. W. Bamforth. 1951. Some social and psychological consequences of the Longwall method of coal-getting. *Human Relations* 4: 3–38.

Trist, E. L., G. W. Higgin, H. Murray, and S. B. Pollock. 1963. *Organizational Choice*. London: Tavistock.

Vaillant, G. 1977. *Adaptation to Life*. Boston: Little, Brown.

Van de Ven, A. H. 1989. Nothing is quite so practical as a good theory. *Academy of Management Review* 14: 486–489.

Van Maanen, J. 1983. *Qualitative Methodology*. Beverly Hills, Calif.: Sage.

Webb, E. J., D. T. Campbell, R. D. Schwartz, and L. S. Sechrest. 1966. *Unobtrusive Measures: Nonreactive Research in the Social Sciences*. Chicago: Rand McNally.

Weick, K. E. 1979. *The Social Psychology of Organizing*. Reading, Mass.: Addison-Wesley.

Weigl, E. 1941. On the psychology of so called processes of abstraction. Translated by M. J. Rioch. *Journal of Abnormal Psychology* 36: 3–31.

Wertheimer, M. 1959. *Productive Thinking*. Enl. ed. New York: Harper and Row.

Whyte, W. F. 1943. *Street Corner Society*. Chicago: University of Chicago Press.

Whyte, W. F., and E. L. Hamilton. 1967. *Action Research for Management*. Homewood, Ill.: R. D. Irwin.

Yin, R. K. 1981. The case study crisis: Some answers. *Administrative Science Quarterly* 26: 58–65.

Yin, R. K. 1989. *Case Study Research: Design and Methods*. Newbury Park, Calif.: Sage.

Zeigarnick, B. 1938. On finished and unfinished tasks. In *A Sourcebook of Gestalt Psychology*, edited and translated by W. D. Ellis. London: Routledge and Kegan Paul.

Index